Behavior Modification
in the
Natural Environment

BEHAVIOR MODIFICATION

IN THE

NATURAL ENVIRONMENT

ROLAND G. THARP

Department of Psychology
University of Hawaii
Honolulu, Hawaii

RALPH J. WETZEL

Department of Psychology
University of Arizona
Tucson, Arizona

ACADEMIC PRESS   New York and London 1969

ACADEMIC PRESS, INC.
111 Fifth Avenue, New York, New York 10003

United Kingdom Edition published by
ACADEMIC PRESS, INC. (LONDON) LTD.
Berkeley Square House, London W1X 6BA

LIBRARY OF CONGRESS CATALOG CARD NUMBER: 75-91418

Second Printing, 1970

PRINTED IN THE UNITED STATES OF AMERICA

Preface

This book relates the experiences of the Behavior Research Project. We believe that many people who occupy the roles or professions of helping will find these experiences of interest, because we have been on a mapping sortie of the land which most social actionaries believe to be promised. Three major thrusts comprise the perceptible future direction of the helping enterprises: use of the natural environment, reliance on the nontraditional worker, and behavior modification. The Behavior Research Project combined these elements, in rather pure form, and observed the results. These results are encouraging and frustrating: the land has bees, as well as milk and honey. Our goal is to relate what we found, to explain what happens when using nontraditional workers to implement behavior modification techniques in the natural environment. We will discuss our failures as well as successes.

It is no accident that the Behavior Research Project is located in southern Arizona. Tucson is a rapidly growing city of 350,000 located in the desert mountains and flatlands near the Mexican border, a commercial, banking, and supply headquarters for the ranching, mining, and farming areas surrounding it. Thirty years ago it was a small guest-ranch locale on the Southern Pacific line. Population burgeoned; tourism, light industry, and military activities brought people together more quickly than social services developed. In 1965, only one institution for adjudicated delinquent boys existed: Fort Grant, located in the barren foothills of the Graham Mountains. No state institution for delinquent girls existed, then or now. A very small children's program had just been initiated at the State Hospital. One Child Guidance Agency was supported by UCC contributions in Tucson; their treatment waiting list extended for a year. A few private residential centers for delinquent girls were located around the state, but these agencies were geared for girls who were not psychotic, seriously antisocial, or runaway threats. Neither the Family Service Agencies nor the Southern Arizona Mental Health Center had organized children's services. Due to the paucity of existing social and mental health facilities, it was much easier to establish the new (and radically different) service which the research required. We do not mean to imply that institutional and "establishment" pressure was not felt; but we did manage to escape the bitter agency wrangling which can characterize innovation in more highly organized cities.

New services were particularly welcome in the outlying regions and towns of southern Arizona. In small communities which have no resident of any of the mental health professions, even an unusual program is pleasing. Perhaps because the authors are westerners, the problems of serving the population-distribution patterns of the western states remains a central concern. In this, southern Arizona is paradigmatic: many tiny to modest communities scattered throughout the mountains and deserts developing the same problems as people do everywhere, but too many miles from the metropolitan area to commute to a social worker, and too poor and mild to ever attract a resident psychiatrist. It is patent that some form of consultation, deriving from the cities but not depending upon resident professionals, must be devised to serve the rural populations of Arizona, New Mexico, Colorado, Nevada, Utah, Wyoming, Montana, Idaho, Oregon, Washington, and, indeed, Maine, and West Virginia, and a large part of the world. We have applied the Behavioral Research model to problems in Alaska and Hawaii, as are reported here, and find the model continues to hold promise. But the issues of long-distance consultation—though we have experimented over such distances as from Tucson to Nome—were basically derived in the romantic, but not very glamorous, Arizona towns of Tombstone, Bisbee, and San Manuel.

One further word about our locale: there is something about the western character that expects self-reliance; perhaps necessity teaches. But the "BRP" model is definitely a self-help one, and a population which is not characteristically agency dependent made our task an easier one.

Thus, we made life and work as simple for ourselves as possible, at least in organizational issues. These decisions have served us well; only with this kind of setting could there have developed an organization which moved from nonexistence to 147 cases studied in a period of 24 months. For the population of problem children, however, we attempted a stern challenge. It will become clear to the reader that we do not believe any of our procedures or theory to be specific for the predelinquent child *only*. We chose him because he is a stepchild, unpopular with mental health workers; because he is a challenge, traditionally unchanging; and because, if he is not changed, his life is a misery to himself and his society.

We have acknowledged our gratitude and admiration to the Behavioral Analysts—our nontraditional workers—in as clear a way as we know. But the list of others who have contributed to this program is long and impressive.

We cannot overacknowledge the contribution to this volume made by

Gaylord Thorne, Ph.D., whose elevation to his current position of Administrator, Research and Program Evaluation Division, State of Oregon, prevented his participation in actual authorship. Dr. Thorne served as Executive Director of the Behavior Research Project for a longer period than any other person, and the ideas and operations reported here could not have been eventuated but for his diligence and intellect. In addition to the authors and Dr. Thorne, supervising psychologists on the Behavior Research Project included William L. Simmons, Ph.D., and Rachel Burkholder, Ph.D.

The Office of Juvenile Delinquency and Youth Development of the Department of Health, Education, and Welfare supported the Project both through its grants and its excellent consultants, Ralph Susman and Martin Timin. Financial and moral support also came from the Heller Foundation, whose seed money yielded office facilities. The Arizona State Hospital Board, and especially Mrs. Ruth Irving of Tucson, has been loyal and vigorous and indispensable. Robert Shearer, M.D., and his successor Robert I. Cutts, M.D., as Directors of the Southern Arizona Mental Health Center, have distinguished themselves for their imagination in a field where imagination is vital. Montrose Wolf, Ph.D., helped in the early days of planning; and Ronald H. Pool, Ph.D., helped in the late days of conceptualizing what happened.

People in unlikely places have participated, and without them the achievement would have been the less: Keith Anderson of the Alaska Youth and Adult Authority, Juneau; Robert Davis, Chief of the Northwest Alaska Division of the Bureau of Indian Affairs; Lee Ashe, caseworker *par excellence* of the State Welfare Office of Graham County, Arizona; Jerome Levy, Ph.D., of the University of New Mexico Medical School; his current colleague, Gerald Otis, Ph.D., who as a graduate assistant helped to invent the whole thing; Judge Holmes and Ivan Schier of the Boulder Colorado Juvenile Court; Jack Nagoshi and Robert Omura of the University of Hawaii.

Psychology graduate students have served a tour with us and contributed. This is a list of which we will be proud: Michael Morgan, Roger Vogler, Marian Martin, Joe Willis, Barry Kinney, Ray Sanders, Roy Welsandt, Jay Mann, Victoria Hurston, and Mary Leslie.

We were blessed with two extraordinary office managers, Karen Fox and Myra Lehmann. The preparation of manuscripts, documents, and the many graphs could not have been executed without Jessie Carpenter, Jackie Curtis, Joyce Broadbent, Mildred Frank, Linda Murphy, and especially Lynn Sweeney. We are grateful to Dr. Mary Wetzel and Dr. Ronald Gallimore for their reading of the manuscript.

ROLAND G. THARP
RALPH J. WETZEL

August, 1969

Contents

Behavior Modification
in the
Natural Environment

Overview

The winds of discontent are gusting over the lands of the helping professions. Psychology, social work, corrections, psychiatry, education, rehabilitation, nursing; hospitals, clinics, schools, prisons; psychotherapists, pas-
toral counsellors, teachers, probation officers; criticism, self-examination,
and the hard facts of research evidence bring to each of these the courage
to change and the anxiety of ambiguity. The dogmas of the last century's
orthodox psychology do not stand before the challenge of this century's
human condition. The mental health professions are not content with
themselves, and society balks before their unfulfilled promises. The helping
professions of education and sociology are impatient with their virtual
lack of theory, but they are even more discontent with the imposition
of models derived from speculation concerning the mentally ill. Certainly
among us there is much self-satisfaction and reluctance to disturb the
comforts of routine and old habits. But beyond that, the thrust toward
excellence and the dedicated desire to extend help is discernable—to au-
thentically extend the helping enterprise in ways that are more effective
for a much broader portion of the spectrum of human misery.

The conception of human misery as intimately linked with mental illness
must be radically reexamined, if we are to progress. The mental illness
model has failed to produce a technology for cure which is sufficiently
reliable. More seriously, it has failed to provide a useful action model
for the helping enterprise as most broadly conceived—the enterprise of
education and rehabilitation. It will not be argued here that the mental
illness model is "untrue." Certainly it meets some of the criteria for
"truth"; there is a good measure of internal consistency in its positions,
and there are many points at which its predictions are valid. The model's
inadequacy, rather, resides in its limited applicability, and in the stultifica-
tion of the organizations which its implementation generates.

It is widely recognized that if the full potential of society is to be
mobilized for the help of its less fortunate members, then the helping

enterprise must be despecialized. The hyperprofessionalization of the mental health professions militates against the use of society's greatest resources: the client's natural relationships, with their extraordinary potential power for generating behavior change; and talented subprofessionals, with their energy and idealism. The conception of mental illness bears with it the burden of the medical model (the disadvantages of the medical conception will be explicated in some detail) but perhaps its greatest handicap is not intellectual, but practical. The medical model for organization generates action patterns which promote hyperspecialization, and thus it disqualifies society's greatest potentials for help.

Thus it can be seen that two vectors are converging upon a single current of hope. This hope is for the promise of the theory and techniques of behavior modification to be realized. One vector is the accumulating evidence of research. At this time, there is every reason to continue to explore the utility of behavior-modification constructs. Their heuristic promise is extraordinary. The other vector is that already detailed: the need for an organizational model which can avail itself of the full helping potential of the individual's social environment.

The learning theories, which underlie behavior modification, attempt to specify the relationships between an organism's behavior and his environment. As the environment changes, according to the several laws of learning, so will behavior change. Thus behavior modification assumes that the appropriate locus for intervention in effecting behavior change is the individual's environment. Attempts at amelioration, then, occur in the environment, and generate organizational patterns which automatically use and involve environmental resources. Thus despecialization is not merely imposed, it is an integral aspect of the helping enterprise.

The information and observations contained in this book derive from the authors' experience with such an organization and enterprise. The organization sprang fully from the logical operational extentions of behavior modification assumptions. There is a coherent alternative to the mental illness model and the medical organizational pattern. The value of the alternative can now be judged by the reader.

Not all the techniques of behavior modification have been employed in this demonstration. There are many techniques, and they stand at different stages of refinement. This report centers upon the technique of *contingency management,* which may be defined as the rearrangement of environmental rewards and punishments which strengthen or weaken specified behaviors. Reinforcement theory, which details the course of behavior as it is affected by environmental response, forms the substratum for contingency management. For purposes of this overview, the basic assumption of contingency management may be stated simply: undesirable behavior may be weakened by not rewarding it, and desirable behavior may be strengthened by following it with reward. Each case to be reported here was treated according to this basic paradigm; and the entire organization and all its operations were derived therefrom. The paradigm is simple, but the environment is not, and the operations are extraordinarily complex.

Reinforcers are those consequences of a behavior which strengthen and weaken it as they are presented and withdrawn. Reinforcers lie within the environment of the individual, and are embedded within his social nexus: whether the reinforcer is a smile or a candy, a bicycle or a slap, reinforcement is frequently dispensed by people articulated into the individual's social environment. If the environment is the hospital, these people are the nurses, doctors, or other patients; if the environment is the school, they are the principal, teachers, or other pupils; if it is the family, they are siblings, the spouse, or the parents. These people control reinforcers, in that they may either administer them or withhold them. Depending upon the pattern of control, they may modify the behavior of the individual by strengthening it or weakening it. Thus it may be seen that the potent reinforcers for an individual ordinarily lie within his natural environment, and these reinforcers are controlled by those people to whom he is naturally related. The task of contingency management comes to be the reorganization of the patterns of reinforcement control exercised by the people of an individual's environment. The task of the contingency manager in the complex social environment is thus to specify the correct pattern of reorganized control, and to modify the behavior of the controlling people so that they will correctly reorganize, for the ultimate benefit of the deviant individual.

In this model, then, the direct contact individual—the dispenser of the reinforcers—is not the professional specialist, but is rather some person naturally articulated into the social environment of the deviant individual, some person who, by virtue of an important role relationship to him, has control over his reinforcers. Thus the "treater" is rarely a psychiatrist or psychologist or social worker, but is rather the individual's parent or teacher or spouse or ward attendant or sibling or friend or employer. We have chosen the term "mediator" to describe this function, because he occupies an intermediary position between the deviant individual and the consulting contingency manager.

The medical model despairs of the use of the mediators because of their unpredictability, their past history of deleterious effects upon the patient, and their lack of professional knowledge. Thus the medical model requires that a new and artificial relationship be built with the psychotherapist, and this relationship must be strengthened until—in learning theory language—the therapist possesses, in the form of his own approvals and disapprovals, the patient's reinforcers. This procedure is patently wasteful, if there is indeed an alternative form of intervention which mobilizes the potential power of the mediators. The intrusion of the artifical therapeutic relationship often has other ignominious consequences: the disruption of natural relationships—whether marital, parental, or community—as a consequence of pscyhotherapy is a well-known embarrassment of the mental health professions. For both of these reasons, it is well to explore the limits to which natural relationships can be solely employed. The demonstration reported here pushed this limit rather severely: the "patient" was never seen for treatment by any member of the staff. All contact was with the mediators (with the single exception of one brief assessment interview prior to intervention). Staff work was confined to consultation with the mediators.

A further aspect of deprofessionalization was also demonstrated. Because the principles of learning theory are clear and precise, and in some of their elements simple as well, a nontraditional pattern of training for the helper would seem appropriate. Here then is a clear opportunity to test the limits of the widespread call for deprofessionalization. Carefully selected Bachelors of Arts were specifically trained for the task of consultation with mediators in contingency management: thus Behavior Analysts (BA's) were created. To clearly demonstrate the effectiveness of this organizational pattern, the professional psychologists (who supervised the Behavior Analysts) did not see the mediators or the patients. The contact sequence thus becomes: supervising psychologist—Behavior Analyst—mediator—"patient."

And as one last reminder to all concerned (including the authors) that the appropriate role relationships and action patterns were to be dictated by a model radically different from the medical-illness one, a new term was employed to replace that of "patient": the identified problem individual was referred to as the *target*.

Behavior modification is an activity appropriate to almost any setting; indeed, its first applications have been made in institutions for the retarded, the mentally ill, the criminal, and the delinquent. Our own research has been carried out entirely in the natural environment. The natural environment is the more difficult field because controls are more tenuous, but it is the field which must be investigated if the work of preventative amelioration is to be perfected. Organizational and operational solutions to the problems of the free environment should find ready translation into the more structured environment of institutions; thus we would hope that hospital and prison workers will be as interested in this demonstration as social workers or school counsellors.

To those trained in the traditions of mental health work, and to those who have been influenced by it, behavior modification brings another challenge and another refreshment: the laws of learning, like the rains, fall upon us all. There are no separate principles for abnormal behavior and for normal, and the "mentally ill" are no longer supposed to behave, or to learn, by different rules than their brothers. In this way, principles for intervention find application as readily to the delinquent as to the neurotic, and as appropriately to the slow learner as to the school phobic. Thus the helping professions can extend their concern to the stepchildren: the delinquent, the culturally deprived, the behavior disordered, the socially disarticulated—that vast sea of problem-beset individuals who are considered by psychiatrists as "unmotivated." In behavior modification "unmotivated" is not presented as a diagnosis; rather, the creation of motivation is the kernel of the enterprise.

For these reasons also, we have chosen to conduct this demonstration with a group of those very stepchildren: the behaviorally disordered, underachieving, pre-dropout, delinquent, and predelinquent youth. Indeed, since the publication of the Lee Robins work, *Deviant Children Grown Up* (1966), it is possible to assert that the behaviorally deviant child should be the principal target for the helping professions, since mental disorder and social deviance are both predictable from childhood behavior disorders; whereas those children manifesting the signs which alarm the mental health professions—shyness, social withdrawal, nervousness, etc.—seem to be those children who "get well" spontaneously. These, then, are the children who become problem adults, and they are the targets for the interventions reported here.

Following the presentation of the detailed argument, the review of relevant prior research, and the articulation of the theoretical material, this book becomes, for awhile, a "how-to-do-it" manual. In Chapters V and VI, we have attempted to share with the reader a wide variety of techniques, sample intervention plans, and many many case studies. Although there are certainly no fixed or limited number of intervention techniques, the three-year experience of the authors and their associates may provide some starting points for the reader's own creativity. In Chapter VII, the difficulties and pitfalls inherent in this enterprise will be detailed, as will those of our mistakes.

In Chapter VIII the book reverts to that hard substance which is the core of the behavior modification activity: the examination of data. As will be seen, behavior modification and the documentation of that modification are inseparable. The presentation and analysis of the research data will allow the reader to judge the magnitude of those behavior changes which were achieved, as well as their value. The results appear to compare quite favorably with any heretofore presented on such a population.

In the final chapter there is a small procedural manual for those who will want to begin a behavioral program. Research implications are reviewed also, and finally we address ethical and professional issues. For a time ethical charges and countercharges were hurled between the trenches of behaviorists and traditionalists. That debate as to whether behavior modification is "ethical" is no longer interesting. Such phrasing has been used to justify the political territories of the traditionalists, and has been used equally sanctimoniously by the modifiers. By Chapter IX we believe it will be clear that the issue of the ethical qualities of human control can be viewed, not with reflexive flight, but with a responsible and informed awareness that human interdependence is an existential condition, and requires the clarity and courage of true ethical choices which are only allowed when a technology presents the actual possibilities of good and evil.

At the end, the discontent of the helping professions may not be allayed, but only clarified, or replaced. The aim of science is to answer old questions, of course, but more truly it aims toward the formulation of new questions, new discontents. This process is called research.

Reference

Robins, L. N. *Deviant children grown up.* Baltimore, Maryland: Williams & Wilkins, 1966. 351 pp.

CHAPTER I

Helping: The Professional Decline and Reorganization

No field of treatment or rehabilitation, no organized attempt to alter human behavior, is without continual confrontation by evidence that the environment in which the individual is embedded is principally responsible for the organization or disorganization, the maintenance or change, the appearance or disappearance of any behavior. A persistent theme in any account of mental health work is the failure of treatment techniques in the face of an adverse environment. How often the therapist reports treatment setbacks as the patient renews an old relationship. A common lament of mental hospital personnel is the disappearance of improved behavior with the patient's return to his natural environment. The environment, in fact, is usually regarded as the principal source of recidivism. The child case worker can recount many instances of the undoing of his therapeutic work by a mother who in one way or another punishes the child for his new behaviors or rewards him for returning to the old. The school counselor knows of the teacher who belittles the students' academic attempts or fails to attend to fledgling approaches to classroom adjustment. The discharged and "reformed" adolescent is soon apprehended by the local police as he rejoins his old delinquent group. The alcoholic falls by the wayside as he is tempted by well-meaning cronies or pressured by a wife or boss.

Therapeutic failure in the face of counteracting natural influences, though common, is largely undocumented. Only recently have the professions faced it as phenomenon. Most surprising, however, has been the failure of the professions to develop ways of directing the forces of the natural environment toward therapeutically congruent ends. Rather than involve the environment in therapeutic reorganization, and, hence, harness the enormous influence on behavior available there, the professions have established the natural environment as the enemy of therapeutic intervention. Although the interaction of the individual and his environment is enormously complex, and discouraging to the therapist charged with helping the patient modify his behavior, the neglect of the natural environment as a force in therapeutic programs is serious. Only recently is this oversight being corrected by gradual changes in professional outlook, research, and community effort. The report of the Joint Commission on Mental Illness and Health (1961), for example, represents significant recognition of the importance of environmental forces in helping efforts.

The Joint Commission on Mental Illness and Health was established by Congress under the Mental Health Study Act of 1955. The recommendations of this Commission followed five years of study and were instrumental in the enactment of the Community Mental Health Centers Act of 1963 which provided federal aid for the establishment of comprehensive community centers (Smith & Hobbs, 1966). Only recently has the full significance of both the study and the Act begun to be realized. It is recognized socially, politically, and professionally that the real potential for helping and for behavioral change lies in the natural environment. Treatment in the community, by the community—this is the central theme of the Joint Commission's report.

The removal of the individual from his social surroundings and his placement in a large hospital has not been a successful form of treatment. The reasons are many. Most obvious is that the hospital frequently disrupts the social relations of the patient without replacing them, or else it replaces them with a social milieu foreign to the individual, bizarre by outside standards, or inadequate as a relearning device. The patient who sits in the ward for long periods of time and watches television, attends occupational and group therapy, and interacts exclusively with other patients and ward staff simply is not acquiring those skills which would help him reintegrate with his family and friends and develop control over the environment which sent him to the hospital originally. The natural result of hospitalization often is increased disorganization of social behavior rather than its acquisition or reorganization.

In many instances there is an intensive attempt on the part of a hospital administration to establish a "therapeutic milieu" which will teach the patient social and occupational skills. These programs, however, can seldom prepare the individual for his particular social life, his particular family, his place of employment, and his community. Sometimes the inadequacies are obvious. An example is the hospitalized Southwest Indian who is surrounded by an environment which is designed to develop middle class urban behaviors and who must return and reintegrate into reservation life. But analogous discrepancies exist between the hospital milieu and the waiting community for almost any patient.

The parallels with any institutional setting are obvious. The youth sent to the state industrial school frequently returns as a more skilled delinquent. The behaviors which he acquires in the formal treatment program are not ones that are useful in helping him maintain nondelinquent behaviors in a delinquent culture. His academic progress, his shop skills, his deportment record, and all the other advances which contribute to his release fall before the forces of the environment to which he returns. Frequently, in fact, his institutional experience may enable him to assume a more rewarding and influential position in his delinquent peer culture.

It is not difficult to discover these inadequacies of institutional treatment; it is not surprising that the Joint Commission recommended the abolishment of large institutions at great distances from the home of the patient and suggested that the treatment of behavior disturbances should take place in the natural environment. It is the comprehensive community mental health center which was charged with bringing all the forces of the community to bear on the treatment, education, and training necessary to reintegrate one of its own members (Smith & Hobbs, 1966). The establishment of such centers across the land has been slow, however, probably due to the failure of community and professional leaders to recognize the important implications of the community mental health center concept.

M. Brewster Smith and Nicholas Hobbs (1966), in an article entitled "The Community and the Community Mental Health Center," clarify the characteristics of the community center concept and the professional reorganizations necessary to implement it. They suggest that if the place and personnel of therapeutic intervention are not to be separate from the community, if the "continuity of concern" is to be maintained, if disordered behavior is to be approached through the social system in which the individual is embedded, then it will become imperative that large numbers of people not now considered to be mental health workers nor "professional" people, in the mental health sense, be recruited and trained to join the helping force. The Smith and Hobbs paper calls for the deprofessionalization of the task of helping. These authors recognize that the Mental Health Center Act is likely to require a revolution in traditional professional treatment and organization if it is to be truly implemented.

Thus the mental health professions have been given a charge which they are ill-prepared to implement. They are being called upon to make the environment of the individual a principal focus of intervention, when tradition has practically ignored it. Techniques for using and training nonprofessionals have hardly been developed, and perhaps the most serious handicap to reorganization is the basic concept of "mental illness." The physical illness model of human experiential and behavioral problems does not readily support either environmental intervention or deprofessionalization. Thus the notion of mental illness may well be preventing its own "cure."

THE ILLNESS MODEL AND ITS CONSEQUENCES

The illness model applied to behavior results in a concept of behavioral origins concealed within the individual. Abnormal behavior, in particular, tends to be interpreted as deriving from a set of internal conditions (anxieties, thoughts, wishes, impulses, desires, etc.) much as physical illness is regarded as the result of viruses, germs, organic conditions, and the like. Such a concept has worked well in physical medicine and, indeed, a science of physical medicine has developed providing concrete data on internal conditions and the techniques of their modification. The model of treatment of the individual, no matter what his particular symptoms, usually begins with the modification of the internal conditions causing the symptoms. The environment is treated only to prevent further occurrence or reoccurrence of the disease. For example, an individual may come to the physician with symptoms which lead the physician to believe that the body of the patient has been invaded by *Treponema spirochetes*. Although he knows the source of the disease is somewhere in the external environment, the treatment of the individual must begin independently of the contributing source. His internal condition must be modified before the overt symptoms will disappear. Hence, though the illness originated in the environment, the internal condition of the individual is the most effective point of intervention. The physician might then report to public health officials, who, in turn, might attempt to modify environmental conditions in order to prevent further outbreaks of syphilis in the population, or reoccurrence in the individual patient.

Traditionally, the mental illness therapist begins in the same way. He alters the internal conditions of the patient (e.g., reduces his anxiety) and relieves the overt symptoms. The method, however, is not as sensible as in the case of physical illness. First, there is little data on the internal conditions accompanying the overt behaviors. Second, there is little relationship between the treatment method and the actual internal conditions. Finally, there are no antibodies, serums, prophylactics, medicines, injections, or operations protecting the individual from the debilitating aspects of the unhealthy environment.[1] In short, the most effective point of inter-

---

[1] We of course recognize that certain bodily dysfunctions affect behavior adversely and that all behaviors have their physiological concomitants. We do not wish to argue with medical science but with the pseudomedical models in much of contemporary mental health.

vention with the individual displaying behavioral disturbance is most likely the disturbing environment rather than the disturbing set of internal conditions.

The prevalent, almost exclusive tendency of the mental health professions to rely on the medical model of treatment, has also involved the reliance on personnel, procedures, and organizations which derive from medical practice, and thus deemphasize the importance of the environment as a locus for treatment. These professions have borrowed from the scientifically and technically based medical model the attitude that the modification of behavior must take place in a professional location (office or hospital) at the hands of a trained professional. They also have indicated clearly that involvement of individuals in the natural environment is not only undesirable but probably dangerous and unethical. Parents have been so threatened with the dire consequences of attempting to change behaviors of their children that many are afraid to maintain even the natural controlling relationships necessary for proper execution of their parental role. Teachers have been so warned about the "mentally ill child" that they frequently avoid subjecting certain children to the natural consequences of classroom behavior and omit them from the learning situation. Soon such children do indeed begin to exhibit the symptoms of their suspected mental illness. From the illness point of view, the sophisticated individual in the natural environment is one that recognizes early symptoms, and quickly refers the individual to the professional person. The doctor and his helpers then quickly exclude members of the natural environment from the treatment process.

Even if the excluded laymen were to attempt ameliorative action, there is an alarming lack of theoretical orientation to guide them. Most theories of therapeutic intervention are intrapsychic in nature. The controlling variables of behavior and the locus of professional help are held to be in the mind.

Theories of personality and mental functioning are of little value to the layman, who finds theory, when available, to be technical, difficult, and esoteric. Intrapsychic theory, and particularly psychoanalysis, seldom help men to deal effectively with their fellowmen on a day-to-day basis, and more often are sources of humor and incredulity.

Techniques of psychotherapy have also been of limited utility to the lay public. Psychotherapy does not involve concepts or terms related to everyday human experience and, in fact, often contradicts what is "common sense" about human behavior. Further, therapeutic techniques are largely developed for use in a professional relationship and hence have no bearing on real life settings and issues. Where in psychotherapeutic technique, for example, can a parent whose teenage son is refusing to stay in at night and is skipping school find concrete advice? Should he listen and try to reflect and clarify the underlying emotion, hidden meaning, and attitude? Should he try to interpret the behavior and reassure the boy of his love? Most parents would find such advice difficult to understand and contrary to their inclinations.

The weakest aspect of contemporary therapeutic theory and technique, however, is not this. Rather it is the failure to guide the non-professional person in helping people. Professional mental health personnel simply do not know what to tell people to do. They neither have the data at hand on which to make clear-cut recommendations, with faith in the outcome, nor do they have strong theoretical principles dictating specific lay behavior. There has developed in most therapeutic techniques a strong prohibition against giving direct advice and telling a patient what to do and how to manage his life. There are several theoretical rationales for this. The probable reason, however, is that no techniques produce a reliable outcome. The net result is passivity in therapist behavior. We are very ill-prepared indeed to begin helping communities and people in the natural relationship assume the responsibility for therapeutic reorganization.

If we are to bring the powerful influences of the natural environment to bear on the behavior of the so-called disturbed person, if we are to have community involvement and real community-based treatment, and if community clinics are really to function as community organizers, then we must recognize the weaknesses of some cherished attitudes and procedures. We must be willing to abandon and modify some of our most admired concepts. One of these, and the one which most effectively prohibits progress in environmental involvement, is the concept of mental illness.

For decades it has been argued that the concept of mental illness has made major contributions to the humanizing of man's treatment of man. Indeed, the history of societies' treatment of their deviates has been a gruesome one. Harsh, punitive, and inhumane practices both within institutions and in the free environment were characteristic reactions to the behavior deviate at the time that the mental illness concept was developed. The redefinition of the deviate from one who is wicked, to one who is ill, has made for greater "kindness" toward him. The deviate who is "sick" thus obtains all the perquisites of the physically ill person: less is expected of him in terms of energy and responsibility. He is not expected to work as productively, he is allowed rest and indulgence, and a period of convalescence (with its attendant dependency) is granted. A man is not to be faulted for contracting a disease, and even though isolation or ostracism may be necessary he is to be pitied rather than punished. Most behavior deviates would prefer such treatment to exorcism or incarceration, and the mental illness concept is generally credited with establishing more humane attitudes and behaviors toward those exhibiting a greater range of deviation from cultural norms.

This belief, however, will not bear total scrutiny. The definition of the deviate as sick is not nearly so kind as it first appears. While it has generally eliminated harsh methods, many have been changed only by definition. (Electroconvulsive shock treatment is now therapy, rather than torture.) Beyond such false gains, however, there are two major consequences of the illness concept which are far from kind. The first of these is the gross dehumanization of the "mentally ill."

In many ways, it is more degrading to be removed from responsibility for one's behavior than to be punished for it. Millions of mentally ill have been persuaded that their own behaviors and experiences are distorted manifestations of their diseased minds. This persuasion is a vital component of psychotherapeutics; a deviate must be brought to acknowledge his own illness before he can be treated. He must admit his own incompetence and seek the "help" of others. All psychotherapists know that a patient cannot be treated unless he "wants help." In other words, he must renounce his independence and self-sufficiency, and acknowledge his helplessness. Not only do mental health professionals typically require such a reduction of the patient's self-regard, but active realistic steps are taken to ensure that patients do indeed earn their newfound loss of self-respect. In many states, the mentally ill are not allowed to operate motor vehicles; in others they are not allowed the vote! Employment opportunities may be forever restricted for those undergoing a period of mental hospitalization. Hospital staffs must continually "prepare" the patient for the stigma which the concept of mental illness has so kindly provided for him. The flagrant abuse of civil liberties which the court-committed patient undergoes is without parallel in criminal corrections, and frequently involves incarceration without adequate counsel or confrontation of the accuser, open-ended "sentencing," and the like. These practices are widely accepted and are derived consistently and logically from the disease model of deviance. The sick mind cannot assume responsibility for itself; it must be cared for.

The second major misfortune which devolves from the illness model is that the socially prescribed behaviors for the sick person are those very behaviors which intefere with the correction of the problem. For example, surrounded by social stimuli which call forth dependent behaviors, the patient is hard pressed to emit responses of assertion and independence which define mental health. Many students of psychopathology suggest that the most salient single feature of the behavior of the mentally ill is that of self-centeredness; yet a pattern of self-indulgent behavior, appropriate to the convalescent physically ill individual, may prevent the development of new skills in interpersonal relationships which would foster the reentry into a reciprocating social environment. Examples abound; suffice it to say that "sick" role behaviors which treatment requires are often antagonistic to the "well" behaviors which treatment seeks.

None of this present argument should be construed as a denial that physical disorders of structure and function can affect behavior, nor that such disorders are the cause of some deviant behaviors. Endocrinological and nervous system disorders bear well-documented relationships to some patterns of behavior disturbance, and it is certainly unwise and irresponsible for any of the helping professions to ignore these potential components as their helping techniques are formulated. It is, however, equally unwise and irresponsible to assume that because a few behavior disorders require physical intervention, all, or even most, disorders of behavior should be managed by the same conceptual and operational model.

The proof is in the pudding; and although it is outside the province of this volume to report on the decades of evaluation studies of the psychotherapeutic effort, it has become very clear that the promise of the medical model has been greater than its achievement.

In the past two decades, a science of behavior quite distinct from the medical model has come into existence. We are beginning to recognize some advantages of understanding deviance from an alternate point of view. For example, let us return to the challenge of deprofessionalization of the helping enterprise. The marshalling of the community in the therapeutic endeavor amounts to the delegation of responsibility in prevention, detection, and treatment. The illness model will not allow for such delegation. The very words themselves, illness, health, disease, therapy, treatment, and detection, suggest that anything but professional action is inappropriate. On the other hand theories of disorders which view behavior largely as a function of the external social environment implicate nonprofessional involvement much more satisfactorily. As yet, we have not developed a language for talking about mental health issues in anything but medical terms. The professions which propose to involve the total community in therapeutic work will have to develop new techniques, new professional roles, theory, and language. Then the community will be able to disperse responsibility to individuals and agencies not traditionally part of the helping profession: family members, teachers, recreation directors, ministers, bartenders, police, courts, unions, gang members, and all other individuals and agencies that constitute the social ecology of the individual. The role of a professional in a so-called center or clinic is that of a coordinator of these natural therapeutic forces. Treatment in the form of a one-to-one relationship between therapist and patient cannot be maintained as the basic model for operation in such a system.

There have been some pioneer explorations in mental health deprofessionalization. Rioch (Pines, 1962) trained housewives to function as psychotherapists in a large eastern city. These were bright, young college graduates who readily profited from training sessions in basic therapeutic principles. Bartenders in a midwestern city were trained to recognize certain symptoms of disturbance in their customers and to refer them to appropriate sources of help. Clergy, teachers, and others are often given some training in how to deal with certain rather simple problems, how to recognize the more serious ones and how to refer persons to the appropriate sources of treatment.

The principle impetus for these explorations has been the severe shortage of traditional mental health workers. It is apparent that the current demand for trained professional workers far exceeds the supply, and that the disparity is growing. A response to this situation has been the intensification of efforts to produce "qualified professionals," but there is no evidence that this effort is successful. In fact, many training institutions are turning away from the task of training workers in order to focus their efforts on producing theoreticians and researchers (Gordon, 1965). Under this pressure, stop-gap measures have been introduced and some of the traditional professional responsibilities have been handed over to nonprofessional workers in special training programs.

These attempts to use nontraditional workers have not produced many new concepts of theory and organization into mental health work. The bartender is taught to recognize certain serious behaviors, but he is still taught that they are symptoms of underlying illness, he is still told that they would be dangerous to deal with himself, and he is still instructed to refer the customer to the trained professional individual. The role which he has been taught to assume and from which he relieves the professional is *diagnostic screening*. He is acting as an intake worker and performing initial psychiatric screening in the cocktail lounge. This does little to relieve the problem. The mental health field is not suffering from lack of diagnoses. The real problem is what to do about the behaviors once they have been given some diagnostic label. The bartender is cautioned not to attempt to enter into any therapeutic relationship himself. In other words, he should not attempt to counsel the customer except to refer him to a professional helper. This is wise because we do not yet know of any way the bartender might help. We have nothing to tell him to do, and it is easy to imagine him doing something that will not help and might even harm the patient.

The housewife may be trained in certain concepts of psychotherapy. She is relieving the therapist and the "treatment need." Still her training is based on therapeutic conventions, (such as being a good listener) which are usually known to help occasionally, and at least not to harm. But she is entering into an artificial relationship by virtue of having the qualifications necessary to take over the role functions of the traditional therapist.

It must be emphasized that the solution does not lie in encouraging the layman to go ahead and see what he can do with the patient. This would be folly. Rather we are suggesting that the natural environment contains potential for therapeutic effect and that this potential does not lie in the capacity of persons in the environment to assume traditional therapeutic role functions. This can not only interfere and detract from their natural function, but also would seem to result frequently in watered down and weakened forms of traditional technique. The therapeutic potential of natural relationships lies within their natural effectiveness and relationship to the behavior of the patient. What is needed to harness this therapeutic force are new concepts of therapeutic organization and technique. How does bartender behavior affect customer behavior? How does housewife behavior affect child behavior, husband behavior, neighbor behavior, and club member behavior? The answers to these questions bear on environmental therapeutic effectiveness.

It is the role of the mental health professions to develop these much needed techniques, to develop ways of working with the natural environment in areas of training, supervision, and general management. The professions must do something more than attempt new roles and new careers based on old concepts.

A very substantial beginning in the development of environmental intervention techniques has grown out of the applications of learning theory to human behavior. These studies are frequently designated inclusively as "behavior modification studies" and the techniques as "behavior modification techniques." For the most part they have not been a product of clinicians or mental health workers in general. As a matter of fact, they have only recently begun to be known in, and have any impact on, the mental health fields. Nevertheless, they are a promising development for mental health at a time when new approaches are badly needed.

A ROLE FOR THE ENVIRONMENT: LEARNING THEORY

A characteristic of behavior modification techniques, with particular implications for the helping professions, is the frequent reliance upon persons in the natural environment of the subject to be the effective agents of change. This is a direct result of a salient feature of learning theories themselves: the specification of the relationship between behaviors and controlling events in the environment. In fact contemporary learning theories which are central to the science of behavior are to a very great degree a series of statements about the relationships between behaviors and the surrounding environment. A portion of the surrounding environment that obviously has great influence on human behavior is the surrounding social environment, i.e., the behavior of other people.

It has never been a stated aim of the workers in behavior modification to deprofessionalize mental health techniques. Rather it has been their aim to show that human behavior is controlled by the environment and that certain reorganization of the relationships between human behavior and the surrounding milieu will result in changes in behavior. It so happens that other people are, to a large extent, the environmental events which affect human behavior, so that the researchers exploring ways of demonstrating environmental control of human behavior very frequently work with the human aspects of the subject's ecology. Likewise, there has not been a strong preference to work with disturbed behaviors although many researchers do. However, problems for which there are no good solutions are likely to be the subject of research so that behavior modification techniques have been developed around a wide range of behaviors which in the medical model would be labeled "pathological." Of course, learning theories have also led to the study of the variables controlling normal as well as abnormal behaviors since there is no distinction between the two classes of behavior in learning theory. Learning theories tend to specify the functional relationship between behavior and the environment, and application to human behavior often results in hypotheses about the way an individual's behavior is some function of the behavior of another individual in the environment. Behavior modification techniques thus tend to specify roles which individuals in the environment of the patient may play to modify the patient's behavior. Since these derivatives of learning theory specify the behavioral role of an individual in the natural environment of the patient, a theoretical model is becoming available for determining specific appropriate behaviors for individuals in the natural environment of the subject. Learning theories thus hold much promise for the development of models of environmental intervention and consultation to the natural environment.

PRINCIPLES OF BEHAVIOR MODIFICATION

The proposition that the behavior of an organism is a direct function of the environment is most clearly and vigorously set forth in the writings of B. F. Skinner (see, for example, Skinner, 1953). A substantial proportion of the behavior modification work is based on the operant conditioning principles which Skinner specified and systematized. Other researchers have drawn their guiding principles from the writings of Pavlov (Salter, 1961), Hull (Eysenck, 1960), Guthrie (Patterson, 1965), and others. In general, however, the bulk of the work falls into two categories: those studies based on classical conditioning in which the behavior in question is regarded to have reflexive properties and those studies in which the behavior is regarded to be nonreflexive and to have instrumental properties. The principles of classical and operant conditioning have been defined and expanded in several writings (Skinner, 1953; Reynolds, 1968) so that only their general characteristics will be described here.

The classical conditioning group is best represented by Wolpe (1958) who has demonstrated the modification of several classes of behavior with his techniques. Although he and his colleagues have made use of individuals in the natural environment, such a focus is not central to their work. The behaviors which hold central position in the Wolpian approach are the responses of the autonomic nervous system which follow, theoretically, the laws of classical conditioning. Current concepts of anxiety regard autonomic nervous system responses as, for the most part, the physiological concomitant of anxiety. Since it is the arousal of anxiety by certain stimuli in the environment (the fear-producing stimuli) which cues or sets off the disturbing or disturbed behaviors, anxiety occupies the central position in Wolpian concepts. The patient is "disturbed" by his anxiety plus whatever avoidance behavior it may set off. As long as a situation elicits anxiety states (intense autonomic nervous system activity) the patient will be disturbed and may exhibit other maladaptive escape behaviors. The key to intervention in the Wolpian technique is to arrange for the anxiety to occur at very low, and hence manageable levels, which will not prevent the individual's engaging in adaptable behaviors. The general technique for avoiding anxiety in a specified situation is to condition a response incompatible with anxiety. A commonly chosen incompatible response is relaxation. Patients are taught to relax, sometimes with hypnosis, as part of the counter-conditioning technique. In the process of desensitization, an anxiety hierarchy, that is, a list of anxiety producing situations, is constructed for the patient from least to most anxiety producing, and the incompatible response conditioned to each. Wolpe and others have made some use of individuals in the natural environment of the patient to effect the desensitization process and several important suggestions for environmental intervention techniques can be derived from desensitization procedures.

Behavior modification techniques based on operant conditioning principles usually represent attempts to deal with maladaptive behavior directly, rather than with underlying events, such as autonomic nervous system behavior or anxiety. All behavior, of course, has its neural concomitants which might conceivably be the focus of intervention. The focus of the operant conditioning techniques upon the external environment is not so much a denial of underlying processes as it is a choice dictated by theoretical consistency, practical considerations, and the emerging evidence for the value of the operant assumptions.

Operant theory as a body of axioms and principles is a very complex collection of information of which only a small part is used in techniques of behavior modification. The relationship central to most studies of application is that between behavior and the events which follow it, that is, between behavior and its consequences. In fact, "operant" can be defined as a behavior which "operates" on the environment and produces some change in it. The collection of principles dealing with behavior and its consequent events is often called *reinforcement theory*. Although there are other environmental events which exert a controlling influence on behavior, besides those consequent to the behavior, reinforcement theory remains the predominant theoretical orientation of most techniques of behavior modification.

The fact that reinforcement theory emphasizes the relationship between behavior and its consequent events often makes the theory seem commonsensical to one hearing it for the first time. The consequences of behaviors, of course, encompass the system of rewards and punishments in which the behaviors are embedded. The principles of reinforcement are concerned with rewards and punishments, and the enormous influence which they have on behavior. All individuals have first hand acquaintance with the effects of reward and punishment, and the culture itself contains many beliefs and customs organized around common consensus about the effects of the consequences of behavior on the behavior itself (e.g., spare the rod and spoil the child). Some of these beliefs are congruent with the data of reinforcement theory; some are not. But whether they are or not, no one who has intentionally attempted to influence the behavior of someone else, or who has been so influenced, can be without some experience concerning the powerful influences exerted on behavior by its rewarding and punishing consequences. Though reinforcement theory has been scientifically and professionally generated, it is highly related to common human experiences and can be useful in providing effective consultation to persons in the everday world.

We shall describe some of the principal tenets of reinforcement theory which are involved in demonstrations of application. Several excellent discussions of operant learning theory are available elsewhere (Bijou &

Baer, 1961; Skinner, 1953; Reynolds, 1968) and anyone seriously interested in the development of behavioral control must necessarily acquaint
himself with these. Here we will describe those principles in common
use in behavior modification techniques and ways in which they may
be applied.

Reinforcement may be described as that event following the occurrence
of a behavior which alters the frequency of the behavior. This, of course,
is exactly what rewards and punishments do. We reward or punish certain
behaviors of the child because we wish to influence the frequency with
which these behaviors occur, i.e., either increase or decrease the frequency
of occurrence. Those events in the environment of an individual which function to modify the frequency of behaviors are reinforcements, by definition.
Some events will increase the frequency of behaviors they follow. We call
these, commonly, rewards and, in the more precise language of operant
reinforcement theory, *positive reinforcers*. Other events will increase the
frequency of behaviors if they are removed following those behaviors.
These are called *negative reinforcers*.

One could probably make a list of the events in his environment which
function as positive and negative reinforcers. They are the events which
control the frequencies of various classes of behavior. We can think of
common reinforcers which control the behavior of children and, indeed,
can imagine the process of maturation to include a broadening of the range
of reinforcing events which influence behaviors. For the infant the range
of reinforcers is relatively narrow. We usually think of food, water, and
comfort as the positive reinforcers. He is not influenced by praise, money,
nice clothes, and opportunities to attend parties. The infant's negative
reinforcers are largely pain-related: open safety pins, food deprivation,
temperature extremes, and uncomfortable positions. He is not affected
by verbal scoldings, fines, threats, and scowls. As the child grows older,
however, more and more events acquire the reinforcing function. Smiles
and other facial expressions, the appearance of certain people, favorite toys,
and many other events become reinforcers. When he begins to talk, words
acquire the positive reinforcing function, i.e., they can increase the frequency of behaviors they follow. One can begin to say "good boy" and
"that was very nice" following behaviors one wishes to increase in frequency
and maintain. One of the most powerful developing reinforcers is attention
from both adults and peers. We commonly talk of "attention getting behaviors" by which we mean behaviors which are maintained by the attention of other people. Everyone is acquainted with the reinforcing function
of adult laughter on child behavior. One laugh following a behavior may
produce a large number of repetitions of that behavior, much like the
adult who continues to repeat the punchline of a joke which has brought

laughter from the audience. However, it is important to recognize that positive reinforcers do not always come in the form of formal rewards or praise. There are many events which may have this function for any given individual. They may be social reinforcers, i.e., come from the behavior of other people, or they may be events in the nonsocial world, such as a block tower falling over, or a beautiful view rewarding the climber.

Two important points are that people vary concerning the number and range of events which function as reinforcers for them and that events gain and lose their reinforcing function. A central issue in learning theory is the process by which reinforcers develop, a subject also important to those working with these principles in applied situations. It can be seen that if an individual is to become socialized he must be reinforced by the events which society uses to increase and maintain target behaviors. A child for whom words do not have reinforcing value is at a distinct disadvantage, for example, because society frequently reinforces in the form of words.

A common reinforcer in the adult world is money—a most interesting one because it is what frequently is called a generalized reinforcer, in this case a "token reinforcer." Money in itself is not particularly reinforcing. Its value derives from the fact that it can be exchanged for other events and things which are reinforcing. One of its advantages is that one need not know what the specific reinforcers for an individual are to be able to maintain certain of his behaviors. The factory manager need not know what a given line worker's particular reinforcers are to be able to maintain his work behavior. Examples of token system management of behavior are increasing in the behavior modification literature (e.g., Birnbrauer *et al.,* 1965; Martin *et al.,* 1967). The technique is the use of reinforcement which comes in the form of a token, which can then be exchanged for another reinforcer. School grades are often of this nature.

Although the preceding discussion emphasizes positive reinforcers, the same sort of analysis is possible for negative reinforcers. The processes of maturation and socialization may involve coming under the control of events that increase the frequency of behaviors which terminate the events. Frowns, threats, traffic tickets, restriction of privilege, and many other events acquire the negative reinforcing function, and as with positive reinforcers, people differ according to the events which bear this functional relationship to their behavior.

In operant theory, reinforcement is an event which follows a behavior; the behavior operates to produce the reinforcement. There is, thus, a contingent relationship between a behavior and its reinforcing events. The reinforcement is produced by the behavior and does not become available except through the behavior. The concept of contingency between behavior and reinforcement is the key concept in behavior modification techniques based on operant principles. Homme (1966), in fact, has described behavior modification work as the management of contingencies between behavior and reinforcing consequences rather than operant conditioning. It is certainly true that many studies involve arranging conditions so that certain reinforcing events occur as a consequence to (and only as a consequence to) certain behaviors.

What sorts of contingency relationships can exist between behavior and reinforcing events? Not as many as one might think. Four different relationships between behavior and reinforcement can be described. Although not an exhaustive list, they constitute the principal operations performed in operant behavior modification work and their outcomes can be theoretically defined. These contingencies are based on the presentation and removal of positive and negative reinforcing events.

Behavior may result in the *presentation of a positive reinforcer* (smiles, money, food, privileges, etc.). One would say that a positive reinforcer was contingent on that behavior. The behavior produced it and it does not occur unless the behavior or certain behaviors do occur. Salary is contingent on work; no work, no salary. This is the common concept of reward. We may reward our child for a good job by adding a bonus to his allowance contingent upon the job. The mother who holds out a cookie to her toddling infant to tempt him to cross the room is entering into the contingency management business and making cookies contingent on walking.

A behavior may result in the *presentation of a negative reinforcer* (pain, frowns, threats, ridicule, etc.). One would say that a negative reinforcer is contingent on this behavior. The behavior produced it, and it would not occur unless the behavior occurred. This is the common concept of punishment. The mother spanks the child for running into the street. She is establishing a contingency between running into the street and pain.

A third type of contingent relationship between behavior and reinforcing events is also commonly regarded as punishment, though it is a different sort of operation. A behavior may result in the *removal of a positive reinforcer* (removal of TV, money, smiles, bicycle, or being allowed to stay up late, etc.).

The fourth type of contingency involves behavior and negative reinforcers. A behavior may result in the *removal of a negative reinforcer* (termination of threats, scoldings, restrictions, pain, etc.). This contingency is often overlooked and is usually not regarded as rewarding even though the behavior may be affected in the same way that rewards affect it.

A mother may threaten her child with all sorts of painful events until he cleans up his room. When he cleans his room she stops threatening or nagging. Hence, the removal of this negative reinforcer is contingent upon room cleaning. Behaviors which are maintained because they keep away threats, scoldings, pain, and other negative reinforcers are often called *avoidance behaviors* because they function to remove or avoid negative reinforcers which are contingent upon not engaging in these behaviors.

There is one other condition which needs to be defined. When a behavior is being maintained by some reinforcing event, it is possible to reduce the frequency of the behavior by disrupting its contingency with the reinforcement, e.g., removal of the salary contingent on work; taking away praise; eliminating the privilege for which the teenager is mowing the lawn. There are many possible examples. This principle is the arrangement of conditions so that the reinforcing event which has been maintaining a behavior no longer occurs, or is no longer contingent. The behavior will decrease in frequency. The antics of the attention-getter decrease in frequency when they no longer pay off in attention. The gradual reduction in the frequency of behavior following removal of maintaining reinforcement is called *extinction*. When the behavior no longer occurs or occurs at low frequency for lack of reinforcement, it is said to be extinguished.

All techniques of behavior modification based on operant principles make use of one or another of these contingent relationships and their effects. To summarize, behavior can be increased in frequency and maintained by the addition of positive reinforcers and/or the removal of negative reinforcers. Behavior can be decreased in frequency by the contingent removal of positive reinforcers and/or the addition of negative reinforcers. Behavior can be decreased in frequency and even removed from the repertoire of an organism due to lack of any contingent reinforcing events. If one were to describe many behavior modification techniques, in the simplest way, it would be: arrange and manage reinforcement contingencies such that desired behaviors are increased in frequency and maintained, and undesired behaviors are decreased in frequency and/or removed from the repertoire.

There are aspects of reinforcement theory other than those described above, many of which are important in behavior modification and which will be defined later. For the present, two additional concepts will be introduced. One is the concept of *reinforcement schedules*. Our experience tells us that we are not reinforced every time we engage in behavior, even for high frequency behaviors like work behavior. Reinforcement does not follow every occurrence of a behavior. The schedule according to which the reinforcement does occur is important to the development and modification of behavior and the topic of schedules of reinforcement is a complex one. There are several adequate discussions available (e.g., Reynolds, 1968). The second concept in reinforcement theory is that of differential reinforcement or *shaping*. This is related to the concept of *goal-setting*, or the selection of the behavior to be reinforced. In principle, the shaping technique involves reinforcing only behaviors which resemble the goal behavior in certain characteristics. There is gradual selection through reinforcement of behaviors that approximate the final behavior more and more closely. For example, we reinforce early the young child's attempts at talking even though they are not perfect and only gradually reinforce those performances which are more and more like correct speech. Shaping is a crucial concept in the learning of new behavior. It is also important to behavior modification techniques and will be described in detail.

There are many other principles and techniques which can be used to analyze and to modify behavior; the alternatives are many, and different contingency combinations can be brought into play. The choice between techniques is not always determined by reinforcement theory or other operant principles. The researcher must assess the environment of the individual for potential reinforcers, assess the total repertoire of the person, and take into account the total situation before he decides to try a particular approach in the modification of the behavior. The skills of the clinician (psychiatrist, clinical psychologist, social worker, etc.) are often useful in this process of assessing the total situation and the potentials for establishing certain conditions. Hence, one characteristic of behavior modification work is that it uses, but is not entirely dominated by, learning theory. Not all decisions in a modification program are based on learning theory. Clinical skills need continued refinement and incorporation into intervention techniques.

A behavioral analysis of clinical skills cannot as yet be totally provided, and the enterprise of human helping remains partially an art—which is to say that it has not yet been verbally conceptualized. But certainly many aspects of the skill of the clinician, whether in psychotherapy or behavior modification, involve his ability to identify the reinforcers of his patient, his ability to understand the contingencies which affect the behaviors, and his cognizance of his own contingent responses to the "sick" and the "healthy" behaviors which his clientele emits. The ability to predict behavior and to predict the ramifying consequences of contingency managements requires experience both in practice and in living. The ability to form open, trusting, and accurate relationships is of a value as great in contingency management as in psychotherapy; rapport and empathy will serve the contingency manager well in his efforts to understand the complex articulations of a social environment.

References

Bijou, S. W., and Baer, D. M. *Child development.* Vol. 1. *A Systematic and Empirical Theory.* New York: Appleton, 1961.

Birnbrauer, J. S., Bijou, S. W., Wolf, M. M., and Kidder, J. D. In L. Ullman and L. Krasner (Eds.), *Case studies in behavior modification.* New York: Holt, 1965, pp. 358–363.

Eysenck, H. J. *Journal of Consulting Psychology,* 1952, **16,** 319–324.

Eysenck, H. J. (Ed.) *Behavior therapy and the neuroses.* New York: Pergamon, 1960.

Gordon, J. E. *American Psychologist,* 1965, **20,** 334–343.

Homme, L. E. *Clinical Child Psychology, Newsletter* **4,** 1966.

Joint Commission on Mental Ilness and Health. *Action for mental health.* New York: Basic Books, 1961.

Martin, M., Schwyhart, K., and Wetzel, R. *Journal of Reading,* 1967, **11,** 111–121.

Patterson, G. R. In L. Ullman and L. Krasner, (Eds.), *Case studies in behavior modification.* New York: Holt, 1965, pp. 279–285.

Pines, M. *Harper's Magazine* 1962, **224,** 37–42.

Reynolds, G. S. *A Primer of operant conditioning.* Glenville, Illinois: Scott, Foresman, 1968.

Salter, A. *Conditioned reflex therapy.* New York: Putnam, 1961.

Skinner, B. F. *Science and human behavior.* New York: Macmillan, 1953.

Smith, M. B., and Hobbs, N. *American Psychologist,* 1966, **21,** 499–509.

Wolpe, J. *Psychotherapy by reciprocal inhibition.* Stanford, California: Stanford Univ. Press, 1958.

CHAPTER II

Behavior Modification and the Natural Environment: Clinical Implications

Behavior modification techniques are not an organized body of instructions and principles for changing human behavior. The body of work which one might demark as the behavior modification literature varies enormously. One might imagine a continuum ranging from highly controlled laboratory explorations at one end, to a search for means of controlling complex human behavior in the natural environment of the subject at the other. At the laboratory end, for example, one might find studies of the effect of reinforcement schedules on the lever-pressing responses of children (Long, 1959). At the other end may be studies on the effect of reorganization of contingencies on delinquent behavior of gang members (Schwitzgebel, 1964). The work in between varies in the complexity of the response studied, complexity of the environment, the degree to which control is exercised over the environment, the degree to which functional relationships between the environment and the behavior are demonstrated, and the goal of the researcher.

We often hear advances in the behavioral sciences described in ideal form as a logical progression from one end of this continuum to the other. That is, principles can be discovered in the laboratory and control established over simple and basic processes. Gradually the analysis can be extended into more and more complex situations and interactions with "real life," with these complexities understood in terms of the more basic processes (e.g., Bijou and Baer, 1961; Skinner, 1953). No such orderly progression is taking place. Work has not proceeded along the continuum, but rather attempts to study human behavior have emerged rather simultaneously at all points. This fact robs behavior modification literature of the characteristic of order.

There is much disagreement among workers. Many laboratory researchers view the work in the natural environment as uncontrolled, even irresponsible, "fooling around." They regard the attempt to extend learning principles to the natural environment as premature. At best, it is not research since the demonstration of a basic functional relationship is frequently absent and nothing new added to basic principles. Many laboratory workers resent the license exercised by some "clinicians" who seem to distort their hard won principles and techniques and pass them off as research. The clinicians, on the other hand, resent the laboratory snobbishness with which their explorations are treated. There are arguments about the interpretation of findings, warning about moral and ethical issues, critiques, and countercritiques. Behavior modification is an area surrounded by professional ferment, confusion, and discord. In short, it has all the characteristics of scientific advance.

What, then, is the common element defining the continuum of professional output? It is probably a quality of the worker rather than of his work. These researchers are held together by the belief that a science of human behavior is somehow possible. They believe that, to some degree, human behavior is lawful and lawfully related to the surrounding environment. They believe that, to some degree, human behavior changes as the surrounding milieu changes and that human behavior can be modified by modifying that milieu. They rely upon some form of contemporary learning theory to provide insights into the way human behavior and the environment interact. They manage to communicate and they are aware of the professional difficulties.

RESEARCH IN THE LABORATORY

The laboratory end of the continuum blends imperceptibly into basic process research and animal work. These form the foundation for applied work. Some researchers have demonstrated that controlled laboratory work with human subjects can yield valuable information about basic processes, and that animal findings can be replicated at the human level. Long, for example, developed a laboratory technique for exploring the effects of reinforcement schedules with children, and demonstrated lawful relationships between changes in the rate of a simple response and changes in the schedule of reinforcement (Long, 1959). Bijou and Sturges (1959) explored the effects of different kinds of reinforcement in the laboratory while Azrin and Lindsley (1956) demonstrated laboratory control of a cooperative response between pairs of children. These studies explored the extension of laboratory techniques, including simple responses (bar press, lever pull, marble drop, etc.), to the control of behavior in normal human subjects.

Basic laboratory findings took on broader professional meaning and social significance as researchers demonstrated that the behavior of so-called abnormal subjects in the laboratory was lawful and subject to the same kinds of control as the behavior of normal subjects. New ways of defining the abnormal characteristics of behaviors developed. On the basis of laboratory work with autistic children (Ferster & DeMyer, 1962), Ferster was able to develop a framework for analysis of the interaction of autistic behavior and the natural environment; Ellis *et al.,* (1960) and Bijou and his colleagues studied basic processes with retardates (Bijou & Oblinger, 1960; Bijou & Orlando, 1961), while Lindsley studied the behavior of schizophrenics in a laboratory setting (1956).

The laboratory also contributes to behavior modification literature through the controlled study of socially significant behaviors rather than simple responses chosen for research convenience. There is a relatively long history for this sort of work, which includes studies such as Watson and Rayner's study of phobic behavior (1920). More recent examples include experimental control of stuttering (Flanagan *et al.,* 1959), thumb-sucking (Baer, 1962), imitative behavior (Baer & Sherman, 1964; Bandura, 1963), aggression (Bandura & Walters, 1963), smiling (Brackbill, 1958), and many other behaviors not mentioned here since this is not intended to be an exhaustive review of literature relevant to behavior modification techniques.

RESEARCH IN RESTRICTED ENVIRONMENTS

Further along the continuum, some restricted environment becomes, in essence, the laboratory. Mental hospital wards, juvenile institutions, custodial homes, and classrooms all constitute limited environments in which it is possible to control the amount and variety of stimulation. The work of Ayllon and his colleagues is representative, in that it occurred on the wards of mental hospitals rather than in a specially designed laboratory; mechanical reinforcer dispensers and mechanisms were not used, the target behaviors were ward-appropriate behaviors, and were frequently managed by regular ward personnel rather than researchers (Ayllon, 1963; Ayllon, 1965; Ayllon & Azrin, 1964, 1965; Ayllon & Houghton, 1962; Ayllon & Michael, 1959). In this way, contingency management begins to involve innovations in the training of personnel, techniques of observation and recording, and administration. The success or failure of a demonstration of behavior control rests as much on the researcher's ability to train and administer as it does on the effectiveness of a reinforcing event and its scheduling. If behavior modification work is to be meaningful to mental health problems, pertinent to clinical and educational issues, then the processes of training and administration must be studied as carefully as the processes of contingency management.

The remainder of this discussion of the behavior modification literature will focus on these training and administrative issues, since they become increasingly important as one moves along the continuum toward work in the natural environment. Ayllon's work is a nice starting point relevant to work in environments which are more complex and difficult to control. Although the mental hospital environment may not be thought a "natural" one, it is the only environment for the patient, and Ayllon's techniques involve only the people and events which are natural components of this total environment.

In the selection of personnel for an early study, Ayllon and Michael (1959) chose those individuals who were in most frequent contact with the 19 patients constituting the target population. This group included aides, attendants, and psychiatric and regular nurses. The nurses had a second characteristic important to the nature of the total program in that they enjoyed "a high degree of autonomy with respect to the treatment of the patient [p. 324]." They did not receive psychiatric orders, though the advice of the psychiatric staff could be sought. They administered such things as ground passes, paroles, and even discharges, and they conducted group therapy under psychiatric supervision. They also enjoyed autonomy with respect to research design since they could refuse or discontinue any program suggested by the experimenters.

The first steps in the development of the program were the selection of the target behaviors and the assessment of the environment for potential reinforcers. To accomplish this the experimenters did what may be cruical to technique: they consulted the nurses about the patient behaviors which concerned them the most. In a series of interviews the experimenters sought information about the nature of the problem behaviors, their duration and frequency, the kind and frequency of naturally occurring reinforcement obtained by the patient, and the possibilities of controlling the reinforcement. Problem behaviors included (1) entering the nurses' station and bothering the nurses, (2) psychotic talk, (3) combative behavior.

The experimenters also discussed possible acceptable alternative and incompatible behaviors.

In an effort to measure the frequency of problem behavior, the experimenters developed some recording techniques for the ward staff to use. First, the rate of problem behavior prior to intervention was observed: this is the *baseline* frequency against which post-intervention rate is compared to judge the effectiveness of the intervention technique. Mainly, two recording methods were used. If the problem behavior involved a nurse, she recorded every occurrence. Examples would be meal eating and nurse bothering. If the behavior did not involve a nurse, a time-sampling technique was used. Supplied with a mimeographed record sheet, the recording nurse sought out the patient every half hour and recorded his behavior for from one to three minutes. Ongoing behavior was checked in one of three categories: (1) problem behavior, (2) incompatible behavior, and (3) incompatible behavior that could not replace problem behavior (e.g., eating, sleeping, dressing). Time sampling started after breakfast and ended at bedtime. Between observations the nurse returned to her duties.

Baseline records over the time period desired by the experimenters were not possible because of the newness of this routine to the nursing staff. It was necessary to depend upon the cooperation of the nurses for recording, and since the nature of this procedure was alien to nursing routines, cooperation was poor. At least, adequate baselines were difficult to obtain.

Training of ward personnel began with completion of the initial behavior study. Instruction took place during the ward meetings of the two shifts on duty during the patient's waking hours and was conducted by the experimenter. Training emphasized the general principle of giving and withholding of social reinforcement contingent upon a desired class of behavior. The rest of the instruction focused on specific programs for specific patients. The following illustrates the former: "Reinforcement is something you do for or with a patient, for example, offering candy or cigarettes. Any way you convey attention to the patient is reinforcing [p. 325]." The instructor provided familiar and commonsensical illustrations of the operations of presentation and withdrawal of social reinforcement. Instruction in general principles apparently did not go beyond this, except in the cases of two patients for which nurses received instructions on the operation of aversive control. The following is an example of specific program instruction: "During this program the patient must not be given reinforcement (attention) for her psychotic talk (about her illegitimate child and the men chasing her). Check the patient every 30 minutes and (a) tally for psychotic talk; and (b) reinforce (and tally) sensible talk. If another patient fights with her, avoid making an issue of it. Simply stop the other patient from hurting her, but do so with a matter-of-fact attitude " [p. 327].

At each shift one nurse carried out the time-sampling and recording program. She reinforced behavior according to plan if it occurred during her sampling time. During extinction periods the recording nurse did everything but reinforce. Recording duty was rotated through the nursing staff so that a minimum of 19 nurses were involved in a single program, and more than 100 nurses took part in the total program. The experimenters' duties became almost entirely training and consultation. Rapid personnel turnover required constant training of new staff. Some time was spent in spot-checking nurse behavior (often without their knowledge). Otherwise the experimenter consulted with the staff on record keeping and the techniques of reinforcement and extinction of behavior.

Ayllon has subsequently reported on the shaping by the nursing staff of bathing, dressing, and eating (candy reinforcers were used for part of this, Ayllon, 1965). In a study of food stealing, nurses learned that it is not necessary to verbalize the contingency to the patient (Ayllon, 1963). In studies of towel hoarding and clothes hoarding, nurses recorded verbal behavior of a patient, withheld meals, and collected follow-up data by time sampling over a one-year period. In a later paper Ayllon and Azrin (1964) make a point which is extremely important to behavior modification techniques, though seldom elaborated. Discussing the failure of attendants to cooperate they say: "The results of this study demonstrated that it was necessary to arrange consequences for the patients in addition to providing instructions. This same finding occurred for the attendants. Repeated instructions had been given to the attendant to ensure her making the appropriate statement to each patient. Yet, the tape recording and visual observations revealed that the attendant did not always follow the instructions . . . [p. 330]." The authors comment on the effectiveness of confrontation with this evidence of noncompliance and add, "The results strongly indicate that any procedure that uses attendants to modify the behavior of patients must also provide operant consequences for the attendants [p. 330]."

Tyler (1965) reported on the behavior of a cottage staff charged with recording misbehavior of a delinquent boy in an institution. He pointed out that some of the fluctuations in recorded behavior resulted from the staff's greater attention to contingencies and recording following staff meetings. He also suggested that staff recording of behavior had a reinforcing effect on the behavior itself. Burchard and Tyler (1965) organized the staff of another cottage to maintain an "isolation continency" on antisocial behavior. This staff was instructed as follows: "Whenever Donny displays any unacceptable behavior, he is to be immediately placed in isolation.

Unacceptable behavior is defined as any behavior which would normally require a sanction, verbal or otherwise. If you don't feel the behavior should warrant isolation, then the behavior should be ignored. However, if any action is taken to modify or eliminate the behavior it should be isolation. He should be sent to isolation in a matter-of-fact manner. He should be told in simple terms why he is being sent and any further verbal interaction . . . should be held to a minimum. It is important that you do not become too emotionally involved with Donny. Anyone who feels guilty or for some reason does not send Donny to isolation when his behavior warrants it is not participating in the treatment plan. As long as Donny is fouling up, the more he is sent to isolation, the more effective the treatment program will be [p. 247]."

Wetzel (1966) reports on the training of a child care staff to monitor the stealing behavior of a subject in a children's home. The staff training consisted of four half-hour conferences on general reinforcement principles plus a film on reinforcement. Discussions focused on the applications of these principles to the target's stealing behavior. In this study, the reinforcement consisted of interactions with the cook in the home. No instructions were given her except that she should not interact with the subject if a stealing incident had been reported. She was instructed to say "I'm sorry you took *so-and-so's blank* because now I can't let you come home with me tonight [p. 370]." She was also instructed not to accept or listen to excuse-behavior. The staff entered stealing incidents on a daily chart and reported to the cook. The cook kept a record of sessions missed with the boy because of stealing. As have other researchers, Wetzel reports difficulty in maintaining the program in the institution because of turnover in staff. He also reports inaccurate recording because of staff misunderstandings of the use of the records (e.g, some felt they were turning the subject in) and fluctuations in staff attitude toward the subject (e.g., they became more lenient as Christmas neared).

There are several other descriptions of behavior modification research in restricted settings which rely on persons and events in the environment to manage behavior. Wolf, Risley, and Mees (1964) consulted with the ward staff of a hospital in the management and rehabilitation of an autistic child. Davison (1965) describes a training program for undergraduate college students who would serve as social reinforcers for autistic children. Tharp, Cutts, and Burkholder (1970) describe contingency management in the classroom by the staff of a special education school. In addition, there are many studies which provide excellent material for instituting training programs and programs of behavior modification. The studies of nursery school behavior at the University of Washington (Harris et al., 1964) have many suggestions for nursery school staff in the management, observation, and recording of behavior. The extensive and impressive work of Lovaas and his colleagues (for example, Lovaas *et al.,* 1965, 1966) is indispensible to any program of ward management and the development of social behavior in severely restricted repertoires. These studies differ in the degree to which they rely on usual staff to manage behavior change and the degree to which they report training and administrative procedures when they do use nonprofessional staff. Nonetheless they are a rich source of management techniques.

LABORATORY–ENVIRONMENT RESEARCH

Some important innovations in behavior modification combine techniques and conditions from the laboratory and the natural environment. These studies have important implications for both research and therapeutic efforts. Methods are gradually developing for maintaining a higher degree of experimental control in the natural environment than has been traditional while a new degree of precision and emphasis on evaluation is appearing in therapeutic innovations. One study in particular combined laboratory and natural environment in a very effective manner. It introduced techniques for consultation to the natural environment which have important implications for the organization of services designed to generate and maintain behavioral change. Mention has already been made of the study of Wolf, Risley, and Mees (1964) in training a hospital ward staff to deal with several behaviors in the repertoire of an autistic child. In the later stages of this work the parents were gradually introduced to the techniques and eventually took over the therapeutic role.

Beginning with a one-hour visit, the parents were permitted increasing amounts of time with their child during which a ward attendant observed and instructed them in their handling of specific behaviors. Among the several target behaviors in the repertoire of this subject were the bedtime behaviors of (1) getting up and (2) tantrums. A contingency was developed on the ward involving isolation of the subject for tantrums and room-door-closing for bedtime problems. Parents began by putting the child to bed in the ward under the supervision of an attendant. Later, the subject ". . . spent his first night at home. For a few weeks prior to this, he had been making short home visits accompanied by an attendant. Several days prior to his first night he was taken home in the evening, and after a few minutes of play, went through the routine of getting ready for bed with his siblings. The attendant then brought him back to the ward and put him to bed. Since this trial run was successful, he was sent home to spend the night several days later. He was bathed and put in bed. After about thirty minutes he was heard humming to himself. The mother started to go in to Dicky but the attendant dissuaded her. Fifteen minutes later, Dicky was asleep. Over the next three months, until his release from the hospital, Dicky spent progressively greater proportions of his nights at home. One night a week an attendant went along to observe both Dicky and his parents [pp. 308–309]."

In the same general way, parents learned to handle tantrum behaviors, wearing of glasses, and eating. Under the direction of an attendant they expanded the verbal repertoire which had been initiated in the hospital. Data collected in the hospital and at home attest to the effectiveness of the procedures of both behavioral control and parent training.

This study in many ways is a prototype of several which followed it, as well as of some of the techniques of therapeutic intervention to be discussed later in this book. It combines a controlled laboratorylike situation and the natural environment. The laboratory is used to explore ways of developing behavioral controls and new repertoires. Gradually elements of a broader environment are introduced and controls are extended. Finally the laboratory is used to train persons from the broader environment who have a natural relationship to the subject and who will have principal responsibility for further development and maintenance of behavior. A model of consultation is also developed in the Wolf, Risley, and Mees work. The authors, who served as the "professionals" in this situation, consulted with and trained the attendants on the ward. They worked very infrequently with the subject himself, usually only for training and demonstration purposes. They worked even less frequently with the parents. The parents were trained by the ward staff who also supervised them and collected the data for evaluating the techniques. The amount of professional time involved was greatly reduced from that in traditional work with psychotic children, and the real therapeutic agents were the ward staff and the parents they trained. New skills were passed on to those in the hospital and home environments, skills which potentially can generalize to new situations, behaviors, and patients.

The control of events offered by the laboratory was used by another group of investigators to explore ways of analyzing events maintaining behaviors as well as modifying them. Wahler, Winkel, Peterson, and Morrison (1965) stated the major purposes of their study to be: "(1) to experimentally analyze the mother–child interbehaviors in an effort to specify those variables (i.e., reinforcement contingencies) which may function to maintain the deviant behavior of children; (2) to eliminate these variables in an effort to modify the children's deviant behavior [p. 115]."

Mothers interacted with their children under conditions of controlled observation with the instructions "just play with ——— as you might at home [p. 115]." During these sessions, two observers working in separate observation rooms made written records of mother–child interactions. These records were later used to select the target behaviors and their incompatible acceptable alternatives. The mother's reactions to these behaviors were selected for study both as maintaining stimuli and as possible reinforcers for the alternative behaviors. *Baseline* (prior to intervention) frequency measures were then collected on the target behaviors, the acceptable alternatives, and the mother's reinforcing reactions.

Following baseline sessions, intervention began: the experimenters attempted to change the mother's reaction to her child's behavior. These techniques involved instructions to the mother before and after each session and also used a light in the laboratory playroom to cue the mother's behavior. As the mother improved in ability to follow instructions, the experimenters used the light as a reinforcer rather than a cue. "The mother was now required to discriminate and respond appropriately to her child's behavior without E's cueing [p. 116]." The aim of the procedure was to train the mothers in techniques of behavioral control: extinction of complaint behaviors through ignoring and reinforcement of acceptable behaviors which were incompatible with the complaint behaviors. The mothers were shown the baseline records of their child's and their own behaviors, and the interactions between the two were explained. The concept of ignoring undesirable behavior and reinforcing alternatives were described to her and she was instructed to ignore her child's deviant behavior in further sessions and to respond in an approving way only to his incompatible behaviors. The signal light was described as an aid to help her carry out the instructions. Initially, the mothers watched the light and responded only if it were illuminated; otherwise they were instructed to make no verbal or nonverbal responses to their child. The experimenters illuminated the light following acceptable behaviors. Mothers were eventually trained in effective ways of dealing with their children's deviant behaviors. Several different classes of behavior were defined by these authors and modified by the participating parents. These behaviors were described broadly as commanding behavior, dependent behavior, and stubbornness. (The authors define these behaviors more specifically in their report.) The study included careful monitoring of the effects of the changes in parental behavior and a clear demonstration of parental control by instructing the mother to return to baseline interaction conditions, at which time the behavior returned to baseline.

The laboratory playroom was used by Wetzel *et al.* (1966) to demonstrate to a mother ways in which several behaviors of her autistic child might be controlled and how new behaviors could be developed. In this study the mother, accompanied by a trainer, watched the experimenter's work with her child from a separate observation room. The trainer interpreted for her the techniques being used, discussed applications in the home environment, and suggested specific procedures to be used. The trainer worked closely with the mother, instructed her in techniques for data recording, explained the use of records as a monitoring device, made home visits, and remained in telephone contact. Gradually, through contact with the trainer, the parents were able to broaden the range of their controls and to develop some new behaviors. The authors suggest that laboratory techniques can have an important role in regular clinical work. The aim was to disperse the therapeutic effectiveness into the environment as quickly and as widely as possible. The laboratory was used to explore the functional control of the subject's behavior and to train others who could extend the work to other environments for continued modification and maintenance of behaviors established in the laboratory. Later, the child's special education teacher visited the laboratory to observe him, as did his speech therapist. Thus, in this study, as well as in others, research techniques and therapeutic procedures merge and overlap.

There is a growing segment of behavior modification literature which contains other examples of techniques of controlled training of individuals in the natural environment of a subject. These techniques are aimed at the analysis of the events maintaining the deviant or target behaviors and the exploration of ways to modify them. Russo (1964) had a mother watch therapy sessions with her daughter and eventually take over the sessions herself. Straughan describes a similar approach (1964). Risley and Wolf describe in detail the techniques for developing speech in an autistic child and the procedures by which the parents were trained to maintain and expand the repertoire (1967). Hewett (1965) describes a different technique for teaching speech to an autistic child, the take-over by the parents, and follow-up in a preschool situation. In a sense the work of Wolpe and others, in which a patient is taught a response in the clinical setting by the therapist which can be practiced later in the natural environment, is analogous to the work described above. Wolpe describes cases in which a spouse is given instructions in ways of helping the marriage partner; a patient is given instructions to pass on to others in his environment; the patient learns a new response to be engaged in at other times, for example, relaxation (Wolpe, 1958). Clark, for example, taught a patient relaxation as an incompatible alternative to spasms (1963), while Cooper (1964) taught relaxation as an incompatible response to asthma attacks. The interaction between controlled and natural environments in behavior modification work suggests several ways in which traditional therapeutic efforts might be modified.

RESEARCH IN THE NATURAL ENVIRONMENT

From an experimental point of view, behavior modification in the natural environment is difficult because of problems in the maintenance of control and collection of data. The functioning source of change, should change be accomplished, is difficult to pinpoint and isolate. There are, however, several studies which have attempted behavior modification totally in the natural environment and which contain many implications for the reorganization of therapeutic effort, for training, and for administration. These studies represent the "natural environment" end of the continuum of work output in behavior modification. Boardman (1962) consulted to the parents of a $5\frac{1}{2}$-year-old boy to help them gain control of his running away, lying, and aggressive behaviors. He suggested a punishment contingency. As the therapist, Boardman had only one contact with the boy himself. The remainder of his therapeutic contacts were telephone calls to and from the parents. The therapist at one point telephoned the father and instructed him to go home and aid his wife in the program. In general, Boardman functioned as consultant-administrator of the intervention program. No frequency data are provided in this study, though it reports anecdotally successful behavior modification. Bandura (1962), in a discussion of Boardman's technique, describes the effects of punishment contingencies and suggests several ways in which intervention work in the natural environment based on operant analysis might be effective.

Parents kept records of the duration of screaming and crying in a study to reduce the frequency of bedtime problem behaviors reported by Williams (1959). Parents were instructed to put the child to bed and perhaps talk with him for a little while. After this they were to leave the room, close the door and not return despite tantrum behaviors. This was an extinction program that eliminated the undesirable behavior in about ten occasions. Williams does not report either his training procedures or his record keeping procedures in detail, but the outcome indicates that the parents of the child functioned very well as the therapeutic agents. Lovibond (1963a) instructed both parents and children in the use of an apparatus to aid in the treatment of enuresis. Treatment was closely supervised by telephone and home visits and relevant details were recorded by parents on a standard form. Lovibond does not report his training procedures in detail but about half of the 34 subjects who responded to treatment remained dry for the subsequent two years so that one suspects some real change in both parent and subject behavior.

In a similar study Lovibond (1963b) demonstrated that persons can participate in a complicated research design. Lovibond wished to demonstrate that intermittent reinforcement will affect relapse in enuresis work. Parents were provided with a reinforcement schedule and were instructed by the author to leave the apparatus off when a nonreinforcement interval was scheduled. Parents checked the child before they went to bed, recorded results, checked an "off" on the form, and moved on to the next stage. The study demonstrated that intermittent reinforcement increases resistance to relapse and that persons in the natural environment can function as research assistants in the generation of research data.

To obtain information on delinquent behaviors and experiences Schwitzgebel (1964) went into the natural environments (pool halls, etc.,) to make contact with his subjects. He later established reinforcement contingencies to maintain attendance behavior at tape recording sessions. Several principles were suggested by this author as important to the reinforcement of behavior in the delinquent group. These include the importance of keeping reinforcement "natural" and modest and the sharing of reinforcement between the researcher and subject. The avoidance of punishment contingencies is strongly recommended. No subjects were reprimanded for missing or coming late to a session. Intermittent reinforcement schedules (for example, variable ratio) were also recommended (Schwitzgebel & Kolb, 1964).

There are other reports on the reorganization of behavior in the natural environment. Thorne, Tharp, and Wetzel (1967) report several representative cases and discuss their implications for probation work. Further discussion of work with parents is provided by Hawkins et al. (1966). Bronfenbrenner (1962), in describing methods of Soviet character education, discusses the use of peers in contingency management and systems of reward and punishment distributed on a group basis. He describes the Soviet methods as an important source of research data. Most of the literature on the organization and control of behavior in natural environments, however, is conjectural. Although the learning theory analysis has generated different ways of viewing behavior and its articulation with environments, major changes in treatment and teaching procedures must probably await the development of a sounder research base.

There are several collections and reviews of behavior modification work now available, all containing examples of application of the techniques of the experimental analysis of behavior and behavioral approaches to clinical problems (see Ullman & Krasner, 1965; Ulrich *et al.,* 1966; Gelfand & Hartmann, 1968). The present chapter indicates some of the implications which research has for a model of consultation to the environment and the techniques of implementing contingency management. Work has now proceeded beyond the point where it is necessary to demonstrate that human behavior is under the control of environmental events or that human behavior varies as a function of its consequences. There is ample evidence that human behavior is a function of the reinforcing contingencies with which it is articulated. The contingency is often the simplest element of a behavioral reorganization. The complexity lies in the program of contingency management, the organization of personnel to maintain it, the selection of target behaviors and reinforcers, the methods of monitoring the technique, collecting data, training, and administrative methods. The literature to date is remiss in both the systematic investigation of these procedures and the report of the particular techniques used within given studies. A brief summary of major topics will indicate some of the variations currently in use.

TRAINING

The selection of personnel has not been a research issue in studies of behavior modification. Ward attendants, nurses, cottage personnel, child-care workers, parents, and others have served as the agents of change in modification programs. Personnel variables, of course, bear on the nature of training and the general complexity of the management problems.

Training techniques for the most part are poorly reported. Ayllon and Michael's report (1959) is probably one of the most complete except for studies such as that of Wahler *et al.* (1965) in which modification of parental behavior with respect to the child is an experimental dependent variable. Many studies report nothing by way of instructions to those in contact with the subject. There is much variation in the handling of persons in the environment. Some are not really trained at all and are simply advised (frequently over the telephone, e.g., Boardman, 1962) how to handle specific issues as they arise. Others are given a formal training session about how to handle specific behaviors with specific individuals (e.g., Ayllon and Michael, 1959). Techniques of training vary from instructions about what to say and do (Ayllon and Michael, 1959) to demonstration (e.g., Wetzel *et al.,* 1966) to actual shaping of appropriate reinforcing behavior (e.g., Wahler *et al.,* 1965). Some training programs give formal instruction on the general principles of learning and techniques of behavior modification (e.g., Wetzel, 1966; Davison 1965).

DATA COLLECTION

Some studies do not report data and of course there is variation in the nature of the data and their reliability. When the data are collected by amateur personnel, the researcher is required to train and advise on the techniques and rationale of data collection. This process is seldom reported. Ayllon and Michael probably give the most complete account of the recording process (1959).[2] The form of the recording sheets, the establishment of reliabilities, the training of the recorder, and the distribution and collection systems are all important variables not yet evaluated. The effect of the recording method on the behavior of the change agent and the behavior of the target is also important. Ayllon and Michael describe the effect of their recording technique on the cooperative behavior of the nurses, while Tyler reports the effect of the recording technique on the target behavior (1965). The method of choosing the behavior to be recorded is singularly important, particularly with respect to certain ethical and moral issues. Most often it is done in consultation with someone in the environment who has legal and socially sanctioned authority with respect to the target behavior. Researchers in general, however, seldom report the rationale underlying the choice of behaviors or the process by which the decision is made.

SELECTION OF REINFORCERS

The process by which a reinforcer is selected is often obscure in research reports. Some studies, of course, are designed to demonstrate that a particular event has reinforcing value with respect to a behavior (e.g., the attention given by nursery school teachers in the University of Washington studies, Harris et al., 1964). Others report that it is done through interview with the subject or someone in his environment. Again the process is important for ethical reasons since some of the objections to behavior modification are based not so much on the concept of contingency management as on the choice of reinforcer.

METHODS OF MAINTAINING CONTINGENCIES

The process of administering a program once it is launched is very important to the outcome. Many researchers report spending most of their time training, retraining, and supervising those collecting data (Ayllon & Michael, 1959; Tyler, 1965; Wetzel, 1966). Other researchers say noth-

[2] Recently, researchers have begun to report data collection techniques more adequately. See, for example, Madsen, Becker, and Thomas (1968).

ing about the procedures of maintaining the program. Some apparently maintain contact with the environment by home visits (Wetzel *et al.*, 1966; Williams, 1959), others by telephone (Boardman, 1962). The procedure by which the professional researcher maintains routine supervision is crucial to procedures in clinical work, especially regarding the use of professional time and consultation techniques.

INTERACTION WITH TARGET

Surprisingly little is reported in descriptions of procedures about what is said to the target himself. Surely this is an important variable. What the target is told about the recording procedures, the language of contingency descriptions, labeling and discrimination aids, selection of reinforcers, and the nature of the interaction between the therapeutic agent and the subject must influence the outcome. As yet, these variables are neither adequately described nor experimentally evaluated.

There is much in the literature on behavior modification that is of great relevance to clinical and mental health issues. There are important suggestions relevant to both the nature of clinical research and the organization of service to people needing help. There are three general characteristics of the work discussed here that those charged with behavioral change (e.g., clinicians) should examine most carefully. (1) So-called behavior modifiers frequently do not see the patient himself but work through someone who bears a natural relationship to him. (2) The behavioral approach dictates that the target of change is behavior (not people; not personalities) and usually behaviors are considered individually. Different programs may be established for different behaviors of the same individual. (3) The behavior modifier tells people what to do. He gives specific instructions and, thereby, accepts, or at least shares, the responsibility for the outcome. His decisions are based on a fledgling but growing body of data. Frequently he is not sure of outcome and makes use of research techniques to evaluate his procedures and add to the system of knowledge. Frequently he presents himself as a researcher and his work as research. He believes that human behavior is lawful, that human beings can help each other through the contingent relationship of their behaviors. He is aware that he is participating in a technical and philosophical revolution in the ways that men offer help to one another.

References

Ayllon, T. *Behavior Research and Therapy,* 1963, **1**, 53–61.
Ayllon, T. In L. Ullman and L. Krasner, (Eds.), *Case studies in behavior modification.* New York: Holt, 1965. pp. 73–76.

Ayllon, T., and Azrin, N. H. *Journal of the Experimental Analysis of Behavior,* 1964, **7,** 327–331.
Ayllon, T., and Azrin, N. H. *Journal of the Experimental Analysis of Behavior,* 1965, **8,** 357–383.
Ayllon, T., and Houghton, E. *Journal of the Experimental Analysis of Behavior,* 1962, **5,** 343–352.
Ayllon, T., and Michael, J. *Journal of the Experimental Analysis of Behavior,* 1959, **2,** 323–334.
Azrin, N. H., and Lindsley, O. R. *Journal of Abnormal and Social Psychology,* 1956, **52,** 100–102.
Baer, D. M., and Sherman, J. A. *Journal of Experimental Child Psychology,* 1964, **1,** 37–49.
Bandura, A. *Journal of Consulting Psychology,* 1962, **26,** 298–301.
Bandura, A. *Journal of Nursery Education,* 1963, **18,** 207–215.
Bandura, A., and Walters, R. H. *Social learning and personality development.* New York: Holt, 1963.
Bijou, S. W., and Baer, D. M. *Child development.* Vol. 1. *A systematic and empirical theory.* New York: Appleton, 1961.
Bijou, S. W., and Oblinger, B. *Psychological Reports,* 1960, **6,** 447–454.
Bijou, S. W., and Orlando, R. *Journal of the Experimental Analysis of Behavior,* 1961, **4,** 7–16.
Bijou, S. W., and Sturges, P. T. *Child Development,* 1959, **30,** 151–170.
Boardman, W. K. *Journal of Consulting Psychology,* 1962, **26,** 293–297.
Brackbill, Y. *Child Development,* 1958, **29,** 115–124.
Bronfenbrenner, U. *American Psychologist,* 1962, **17,** 550–564.
Burchard, J., and Tyler, V. Jr. *Behavior Research and Therapy,* 1965, **2,** 245–250.
Clark, D. F. *Behavior Research and Therapy,* 1963, **1,** 245–250.
Cooper, A. J. *Behavior Research and Therapy,* 1964, **1,** 351–356.
Davison, G. C. In L. Ullman and L. Krasner, (Eds.), *Case studies in behavior modification,* New York: Holt, 1965. Pp. 146–148.
Ellis, N. R., Barnett, C. D., and Pryer, M. W. *Journal of the Experimental Analysis of Behavior,* 1960, **3,** 63–69.
Ferster, C. B. *Child Development* 1961, **32,** 437–456.
Ferster, C. B., and DeMyer, M. K. *American Journal of Orthopsychiatry,* 1962, **32,** 89–98.
Ferster, C. B. and Simons, J. *Psychological Record,* 1965, **16,** 65–71.
Flanagan, B., Goldiamond, I., and Azrin, N. H. *Journal of the Experimental Analysis of Behavior,* 1958, **1,** 173–177.
Gelfand, D. M., and Hartmann. D. P. *Psychological Bulletin,* 1968, **69,** 204–215.
Harris, F. R., Johnston, M. K. Kelly, C. S., and Wolf, M. M. *Journal of Educational Psychology,* 1964, **55,** 35–41.
Hawkins, R. P., Peterson, R. F., Schweid, E., and Bijou, S. W. *Journal of Experimental Child Psychology,* 1966, **4,** 99–107.
Hewett, F. *American Journal of Orthopsychiatry,* 1965, **35,** 927–936.
Lindsley, O. R. *Psychiatric Research Reports,* 1956, **5,** 118–139.
Long, E. R. *Journal of the Experimental Analysis of Behavior,* 1959, **2,** 268.
Lovaas, O. I., Berberich, J. P., Perloff, B. F., and Schaeffer, B. *Science,* 1966, **151,** 705–707.
Lovaas, O. I., Freitag, G., Gold, V. J., and Kassorla, I. C. *Journal of Experimental Child Psychology,* 1965, **2,** 67–84.

Lovibond, S. H. *Behavior Research and Therapy* 1963, **1**, 17–21. (a)

Lovibond, S. H. *Behavior Research and Therapy* 1963, **1**, 127–132. (b)

Madsen, C. H., Jr., Becker, W. C., and Thomas, D. R., *Journal of Applied Behavior Analysis,* 1968, **1**, 139–150.

Risley, T. R., and Wolf, M. M. In S. W. Bijou and D. M. Baer, (Eds.), *Child development: readings in experimental analysis.* New York: Appleton, 1967. Pp. 184–194.

Russo, S. *Behavior Research and Therapy,* 1964, **4**, 43–47.

Schwitzgebel, R. *Street corner research: an experimental approach to the juvenile delinquent.* Cambridge, Massachusetts: Harvard Univ. Press, 1964.

Schwitzgebel, R., and Kolb, D. A. *Behavior Research and Therapy,* 1964, **1**, 297–304.

Skinner, B. F. *Science and human behavior.* New York: Macmillan, 1953.

Straughan, J. *Behavior Research and Therapy,* 1964, **2**, 37–41.

Tharp, R. G., Cutts, R. I., and Burkholder, M. A. *Journal of Community Mental Health,* in press.

Thorne, G. L., Tharp, R. G., and Wetzel, R. J. *Federal Probation,* 1967, **31**, 21–27.

Tyler, V. O., Jr. Paper read at American Psychological Association Convention, Chicago, 1965.

Ullman, L., and Krasner, L. (Eds.). *Case studies in behavior modification.* New York: Holt, 1965.

Ulrich, R., Stachnik, T., and Mabry, J. (Eds.) *Control of human behavior.* Glenville, Illinois: Scott, Foresman, 1966.

Wahler, R., Winkel, G., Peterson, R., and Morrison, D. *Behavior Research and Therapy,* 1965, **3**, 113–124.

Watson, J. B., and Rayner, R. *Journal of Experimental Psychrology,* 1920, **3**, 1–14.

Wetzel, R. J. *Journal of Consulting Psychology,* 1966, **30**, 367–374.

Wetzel, R. J., Baker, J., Roney, M., and Martin, M. *Behavior Research and Therapy,* 1966, **4**, 169–177.

Williams, C. D. *Journal of Abnormal and Social Psychology,* 1959, **59**, 269.

Wolf, M., Risley, T., and Mees, H. *Behavior Research and Therapy,* 1964, **1**, 305–312.

Wolpe, J. *Psychotherapy by reciprocal inhibition,* Stanford, California: Stanford Univ. Press, 1958.

CHAPTER III

A Theory for Behavior Modification in the Natural Environment

Detractors of the behavioristic position are fond of the observation that people are not rats in a Skinner box, and that one must not assume that they can be treated in the same way. The human being, who has a large measure of control over his own destiny, who is a symbol-bearing, language-mediating, hyperencephalated creature of plans and pride, exists in a social and cultural world that does not allow for the simplistic analyses and precise control upon which functional analysis rests. Therefore, functional analysis and the real world are mutually exclusive. Because schedules of reinforcement can neither be determined nor controlled, because of the plethora of stimuli in the natural environment, behavioristic theory is inappropriate and offers no basis for the development of a technology.

The laboratory investigator of pure learning processes sometimes agrees that because the free environment does not allow for precision of control and observation, it is deceptive to attempt extrapolation from the principles of learning to a technology of real-world intervention.

Yet this technology is being developed, and the previous chapter documents a considerable achievement. The task of this chapter is to describe the similarities which intertwine these diverse enterprises, and to suggest a set of principles which can and do guide the behavioral "engineer" as he translates learning theory into action in the natural environment.

THE REINFORCING EVENT

The central issue, both in behavioristic research and in behavioral intervention, is the discovery and control of those environmental events which bear functional relationships to the behaviors under investigation. To accomplish this end, science has traditionally restricted environmental events by number. Thus, the animal who learns a maze for a food reward is trained and tested in an environment which restricts the variations of temperature, of light, and of sound, so as to measure more purely the effects of the schedule of reinforcement. For the mouse in the meadow, obviously, this kind of control is not possible. A left turn in the field presents an array of stimuli to him: changes in light, other mice, food, hawks, men, coverage. His discrete responses produce multiple consequences, each having its own functional relationship to his behavior. If we are to predict the paths down which he will wander, we must adopt a different strategy. A strategy which will allow for the simultaneous consideration of those several environmental variations which contribute to the control of his behavior: light and sounds and mice, as well as his history of food acquisition. We can opt for such a strategy while in no way rejecting our knowledge that each discrete stimulus bears a precise relationship to the behavior which it follows.

For the analysis of the behavior of children in the natural environment, this issue is the same. For example, the unit of *history-homework behavior* has many consequences: the teacher's reaction, the sacrifice of television programs, parental approbation, the reactions (positive and negative) of his peer group. It is possible to conceptualize and, under laboratory conditions to manipulate these consequences separately, so that functional relationships may well exist between the frequency of homework behavior and any of these reinforcing stimuli. But it is also possible to view these (and all other) consequences as bearing a sign ($+$ or $-$) indicating their functional reinforcing value. Their combined value may be inferred from the subsequent behavior itself: continuation indicates a plus-combined value, decrease indicates negative consequation. There are some who disclaim "operant conditioning" as the apt description of such analytic processes. Lloyd Homme (1966) for instance, prefers the term "contingency management": "Operant conditioning and contingency mangement are not the same thing. Contingency management is a crucial bit of technology derived from operant conditioning, not operant conditioning itself. The reason this distinction is important is that there are people in our society— parents, teachers, and so on—who have to deal with tremendous amounts of behavior. They have neither the time nor the inclination to learn operant conditioning, but they welcome a small bit of technology which gives them some control over what is going to happen next in the world of behavior." It is possible, then, to gain some control even though we are working at a complex level. We are in full agreement with Homme that the practical management of contingencies requires an analysis somewhat different from that of operant conditioning.

For example, he has suggested "reinforcing event" as the construct which describes the total consequence of a behavior. Thus, the great many things which follow a child's homework behavior can be simultaneously considered. The individual components of the event often are not subject to separate control or even observation, but if the event has regularity, then it is subject to control and to functional analysis. The reinforcing event carries a sign—it may decrease or increase the frequency of the behavior which it follows. The + or − sign may be considered the resolution of the signs of the separate (including the unobserved) components.

THE COMPONENTS OF THE REINFORCING EVENT

The adoption of the "reinforcing event" construct implies that the components are not all subject to control or observation. But it does not imply that we should abandon the effort to understand them, nor the effort to more carefully manipulate the separate sources of variation. For purposes of technology of helping it is useful to consider, for example, the sources of the various components of the reinforcing event, particularly the human sources. Who is it that dispenses the reinforcers? We suggest this approach because the contingency manager—as was seen in the previous chapters—has as his major task the consultation and instruction of those individuals who do the actual dispensing of contingent reinforcers. Thus, in his role as consultant, he is particularly concerned with who is doing the reinforcing. Before discussing ways in which a consultant handles the multiple reinforcer problem, however, let us examine the consultant's relationship to the helping effort.

THE TRIADIC MODEL

In the psychotherapeutic model, the professional specialist interacts with the patient. Various strategies have been invented to purify this dyadic interaction, and, indeed, it is the aim of psychoanalysis to recreate in this dyadic arena all of those behavioral and emotional proclivities which constitute the patient's "mental illness." The therapeutic dyad—doctor and patient—derives from medical organization, and is comfortably consistent with the consulting-room pattern by which disease is treated.

As will be recalled from Chapter II, a different model of practice has emerged naturally from the assumptions of the behavior therapies. In behavior modification techniques, the professional specialist need not have the direct interaction with the "patient." Rather, he may instruct, or advise, or consult to other individuals who bear some normal role relationship to the "patient." This is not always the case, nor need it be, but in the majority of situations we see that the more powerful reinforcers, and the control of those reinforcers, are in the hands of someone other than the professional consultant. The logic of behavior modification dictates that those individuals who do indeed possess the reinforcers should occupy a position intermediate to the consultant and the patient who is the ultimate target of behavioral intervention. Thus for behavior modification the basic model is not dyadic, but triadic. The three positions are those of the consultant, the intermediary, and the target.[3]

The consultative triad, then, may be seen as the organizational convergence of the thrusts of behaviorism, of deprofessionalization, and the utilization of natural relationships. A careful analysis of each of the positions of the triad can guide both organization and the techniques for intervention. Such an analysis is intimately related to the issue of the multiple sources of reinforcement as well.

In this pure form of the consultative triad, as shown in Fig. 1, all effects proceed to the target via the *mediator*, none directly from consultant

FIG. 1. The consultative triad.

to target. This analysis describes functional positions, not the people who occupy those positions. For example, any number of individuals occupying any number of social roles might serve as mediator: father, teacher, sister, minister, mother, employer, friend, and psychotherapist. Indeed, the same is true of the functions of either consultant or target (see the following tabulation).

[3] The development of consultative models has also characterized the operations derived from nonmedical theories other than behaviorism. For example, using social-system analyses, one may deduce that the preferred form of treatment for children or spouses is through consultation with parents, husbands, or wives (Tharp, 1965; Tharp & Otis, 1966).

Consultant	Mediator	Target
Psychologist	Teacher	Predelinquent
Behavior analyst	Father	Mental patient
Social worker	Employer	Employee
Mother	Wife	Husband
Teacher	Psychotherapist	Mother
Anyone with the knowledge	*Anyone with the reinforcers*	*Anyone with the problem*

In examining these possibilities, we see that the sole criterion for the function of consultant is possession of knowledge. As will be seen in Chapter IV, the position of consultant can be occupied by the Behavior Analyst, a nontraditional helping agent specifically trained to provide knowledge concerning behavior modification in the natural environment. In the use of other theoretical systems, for instance, in traditional child-guidance work, the social worker may be consultant to the parent of the patient.

Anyone with the *problem* can be considered the *target:* autistic children, schizophrenic patients, adult neurotics, delinquent adolescents. The target, then, is anyone whose behavior the consultant contracts to modify.

The position of the *mediator* is perhaps less clear. As defined above, the mediator is the individual who is in direct contact with target. He is the intermediary of the consultant. He receives instruction from the consultant, which he uses to affect the target.

But there are five or ten or a hundred potential mediators in the social network of any given target. The mediator(s) will be in contact with the consultant for the purpose of affecting the target. We can immediately see, then, that the selection of the mediators is crucial. An examination of the selection procedures also moves us directly into a discussion of the theory of intervention, because the mediator in fact may be anyone with the *reinforcers*.

THE CHOICE OF MEDIATORS

The basic contingency-mangement technique is simple and immutable: rearrange the contingencies so that desirable behavior is rewarded and undesirable behavior is not rewarded. The reinforcing events and/or stimuli are reorganized so that beneficial contingencies result. Control of the reinforcers becomes the paramount issue. Working in the complex and stubborn natural environment always brings difficulty of control, so that discovering the agent who controls the reinforcers which, in turn, control the behavior of the target becomes essential. Thus is the mediator defined and selected: he must (1) possess the target's reinforcers, and (2) be able to place them on contingency.

Some reinforcers which the consultant may believe to have particular power for the target may not be possessed by the mediator. For instance, the assessment may reveal that a particular predelinquent child might respond most with the reinforcement of cash. This is well and good if the mediator of choice has cash. For many cases, of course, even an extra expense of ten cents per day is simply not possible (and would bring considerable negative outcome from other family members). The lack of availability of the reinforcers is also an issue when the choice is an interpersonal event: it is well enough for the consultant to instruct a mediator to dispense "maternal attention" on contingency, but this instruction is of little consequence if the mother-mediator is a cold woman who does not have it in her repertoire to extend the kind of warmth which is high in the target's reinforcement hierarchy. It is worthless also to suggest to a mediator the dispensing of aversive stimuli consequent on undesired acts (e.g., punishment) if the mediator of choice has a lack of ability to dispense this contingency due to a hiatus in his own behavioral repertoire. Many passive fathers would be unable to carry out such a suggestion.

Other parents are unable to carry out suggestions for dispensing aversive stimuli because of the poor control which they have over hostile outbursts. For these individuals, it would be very unwise to suggest an action which might rapidly escalate to proportions beyond the desire of the consulant. This consideration returns us to the second criterion of mediatorship: the mediator must possess the reinforcer (the material, or the action in his repertoire), but he must also be able to dispense it on contingency, to control it. The "ability to place on contingency" becomes a most complex issue. In order to pursue it with maximum clarity let us now return to a discussion of the multiple sources of reinforcement.

THE SOURCES OF REINFORCEMENT

We may divide the social sources of reinforcement into two: the chosen *mediator* and *others*. By "others" we mean others than mediator. For example, even if a particular plan for behavior modification used a history teacher as the mediator, both the target's arithmetic teacher and his gym supervisor will continue to affect the target's behavior, although not according to any particular instruction from the consultant. As does all the world, these other teachers will be responding to the child's changing behavior, and dispensing their own reinforcers in the usual automatic ways that they have always praised, punished, ignored, etc., any child's behavior. These reinforcers may well be as powerful as those which are being systematically controlled by the consultant and mediator. The distinction illustrated in Fig. 2 is this: the *mediator's* use of reinforcers is

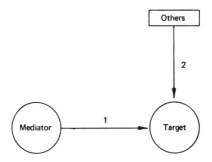

FIG. 2. Target's sources of social reinforcement.

according to specific direction by his consultant; *others* are not in direct interaction with the consultant.

Because of these uncontrolled sources then, we must choose as mediators those individuals who will maximize the control over the target's reinforcers. Multiple mediators must frequently be employed in order to maximize. This is not always practical though, and the use of too many mediators may create organizational difficulties more serious than useful. Although this discussion will become more complex later, let us continue to treat the simple case of the single mediator. He should be chosen in such a way that the resolved contributions from all sources will be in the required direction. Usually this direction should be positive: the sign of the combined reinforcing outcomes from others and mediator should be +. For example, a target who is asked to turn his homework in promptly may have this behavior reinforced by the mother (mediator) with tokens-toward-a-movie-ticket (+); his gym teacher (other) may hear of the child's improvement and praise him (+); and these two positive outcomes may be sufficient to outweigh his sister (other) mocking him for studying (−). If so, the resolved sign of the reinforcing event will be +, and homework behavior will increase.

With this typical example, we can further refine our criterion for mediatorship as follows: the mediators should be those individuals who have control over the most powerful of the available reinforcers, since these mediator-controlled reinforcers must frequently outweigh outcomes to the target of an opposite sign.

If we take seriously the triadic analysis, with its accompanying "sources of reinforcement" concepts, we can immediately see that it must apply to the mediator as well as to the target. Indeed, not only does it apply but it increases one step in complexity.

As illustrated in Fig. 3, the mediators' behavior will be controlled by the same source of social reinforcement as will the targets': (1) that

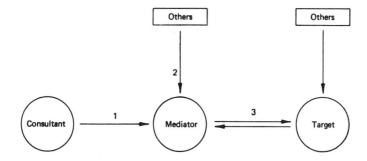

FIG. 3. Mediator's sources of social reinforcement.

reinforcement which is under the control of the consultant; (2) from others surrounding the mediator (his wife, employer, other children, etc.). The identical analysis may be performed upon the mediator as was achieved above for the target: if the *mediating behavior* is to continue or increase, the resolved sign of outcomes for mediating must be in the positive direction.

But when the mediator is the focus of analysis, we see that there is yet a third source of reinforcement to the mediator, and that is from the target. The modification of the target's behavior is a reinforcing event for the mediator. This source must be carefully balanced with the other two, and the resolved sign of all sources must be positive.

In theoretical analysis, it becomes apparent that the central issue must become the maintenance of the mediator's desired behavior. Since the key agent for control is the mediator, the target's behavior is a near-strict function of the effectiveness of the mediation. Therefore, behavior modification in the natural environment stands or falls on the effectiveness of the behavior of the mediator.

THE MEDIATOR AND THE TARGET

It is very important that the reinforcing consequences of actions suggested to the mediator be carefully weighed. This is quite obvious when one has reference to the reinforcing value of a particular stimulus with reference to the target: it is equally important with reference to the mediator himself. The most effective combination, of course, is that in which there would be a *positive–positive* value. This would be the case in which a mediator would be instructed to reward the target with an activity or an object, the presence of which would be equally rewarding to the mediator himself. We have found this particularly effective, for instance, in instructing husbands to reward their wives by taking them out to dinner. This, however, has clear limitations when the financial problems of the family are so severe as to make entertainment outside the home an expense which is punishing to the mediator. A more subtle condition, however, can and does frequently arise. This is the instance in which, although the preferred rewarding stimulus (going to a movie), is also rewarding to the mediator, the *offering* of a reinforcement to the wife is aversive for the husband.

Let us elaborate. Most instances of "disturbed" behavior are so because they are disturbing to society, usually the family. Thus undesirable behavior, when it has persisted long enough to come to the attention of the consultant, has already partially alienated the potential mediators from the target. This is particularly salient in marriage counseling work. A "symptomatic" wife, by the time she reaches the counselor, has in more instances than not managed to make herself aversive to her husband. The mediator–husband might find the act of offering positive reinforcement to his target–wife aversive.

In such instances, we have found it more effective to reverse reinforcement as follows. The withdrawal of reward to the target may be positively reinforcing to the mediator. Of course, if such antagonism existed as would make this statement always true, this relationship would not be a practical one to use for mediating purposes. However, it is frequently possible, through withdrawing the presence of the mediator, to establish this aversive-rewarding combination. For instance, one of the most effective control techniques is that of having the mediator withdraw his presence from the target when undesired behavior is emitted. This has been especially effective in cases in which the wife's negligence or vituperation is the problem under consideration, and we have encouraged the husband (mediator) to withdraw when evidence of this behavior first presents itself. This "leaving the scene," is at the same time aversive to the wife, and positively rewarding for the husband. In many instances his preferred response is indeed "leaving the scene," and by placing this response on contingency much more effective methods of interaction can be established.

These same issues may be considered in relation to any target. When children are misbehaving so badly in the home or in the classroom as to make mediators angry with them, it may be difficult for the mediator to institute a program of positive reinforcement. Many, indeed, are inclined toward punishment. Assessment of the behavioral repertoire of the mediator must take these issues into account. The repertoires of mediators, as of any organisms, are highly individual and will vary with cues given by the target.

Nevertheless, there are certain commonalities of behavior repertoires which may be predicted grossly by use of the concept of *role*. In general, society rewards parental and teacher behaviors which are nurturant and controlling to the child. It would not necesssarily reward the same mediator's behavior if he were nurturant and controlling toward the spouse. Thus that intervention procedure which may be most effective in dealing with the disturbed marriage may not be effective when the relationship at issue is pupil and teacher, or mother and child. Social-psychological role theory provides a framework for classing together behaviors which have a high probability by virtue of the individual's occupancy of a given social position. The same individual may occupy the two positions of uncle and father. If he were asked to mediate in two separate cases, the one target being his son and the other target being his nephew, he might not be capable of the same intervention program in the two instances. Teachers should never be asked to engage in antiteaching behavior; nor should psychoanalysts be asked to take their patients to a movie. But a psychoanalyst–mediator might well be instructed to take his problem daughter to a movie, on contingency. Mediator-behavior which is consistent with role-repertoires is an astute choice of the consultant because it has a high initial probability of occurrence. Of course, any assumptions made about role-behaviors must yield to careful analysis of the specific individual's own repertoire, and a measure of idiosyncracy always exists. Regardless of these variations, however, the wise consultant will rarely ask any individual to violate his own particular role-organized repertoire. The rule is as follows: the consultant should select behaviors which are consistent with the role position which the mediator holds vis-a-vis the target.

In summary, then, the ability to dispense a given reinforcer on contingency always involves (1) the possession of the reinforcer; (2) the presence in the repertoire of the acts of consequation; and (3) the potential presence of a resolved + in the events which follow mediating-behavior.

THE TARGET AND THE MEDIATOR

In the case of the misbehaving child, the consequences to the mediator of the child's behaviors are frequently so punishing that virtually all interaction stops, or great vacillation and alternation of the behaviors of the adult toward the child occurs. In many ways, the child's effects on the parents and teachers serve to modify these mediators' behaviors into a topography which intensifies the child's bad-acting. These processes do not cease upon intervention. The third source of reinforcement to the mediator—from the target himself—continues to modify the mediator's behavior and to affect the ability of the mediator to apply reinforcers contingently.

This source of reinforcement to the mediators' behavior could be described as "not controlled" by the consultant, along with reinforcement from others. Yet, the modification of mediator behavior is crucial to success of enterprises in the natural environment. So even these sources must be brought under indirect control.

INDIRECT CONTROL OF THE SOURCES OF REINFORCEMENT

Let us examine a particular behavior: a mother is chosen to mediate the intervention plan for her child, the target. The child may be exhibiting two undesirable behaviors, refusal to make her bed in the morning, and tardiness to school. The mother is instructed to enter a mark on a wall chart when and only when the child behaves properly, and later to redeem a preestablished number of marks with a mother-daughter excursion. The mother believes this system to be beneath her dignity. The father is disinterested, and mildly pokes fun at the wall chart. The consultant's presence and personality is pleasing to the mother, and she wants to gain the consultant's respect. Thus the sign of reinforcements will be:

$$
\begin{array}{ll}
\text{Other} & - \\
\text{Consultant} & +
\end{array}
$$

A simple inquiry of the mother will disclose the resolved sign: "Will you begin the system?" If she agrees the resolved sign may be hypothesized as a "weak +," or perhaps a "weak −." In this situation, the consultant may have little confidence that mediation-behavior (entering marks and redeeming them) will occur with sufficient frequency. With such a borderline reinforcing event, the third source of reinforcement—from the target—becomes crucial.

We now come to the issue of indirect control. We can arrange that the change in the target's behavior is positively reinforcing to the mediator, creating a resolved sign as follows:

$$
\begin{array}{lll}
\text{Other} & - & \\
\text{Consultant} & + & \text{Resolution} = \text{a strong} + \\
\text{Target} & + &
\end{array}
$$

This indirect control can be gained by choosing an initial behavior in which a change will be immediately and positively reinforcing to the mediator. In our example, we should definitely choose making-bed behavior rather than school-prompt behavior as the initial response to strengthen. To choose "reducing tardiness" (1) would not be as visible to the mediator, (2) would require the establishment and perfection of a complex notification system from school to home in order for the mediator to perceive the effects, and (3) would remove less "sandpaper" from the mother–daughter relationship than would the choice of bed-making. The latter, we might suppose, is a source of irritation and additional work for the mother. Even one morning's made bed could make for a more pleasant day for our mother-mediator.

The reinforcement from the target can be brought under control, albeit indirectly, by the astute choice of targeted behaviors. Once mediating-behaviors have been shaped and increased in the mediator, the mediating repertoire can be expanded. Once the mother is "hooked" on modification techniques by the reinforcing value of bed-making, she will persist more in mediating other plans, including that of tardiness-reduction.

This strategy is also exemplified by the work of Ayllon and Michael, as was described on page 29, Chapter II. Out of the wealth of problem behaviors of the schizophrenic patients, those of most concern to the nurse-mediators were initially chosen for modification.

The reinforcement from others is also subject to this same kind of indirect control. The possibility for punishing responses from others exists as a consequence of the mediator's responses to the consultant's instructions. Two examples: A teacher may be reluctant to reward a child's school achievement with poker-chip tokens because other teachers would mock her, or because the principal might frown at such an "irregularity." At a child's home, a mother might be constrained from rewarding her daughter by spending some time in teaching her sewing skills, because the father would be jealous of time spent away from himself. The careful consultant will design an intervention plan which will contain a minimum of such punishment. If a token system is needed, it must be created with the participation and approval of the principal, and with a minimized likelihood of mockery from the mediator's associates. With attention to such issues, they can ordinarily be solved with a minimum of compromise. Beyond that, there is yet another strategy for achieving indirect control which the second example can illustrate. The modified behavior of the target should be made reinforcing to those others who control the reinforcers of the mediator.

In Fig. 4, if source A is positive, source 2 is more likely to also be positive. If the daughter's improved behavior allows the father (other)

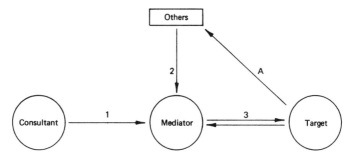

FIG. 4. Indirect sources of reinforcement to the mediator.

to sleep more easily at night, then he will be more likely to positively reinforce (encourage, not obstruct) the mother's desirable behavior (spending the reward-time with the target). Therefore the consultant should choose behaviors which will produce a + sign from sources 2 and 3. He must give this same consideration to source A.

Ideally, then, sources 2, 3, and A are all positive. It will occur to the reader that one is seldom so fortunate. The critical source of reinforcement, the one that most often will tip the balance toward one resolved sign or the other, is source 1—reinforcement from the consultant.

THE MEDIATOR AS THE TARGET

We have referred to source 1 as controlled; that is, the consultant who designs the intervention directly interacts with the mediator, and directly consequates the mediator's mediating behavior. The consultant praises the mediator, ignores him, gossips with him, or gives him some assistance, or a piece of gum, or a letter of recommendation. Through a process of shaping and stimulus control, effective mediation must ordinarily be taught to the selected mediator, and the consultant must employ the standard laws of learning in modifying the behavior of the mediator, just as the mediator must do likewise with the target. As we have previously argued that the target's modification is attributable to mediator-effectiveness, so we can now state that the mediator's modification (and effectivness) is attributable to the consultant-effectiveness. It is also clear that if the problem-person is the target of the mediator, the mediator is the target for the consultant (see Fig. 5).

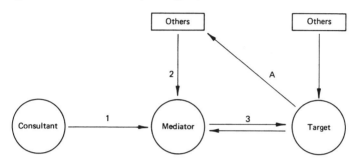

FIG. 5. Indirect sources of reinforcement with the mediator as target.

This is the essence of the triadic model. The professional (consultant) attention is to be directed to the modification of the mediator behavior. The consultant will choose mediator behaviors as goals which will result in the desirable modification of the actions of the target; but the consultant operates upon the mediator, and he must not forget it. If he does forget, and attends directly upon the target, he will have made two serious errors. First, he will have failed to modify the maintaining stimuli for the target's misbehaviors; thus the target would revert to misbehavior upon the withdrawal of the consultant. The second error is much more visible: in all likelihood, the erring consultant would fail to alter the behavior of the target, since the mediator is the individual who controls the reinforcers most powerful for the target.

Such an analysis reveals the inherent limitation upon a dyadic model, such as psychotherapy.

THE CONSULTANT AS THE TARGET

As we have changed focus, we have seen that any individual in the social system can be seen as the "target" of attempted modification. The consultant himself is not excepted, and he must apply it to himself (see Fig. 6). For the modification and shaping of consultant behavior, there are the same sources: the mediator-source (3) is analogous to the way in which target behaviors reinforce mediator actions. If the mediator responds with "good" mediation, that action taken by the consultant which resulted in the mediator improvement, is more likely to reoccur in the consultant. If the mediator improves, the consultant will continue the methods of consultation which preceded it. Sources 1 and 2 are analogous. Various consultant-behaviors will be affected by others (his peers, his associates, and the like).

In addition there may be a source 1 for the consultant as well; in most settings and organizations there are supervisors for those occupying

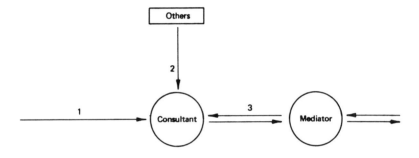

FIG. 6. Consultant's sources of reinforcement.

the consultant role. The supervisor will then become the source 1 for the consultant.

We are now prepared to consider the various elements of the paradigm simultaneously. Thus, we can see that there are the same sources of reinforcement for the supervisor of the consultant as well. Indeed, by extending the diagram off the right side of the page we observe that the target himself will no doubt be engaged in a mutually influencing relationship with some other individual.

The consultative-triad analysis can be applied to any three individuals in the chain. In the diagram, there are suggested individuals who might be represented by the circles above. But it is vital to understand that the (Consultant---Mediator---Target) pattern may be superimposed upon any three consecutive circles in an endless chain, as illustrated in Fig. 7. This superimposition is determined by the problem which locates the target. That individual who, under the direction of the consultant, operates directly upon the target is known as the mediator, and so forth.

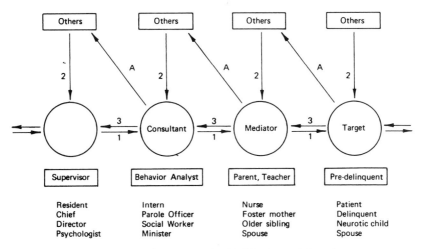

FIG. 7. The consultative triad embedded in the social environment.

CONSULTATION TO THE COMPLEX SOCIAL ENVIRONMENT

It can be observed that the triadic model offers guidance to intervention in the problems of institutions, as well as to those of individuals. For example, a "target" may be considered an entire class of students, an entire hospital ward (as in token economies), or indeed as any unit of a complex organization of whatever size, so long as that unit is boundaried by behavioral commonalities and common reinforcers. In such instances, a consultant to an institution would be guided by the triadic analysis to attend directly, not to the target(s), but to the mediator units (nursing staff, second-level supervisors, Board of Directors, etc.). The Sources of Reinforcement may be grouped as described above, and the same considerations applied to their management. Indeed, the consultation to any complex social environment will require interpenetration of the individual target analysis with modification at the institutional level, as will be seen below.

SUMMARY

In a previous chapter, the principles of learning were enunciated. In the present section, we have suggested a model by which the principles of learning may be systematically applied to the natural environment. The basic technique is contingency management; that is to say, a positively reinforcing event must follow desirable behavior, and must not follow undesirable behavior. A positively reinforcing event is defined as that outcome in which the resolved sign of all sources of reinforcement is $+$. The task of the consultant is to select mediators and behaviors which will maximize the positive resolution. The task can be facilitated by attending to the role positions and the specific available reinforcers for each individual in the chain. Each individual in the chain must attend to the primary task of modifying the behavior of the next individual in the chain, not the target's behavior. That behavior should be chosen for the next individual, which will then ultimately maximize the behavior correction of the target.

References

Homme, L. Contingency management. *Clinical Child Psychology Newsletter,* 1966, **4.** (November)

Tharp, R. G. *American Journal of Orthopsychiatry,* 1965, **25,** 531–538.

Tharp, R. G. and Otis, G. *Journal of Consulting Psychology,* 1966, **30,** 426–434.

CHAPTER IV

Organization: A Program
for Demonstration

Sufficient advance has been made in behavioristic thought and practice, then, to allow the creation of a total program designed to demonstrate, explore, and test the general hypotheses presented in Chapter III. Such a demonstration was attempted by the Behavior Research Project, and we turn now to a brief description of an actual organization derived from the foregoing principles.

The value of such an organization lies in the opportunity for relatively pure demonstration and research. But because this demonstration has organizational as well as case-management implications, a description of the procedures is in order. As will be seen, the line-and-staff patterns and even the day-by-day operations derive from the principles discussed in Chapter III.

The functional organization of the program is illustrated in Fig. 8.[4] Contacts between people occurred only in the pattern described by the diagram. Supervisors did not see mediators, and Behavior Analysts did not see targets, except for training, experimental, or emergency purposes. (The only systematic exception was in the one direct staff contact with the target for purposes of assessment; see Chapter V.)

[4] Of course certain administrative lines for any organization are established by conditions irrelevant to operational issues. For example, primary funding for the Behavior Research Project was provided by demonstration grants (#65023 and #66020) from the Office of Juvenile Delinquency and Youth Development of HEW to the Southern Arizona Mental Health Center of the Arizona State Hospital; the co-investigators were affiliated with the Psychology Department of the Center, and so administrative, fiscal, and personnel practices proceeded in a line through that chain. Operationally, however, these institutions did nothing but facilitate the programmatic integrity of the demonstration organization.

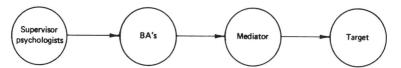

FIG. 8. The organizational pattern of the Behavior Research Project.

THE TRIADIC ORGANIZATION

SUPERVISOR PSYCHOLOGIST

The function of the supervisor was to shape the behavior of the Behavior Analyst in such a way as to maximize the impact for change upon the mediator. In addition, the supervisor provided the theoretical knowledge of learning principles required for an effective program of intervention for the target. The third principal task was to provide the young Behavior Analyst with the supervisor's experience (garnered from clinical and research practice) in predicting and understanding the complexities of child and adult life. The supervisors were the authors and their associates.

THE BEHAVIOR ANALYST

The central figure in the Behavior Research Project was the Behavior Analyst—the "BA"—a nontraditional, "sub"-professional change agent, trained specifically for the position by the supervisors. A major achievement of this project was the success of these behavior modification technicians. Selected specifically for their lack of previous training in any of the helping professions, their requisite characteristics included only intelligence, energy, flexibility, and qualities of personal attractiveness. The "BA's" have included sociology majors, an ex-football player, an ex-stevedore and carpenter, a returned Peace Corps volunteer, a housewife, a cocktail waitress, and the like. Most have been in their twenties, although the coordinator position was held by a man of 45.

After the training period, all case contacts were made by the Behavior Analysts, except for extremely infrequent emergencies. In assessing the achievements of this program, it cannot be overemphasized that the people-contact work was done exclusively by young, bright individuals whose sole training was a three-week seminar and on-the-job training. The materials used in training were generally the books and articles in the reference list of Chapter II, which were available at that time.

THE TARGET

The target population selected was the behaviorally disordered child—one manifesting behavior management problems in the school, the community, or the home. If viewed in psychiatric terms, these cases would have run the full nosological gamut, from character disorder to incipient schizophrenia. This population was chosen to provide a stern test; treatment results with this population have always been poor for they are "unmotivated," and the predelinquent syndrome is one of the nation's most serious current problems. Further, it is a population which concerns virtually every helping profession and agency.

Referrals of problem children were made primarily from the two local participating school districts, which included about 12,000 pupils. In one district, the principals made direct referrals; in the other, referrals were routed through the district psychometrists. Referrals were also accepted—of children in participating school districts—from parents, social agencies, or the juvenile court.

Referral criteria were simple, and chosen to broadly encompass "predelinquency": (1) misbehaviors at school and/or home; plus (2) academic underachievement; plus (3) evidence for an IQ equivalent of ≥ 90. The last criterion was added, not as relevant to predelinquency, but to ensure that some potential was present for improving poor academic performance.

The range of problem behaviors was wide: theft, mischief, runaways, property destruction, classroom disruption, defiance, etc. The mean grade received in school for the year preceding referral was D+; the children were average-to-above in intelligence. They were of both sexes, and from 6 to 16 years old.

OPERATIONS

Upon acceptance of a referral, the case was assigned to a Behavior Analyst and a Supervisor. The Behavior Analyst immediately visited the home of the child, presented himself as a consultant to the school, and interpreted the BRP services to the target's family. If the parent declined the service, no further action was taken. If the parent signed a "permission form," the *assessment* stage immediately ensued (see Chapter V). The BA visited the school, interviewed appropriate personnel, and made classroom contacts. Family assessments proceeded apace, and the target himself was interviewed (not by the assigned BA). Recording the occurrence of problem behaviors was begun. Although the supervisor remained available to the BA during this period, the more experienced Behavior Analysts required minimum supervision until the assessment phase was complete.

At the point of the completion of mediator and target assessment and the achievement of behavioral records (usually one to three weeks), a case conference was held, involving at least the assigned BA and his supervisor. The purpose of the conference was the creation of an *intervention plan* (see Chapter VI). Such a plan included the selection of target behaviors, contingencies, and mediators.

The time between referral to the Behavior Research Project and parental permission averaged eight days (range 0 to 49 days). The time between parental permission and implementation of an intervention plan averaged 38 days (range 2 to 148). (The latter was influenced by many factors, including severity and frequency of referred behaviors, school cooperation, and availability of mediators.)

The BA then visited the selected mediators, and presented the intervention plan to them. Negotiation frequently followed, and an alteration of the plan was not unusual. Implementation began as quickly as possible.

The coordination and liaison function of the BA then became central. Visits and phone calls to the mediators were frequent, often daily. The natural environment was the field of operation; BA's held no office visits, but worked in the schools, in bus depots, on ranches, in grocery stores, in parking lots—in odd places, at odd hours.

The nature of each contact was recorded by the BA in a case file, and graphs or other records were regularly continued. Psychiatric, neurological, and general medical consultation was provided by the Southern Arizona Mental Health Center and by the school systems, although such was necessary in only three cases. Three graduate students in psychology participated in data storage and analysis and in assessment.

Case assignments were made with all permutations of BA's and supervisors; most case-management decisions were made through discussion among these two or three assigned individuals. During the early days of operation, each case was discussed at a weekly total-staff meeting, although each supervisor retained sole authority for management decisions and sole responsibility for the conduct of the case. Later, this weekly meeting evolved into a continuation of in-sevice training for the BA's (and the supervisors); the format varied from presentation of case diffi-culties, to discussion with visitors, to wrestling with complex theoretical issues. These meetings served also to build and maintain spirit and morale.

Thus the theoretical model was transmogrified into an organization. The inbred behaviors of this staff were not systematically studied; this is one of our shortcomings and our regrets, because day-to-day life was very different from that in organizations deriving from the illness model. Not that there was any lack of the usual quarrels and reconciliations, parties and punishments, shifting factions, and friendships. But the model also permeated our interactions with one another, and there was little concern with the self-discovery of staff feeling states which often occupies the time and energy of mental health operations. Things were task-oriented, in the main, as is likely to happen when goal behaviors are clear. But on this we have no data.

CHAPTER V

Assessment

In the natural environment, accurate assessment of the social and behavioral field is of crucial importance. Compared to laboratory conditions, control is at best tenuous. In the absence of accurate data, it may disappear entirely.

In addition, the use of behavioral techniques clearly focuses the eye of the worker on facts. If we are to attempt to modify a behavior, for example, we had best know exactly what the behavior is. If we are to employ reinforcers, we had best verify that the chosen events are indeed reinforcing. This concentration on verifiable data is central to all contingency management; of all our findings, this element of work in the natural environment seems most desirable. *Accurate description,* though unusual in most helping-role work, is the most powerful tool for social problem amelioration. This discussion of the procedures and problems of assessment will only include the modes of accurate description.

The assessment task, simply stated, is this: to assess qualitatively and quantitatively (a) the behavioral repertoire of the target; (b) the stimulus conditions under which the focal behaviors occur (antecedent events); (c) the maintaining stimuli which reinforce the focal behaviors; (d) the reinforcement hierarchy of the target; and (e) the potentials for mediation in the natural environment. Each of these tasks will now be discussed.

THE TARGET'S BEHAVIOR

The first requirement of observation is the selection of a carefully defined category of behavior to be observed. This selection should be preceded by a period of naturalistic observation by the staff and by potential mediators. Theory suggests that an initial focus of intervention should often be those behaviors which are the most immediately irritating to the mediators, regardless of the ultimate importance of the behaviors. Thus, there will be an initial interest in the referral behaviors.

Schools—both teachers and administrators—generally refer children for some sort of special agency handling because they despair of solving the problem internally. Therefore, by the time of referral, relationships between target and school are deteriorated. These are not ideal circumstances for dispassionate observation. For example, typical complaints from schools are that the target is "defiant," "has a poor attitude," "is rebellious." These are important reactions by the school personnel, but are far from being behavioral descriptions. The first task of assessment is clarification of the behavioral referents of, for example, "poor attitude."

This clarification is sometimes difficult, and requires repeated restatement of the issue, "What does the child *do?*" People do not seem to think in behavioral terms naturally; we perceive others' actions in terms of our own reactions. Careful questioning of the teacher may ultimately reveal, for instance, that "poor attitude" of the target means that he will not put his notebook on his desk during notebook-time, instead, he stares out the window. "Defiant" may be the teacher's interpretation of the target's low frequency of homework completion. These behavioral meanings are highly idiosyncratic, but it is vital to the intervention (and beneficial to the mediator) that all referral complaints be specified in terms of the behavioral referents. At home as well as in school, family members perceive in attitudinal categories, perhaps more often than in behavioral ones. Careful conversation with the mediators is most often sufficient to establish the problem-behavior categories.

Whenever possible, the target's behavior should also be observed directly. In the classroom, this is frequently possible, for schools are accustomed to a parade of visitors, and one or two direct naturalistic observations have been simple to achieve and have been nondisruptive in effect, particularly in the lower grades. In homes and in other environments—at work, on the street, in church—direct staff observation is more difficult and can be very disruptive. In these instances, we can often direct potential mediators to accomplish the observation. Careful instruction is required. Narrative written accounts can be requested.

This stage should continue until the staff is satisfied that the principal problem behaviors have been conceptualized into observable units. The period of *baseline recording* can now begin. (See Chapter VIII for a discussion of the rationale of baseline recording.)

Let us consider a simple misbehavior: a third grader who frequently gets out of his seat without permission. (This is not easily borne by the public school teacher.) After having determined that the teacher's initial complaint about the child—perhaps phrased as "hyperactivity"—has get-ting-out-of-seat as the behavioral referent, it is now necessary to establish the operant rate. How often, per unit time, does the child get out of his seat without permission? The teacher will likely assert that it is "con-stantly!" We will want to know, "How many times per hour?"

A staff person can then be assigned the task of recording the frequency of the focal behavior. On a time/unit chart, each instance of getting-out-of-seat is indicated by the observer. (The recorder will also be noting the teacher's response; see the discussion of "Maintaining Stimuli" below.) We have found it adequate to use time-samples, hour or half-hour units at different times of the school day, and over a period of several observa-tions establish a *baseline* (rate prior to systematic intervention). For be-haviors such as getting-out-of-seat, one week's observation (perhaps five to seven recordings) has ordinarily been adequate to establish the typical frequency of the child's misbehavior. For other children and other be-haviors, the fluctuation across time-samples has been more extreme, and more extended sampling has been required in order to assess a mean probable frequency per unit time. Baseline recording should continue until stability of frequency has been established.

This is not always possible. For example in a case where "fire setting" is the referral behavior, we have dispensed, and would again, with the baseline period altogether and instantly intervene. In a case of dangerous acts, we would require only acceptable verification that the behaviors have actually occurred; whether the frequency is once per week or twice per week is a nicety that must be sacrificed. On the other hand, it is a sacrifice, and a baseline recording should not be omitted if at all possible. The effects of intervention cannot be assessed in the absence of some clearly established pre-intervention operant level.

We make this point vigorously, because the natural environment has little patience with "scientific" methodology; the consultant will find him-self under telling pressure for immediate action. The school principal or the parent or the probation officer finds it difficult to understand that before behavior modification can begin, we must stop and count the occur-rences of misbehaviors. They demand action now. In those instances in which we do yield, we pay dearly: functional analyses are vague; assess-ment of the correctness of the intervention is impossible; and success of the management cannot be assayed.

It will have occurred to the reader that a staff person is not always the correct individual for baseline recording. When possible, an expert should be used; the data are more reliable, and the demonstration of recording techniques to potential mediators is of great value. But other experts are often available in the natural environment. For instance, the operant level for "truancy" can be reported with relative accuracy by the high-school attendance officer. "Defiance" in PE class (e.g., refusal to "suit-up" for exercise) can be measured by notes in the coach's daily record book. Tardiness to work can be taken off the punch-clock records.

Expert recorders can also be taught. For the second or third case which he refers, a teacher might well be able to record frequencies as well as the staff members whom she has been watching. Many cooperating teachers have become their own best recorders. A few mechanical aids—a golf-score counter, an umpire's counter, etc.—have been sufficient to allow the teacher to count while teaching.

In many instances, particularly in the home environment, an expert cannot be used, and accurate baseline recording must be preceded by careful instruction to the selected recorder—the parent, the aunt, or the playground supervisor. People vary enormously as to whether or not they understand the principle of counting focal behaviors. Simple as it seems, it goes against many grains.

> A playground supervisor was asked to record, by a simple tally mark, the incidents of *playground aggression* (biting, hitting, snatching, vituperation) committed by #01. The BA was to pick up the week's record from the supervisor on Friday. There was one mark on Monday's column, none in Tuesday's, and for Wednesday the entry was "windy day."

Frequently, the recorder's behavior must be shaped. Baseline level should not be assessed until the recorder's behavior has stabilized.

The tally-mark system is easiest to teach. In homes, it is often possible for the mother to make a mark on a chart each time the boy does not take out the garbage, or each time the daughter makes the bed. Of the two systems, it is preferable to record behaviors rather than nonbehaviors.

During the period of baseline recording, several focal behaviors will no doubt be observed, simultaneously, in different settings. Upon the observation of apparent stability—or when we are satisfied that there is no stability—a highly unusual condition will have been achieved: we will know what the child is doing. In many cases, the period of recording brings about improvements. (See the discussion in Chapter 7.)

ANTECEDENT EVENTS

We should also know when the child is doing what he is doing (i.e., upon what occasions he misbehaves, or does not misbehave). We should discover the events which set the occasion for the focal behaviors.

In the absence of trained staff observers, we have been generally unsuccessful in discerning these antecedent events. Parents and teachers are often reluctant to find any controlling stimuli in their own behavior. Such concepts seem threatening, since they appear to attribute the cause of the misbehavior to the responsible adult. Even with trained observers, some antecedent events are difficult to identify: they are mediated by thought processes, and are idiosyncratic; or they subtly elude our observation skills. BRP intervention plans did employ instructions by mediators as a technique of stimulus control; that is, a technique to increase the frequency of some desirable behavior, so that the behavior may be then reinforced. Although research psychologists are becoming aware of the high degree of control exerted over human behavior by antecedent events, behavior modification techniques have not involved them to a high degree. The potential for manipulation of antecedent events in the natural environment is good and this important avenue of behavior control should be explored by future applied research.

MAINTAINING STIMULI

We must carefully assess the consequences to the child of his focal behaviors. It is a postulate of the behaviorist position that there are now, or have been in the history of the individual, reinforcing consequences to a given continuing behavior. Some of these consequences (the maintaining reinforcing stimuli) are current in the interactions of focal behavior and the environment. Some are not; they are lost in the history of the habit formations. For purposes of assessment, however, it is well to assume that there are currently rewarding consequences to the child's behaviors (and misbehaviors). This assumption keeps the observer constantly alert to the possibility that the functional relationships of focal behaviors and environmental consequences can be discovered. Although it is not always possible, the assumption increases the likelihood.

The search for the maintaining stimuli has as its goal the creation of a functional-analytic hypothesis.

During the period of naturalistic observation, the BA discovered that Case #Pilot 3 underachieved enormously in fourth grade arithmetic. His papers were incorrect and incomplete. The teacher returned them to Pilot 3, who took them home. Each time, the boy's father, upset by his child's arithmetic "stupidity," worked with his son in the evening, carefully explaining the problems and the techniques. These sessions occurred several times weekly, and lasted up to an hour. *Functional analytic hypothesis:* arithmetic underachievement is maintained by the reinforcement of paternal attention.

Naturally, the hypotheses are not always correct, but they are subject to verification through observation and experimentation, and thus to subsequent corrections. Once the hypothesis is created, the period of baseline recording can include the simultaneous recording of hypothesized maintaining stimuli.

Pilot 3's mother was instructed to record on a large calendar those days on which he brought home an unacceptable arithmetic assignment. She was also instructed to record whether or not the father worked with the child at his study-table, and the length of these sessions.

It is imperative that the functional relationship remain undisturbed during the baseline period. This requires that the environmental response to focal behaviors remain as it was prior to observation. However, it never can. The students of science have clearly established that the effects of the observer upon his field of observation are inevitable, but gross alterations can be avoided, by careful instructions to the potential mediators. These instructions should be: no changes in the handling of the problem behaviors should be initiated during the observation.

Pilot 3's parents were concerned immediately with the issue of the father's tutoring sessions, when the BA asked for the recording. They pressed for an opinion by the BA. Should they increase or discontinue the habit? The answer was "do as you have been doing." This was puzzling to the parents.

Indeed, it is puzzling to most people, who are accustomed to action, advice, or interpretation prior to the collection of information. Continuation of the preceeding sequences during assessment, however, can be largely achieved through encouragement and an explanation of the value of careful data collection. It can never be perfectly achieved; even the most cooperative observer cannot help but have his behavior somewhat altered by consciousness and attention to a previously automated behavior. These effects are sometimes lessened by the use of the nonparticipating observer.

In observing the third grade classroom of #06, the BA had hypothesized that the focal behavior (hitting the neighboring-seat children) was maintained by teacher-attention: scolding, standing near, etc.). On a two column chart, the BA entered both the focal behavior frequencies and the teacher's attending-behavior. The correlation of the two events suggested a functional relationship.

On the other hand, the presence of a staff observer in some settings is so disruptive that the natural sequences will not occur; or, such a long period of adaptation to the observer's presence would be required that the technique would be disqualified. For example, the presence of a BA in Pilot 3's home would have been disruptive to the family interaction. The observation would have been of a nontypical sample. The interference produced by parental consciousness of the potential hypothesis would have been less, and was thus chosen.

Whenever possible, the baseline period should include recordings of possible maintaining stimulus events. We will then know when a child does what he does and what happens next.

Often, though, we cannot discover maintaining stimuli. Frequently, too, the observed maintaining stimuli may not be the only potential consequences, and even those reinforcers which are now maintaining problem behavior are not always the most powerful reinforcers for the child.

THE REINFORCEMENT HIERARCHY

Many reinforcers of relatively low power can maintain behaviors. A mildly pleasant consequence may increase the probability of the reoccurrence of some behaviors which preceed it, but some other reinforcer might well have more power in the potential for modification.

We rely upon the concept of *reinforcement hierarchy* to express the notion that reinforcing events can usually be ranked in the order of their hypothetical power to strengthen behaviors. Such relative positioning is vital to the behavioral engineer because some functional relationships to focal problem behaviors cannot be altered in the natural environment.

> Case #SES-4 was in a Special Educational class for early adolescents. Although the teacher was sophisticated in behavioral techniques, and was able to withhold her attention from the boy's stage-whispered obscenities during class, the attention of the boy's classmates—their giggles, egging him on, and the like—provided enough reinforcement to solidify this behavior. It did not appear likely to the observer that sufficient control over the peer behavior could be gained to alter this functional relationship. The assessment task then became the discovery of a manipulable consequence which would be more powerful in the hierarchy than peer attention.

The ultimate task of intervention is to alter the consquences in the environment, so that powerful reinforcing consequences are used to strengthen desirable behavior. It follows that a catalogue of available reinforcers must be created. We have used three basic techniques for gathering the data for the reinforcement hierarchy: the first is observation of response–consequence units, as has been discussed in the section above. Maintaining stimuli would of course find a place in the catalogue. The other two techniques remain to be discussed. They are interviews with the mediators and direct examination of the target.

Interviews with the Mediators

Interviews with the mediators have as their fundamental purpose the evaluation of the mediator, himself; this issue will be discussed in detail below. However, it is a secondary aim of these interviews with the teacher, the parent, the employer, etc., to garner information relative to the reinforcement hierarchy of the target. For example, we would establish the parent's version of the child's reinforcement hierarchy by asking the parents to list—and rank according to their relative reinforcing values—the activities or events that seem to be reinforcing the child. To establish this reinforcement hierarchy, the parents (or other mediators) are questioned about the kinds of things their children like to do or would like to have. The mediators rank these events from the most reinforcing (to the target) to the least reinforcing. We find out how often the target has an opportunity to engage in the activity or how often he may receive the positive reinforcers.

Some powerful reinforcers may not be manipulated. It may be, for example, that the mediator's work schedule is such that he cannot arrange free time for extended contact, for example, camping trips. A reinforcer like father-attention would be inappropriate for use with this child, even though it seems powerful. Occasionally, the availability of the reinforcers (for example, money) is in doubt. If the mediators simply cannot afford to reinforce with money this avenue of reinforcement is obviously closed. Some reinforcers may be inappropriate. For example, a child may want very much to drive a car but is too young to be legally licensed. Many parents and teachers of problem children have attempted to control the child's behavior largely through aversive control. They do not understand the value of positive reinforcement in behavior control and do not know, in particular, the child's positive reinforcers. They have had no need to know or ask. It is remarkable how little the primary mediators of a problem child know about his favorite activities and events. When they do attempt to describe them they are frequently in error.

There are two ways to test the validity of the reinforcer hierarchy listed by the mediator. The first method utilizes the interview with the target wherein the target's reinforcers—as he ranks them—are listed and ranked subjectively by the interviewer. The reinforcers found in this interview are compared with those from the mediator interview, and any discrepancies are generally settled in favor of the target's ranking of his own reinforcers. The second method is even more empirical: the reinforcers listed by the mediator may be placed contingent on desired behaviors in the target's repertoire and their effectiveness as reinforcers determined simply by the presence or absence of a significant increase in frequency of the behavior in question.

DIRECT TARGET ASSESSMENT AND QUESTIONNAIRE

Direct observation of target behavior, while highly desirable, cannot be accomplished for all behaviors. Interview and questionnaire data are valuable elements in the assessment structure. Because the behavioral constructs are simple and direct, direct and simple methods of inquiry can be employed. For example, when one inquires of a target as to those things he likes to do, or likes to get, and from whom and with whom, a minimum of "psychodynamic" distortion will occur. That is to say, because the inquiry is purposeful, the interviewer will not need to rely unduly on his own speculation.

The procedures for such an interview and the structure of such a questionnaire will vary according to the age of the target, the setting in which it occurs, and the perceived relationship of the target to the interviewer. But the general form of the inquiry will be dictated by the information relevant to it: a discovery of the potential reinforcers and the potential mediators. Because mental health workers are more accustomed to an interest in the novelistic aspects of clients' lives, a structured interview format is very desirable: it helps to recall (continuously) the reason that the interview is taking place. Below is a general "case-study": a detailed account of those procedures developed by the Behavior Research Project for direct assessment of the target. This account is not intended as a model for other workers in other settings. Behavioral assessment, as it occurs in other settings and by other kinds of staff, will need to be responsive to the specifics encountered there. Quite different procedures might be followed for assessment of adult psychotic hospital patients, or for outpatient neurotic children in psychiatric practice, or for vocational rehabilitation counsellors in sheltered workshops. But the foci of inquiry will be comparable, and this "case-study" illustrates how one organization met the specific problems of assessment of behaviorally disordered children in the school setting.

DIRECT TARGET ASSESSMENT IN THE BEHAVIOR RESEARCH PROJECT[5]

The one contact with the target, in the BRP model, has been that of assessment. While in some instances the child may have observed the observer observing, that observer did not talk to the child. During the assessment interview, however, detailed and careful conversations take place between the BA and the child.

Two special testing instruments were devised initially to aid in the determination of reinforcers and mediators. These were the Mediator–Reinforcer Incomplete Blank (MRB) and the Structured Thematic Apperception Test Interview Form (TATIF). The MRB is a 34-item incomplete-sentence blank. Items were devised to give pertinent information on reinforcers and mediators. A few examples: (a) "Two things I like to do best are ————"; (b) "I will do almost anything to get ————"; (c) "The only person I will take advice from is ————"; (d) "The thing I like to do best with my father is ————." There has been revision: items which were not evoking significant information on reinforcers and mediators were discarded; revisions in wording were made, and new items added. The completed MRB test is included in Appendix III.

The TATIF is a modification of the Thematic Apperception Test. TAT cards were selected which could be structured by the interviewer to allow direct questioning about the reinforcers and mediators involved in the behavior of characters in the picture. Card I of the TAT serves as an example: (a) "If you were the father (mother) of this boy, how would you get him to play the violin?" (b) "If he still wouldn't play it, then what would you do?" (c) "If you were the boy, which of your parents might be most successful in getting you to play it?" The TATIF was much less useful than other techniques; the procedure was abandoned and is not recommended.

In the BRP procedure, target assessment begins with the interviewer contacting a school official (the principal of the school, his secretary, or the child's counselor) to arrange a time and place for the interview. The school official is asked to say nothing about the interview to the child.

[5] We are grateful to Roger Vogler, Michael Morgan, and Barry Kinney for their contribution to the development of these techniques.

The assessment interview can be divided into three basic parts: (1) introduction, rapport establishment, and semistructured questioning; (2) administration of the tests; and (3) a ranking by the subject of his reinforcers.

Once the child and the interviewer are alone in the interviewing room, the interviewer presents himself to the child as a consultant to the school who works with some of the children who have not been getting as good grades as they probably could, and who have been in some sort of trouble. With very young children it is usually unnecessary to communicate even this, and the interviewer can begin by asking the child how he is getting along at school or at home.

Having defined the relationship, the interviewer usually directs the conversation to what the child likes to do or what he would like to have, and with whom he enjoys his activities. This information is recorded for both the school and the home setting. The child is occasionally asked to describe his daily schedule from the time he gets up to the time he goes to bed, both for weekdays and for Saturdays and Sundays. This provides a record of what he usually does and some idea of the frequency with which he engages in such behaviors.

Throughout the interview, it is important to have the subject clearly describe the reinforcers, and to have him specify referent behaviors of the mediators when he makes a positive or negative statement about them. For example, if a subject says the best reward anyone can give him is "love," he is asked what he would like other people to do to show their love.

Candy has been found most useful as an adjunct to interviewing. The candy is given noncontingent during the early part of the interview, but is made increasingly contingent on responding as the interview proceeds. Somewhat to our surprise, candy worked nearly as well with many older subjects (even 14-year-olds) as it did with younger ones. The effectiveness of making the candy contingent on appropiate responses became clear to the interviewers as they became more experienced. For example, when it became apparent that the child was answering the questions with anything that came to mind just to obtain the candy, the interviewer might say to the youngster that he does not seem to be giving answers that are meaningful, and might then withhold the candy. Then, when the child began to delay his responses and give the question some consideration, the candy again would be dispensed. It is difficult to communicate the subtleties of this technique but it may be said that by means of a variety of cross-checks on the subject's responses (such as variety, latency, frequency, and emotional tone of response), it is possible to get some impression of the sincerity of his answers.

The MRB is administered first and is given orally regardless of the child's age.

Occasionally, the child is asked to name three wishes and to name three things or people he would take with him if he were going to a deserted island. These two questions only take a few minutes to ask, and on occasion have given very useful information. As mentioned above, the child is asked in as many ways as possible about reinforcers and mediators. The redundancy of many of the questions has the advantage of cross-checking the subject's report. Also, the number of times a subject mentions a particular reinforcer or potential mediator and the tone of his voice (such as enthusiasm or lack of enthusiasm) are used by the interviewer in assessing the relative strength and importance to the subject of reinforcers and mediators. At the end of the interview, the interviewer makes a brief survey of the test results, lists all the stated reinforcers and asks the subject to rank them.

The interview data are recorded in a written report. The report follows this general format: (1) a description of the target and behaviors he emitted during the interview, (2) a statement about existing contingencies and the usual consequences to his behavior, (3) a statement on home mediators and external mediators and their relative effectiveness from the target's point of view, (4) ranked listing of positive reinforcers with description and/or potential use, and (5) a ranked listing of negative reinforcers with some descriptive information.

A reinforcer-rating scale was devised to aid in communicating the estimated relative effectiveness of reinforcers. Reinforcers are rated one through nine according to the scale. The scale is reproduced below:

9 Highly reinforcing; rarely fails to be effective
8
7 Quite reinforcing; will work hard for it (or avoid it)
6
5 Reinforces fairly well; moderately effective
4
3 Weak reinforcer; only works sometimes
2
1 Has reinforcing property of a very low or indeterminate power

The interviewer excludes some mediators and reinforcers in writing a report, because they are either unavailable or not manipulable. For example, it may be that a child's favorite mediator is someone who lives out of town, such as a divorced father. Or in the case of a reinforcer, for example, a child of fourteen may find driving an automobile the most powerfully reinforcing event in his environment.

POTENTIALS FOR MEDIATION

Creating of the reinforcement hierarchy can be a fairly simple matter when the reinforcers are objects. Lloyd Homme (1966), for example has devised the reinforcement "menu," a pictorial representation of several desirable objects, from which the child may choose. It is often simple to ask a target if he prefers movie tickets or chits-for-bowling. There are other reinforcing events, however, which are more complex, and intimately involve the *dispenser of the reinforcement.* For some children, going to the movies alone or with someone else (or anyone else) is all the same. For others, going to the movie is only a reinforcer if it occurs in the company of the girl friend. For a young boy, playing-baseball-with-father may be the most powerful reinforcer conceivable to the target; but playing baseball (other than with father) may have little appeal.

The point here is that many reinforcing events are interpersonal events, and that some reinforcers require a particular mediator to behave in a particular way. Thus, we hark back to the issue in Chapter IV: the vital issue in behavior modification in the natural environment is that the mediator must be able to perform the required mediation. The selection of a key mediator is thus crucial to successful intervention. Accurate selection presupposes prior accurate assessment.

A Catalogue of Mediators

The assessor will by this point in the process be able to assemble a list of those individuals in the target's environment who may be considered for mediation. This list will be drawn from (1) complainants; (2) staff observation of the target's associates and interactants; (3) those individuals who occupy family, social, educational, or occupational roles which reciprocate with the child's roles; and (4) other individuals mentioned as influential or desirable to the target, in the interviews with the target or other potential mediators. From this list, the mediator or mediators will be drawn.

Assessment of Individual Mediators

Only two simple questions need be asked in assessing an individual's potential for mediation: (1) Does he possess high-ranked reinforcers for the target? (2) Can he dispense them on contingency? All other information is irrelevant.

The Availability of the Reinforcers

Prior to the preparation of mediator analyses, the reinforcement hierarchy should be available. With the object-reinforcer, at least, possession of the reinforcer by a particular mediator is easy enough to determine. Suppose the reinforcer is cash: does the family have 25¢ per week or not? They can be asked. Suppose the reinforcer is cosmetics: who on the list of available mediators has enough knowledge and money to provide satisfactory cosmetics? In the school setting, the high reinforcer may be playing-football-after-school. Who, then, "has" it? Most likely the football supervisor. These are simple instances.

Reinforcers which are interpersonal events, although complex in the execution-phase, make mediator-assessment all the more simple. For example, the boy who wants to play football with father has already restricted the possession of the reinforcer to father. For the child who wants adult attention during reading class, the choice of the mediator is likely restricted to the reading teacher.

Even though there are relatively few cases in which the determination of the possession of the reinforcer is difficult, there remains the more difficult issue of bringing the reinforcement under control.

The Ability to Dispense on Contingency

By this point in time, the list of potential mediators will be sharply reduced, since it will then contain only people who possess the reinforcers in the child's hierarchy. From this list, those who can place the reinforcer on contingency will be selected. Information relative to this decision may require additional interviews with these potential mediators; on the other hand, the information may well have been gained in the preparatory interviews.

There are many reasons why a given individual may be unable to establish a given contingency between behavior and reinforcement. These reasons will be discussed in detail, with case illustrations, in Chapter VII. Also, the issues which are related to contingency-management–ability have been discussed in Chapter III: for example, role occupancy and family and/or organization constraints. For each potential mediator, these criteria can be applied to those reinforcers which have high rank for the target. Most matchings are rapid and surprisingly obvious.

Case #31: Age seven. Third highest reinforcer, ice cream. Potential mediator, second grade teacher. Potential for consequating: zero. School regulations in this district forbid rewarding children with food.

Although most issues can be settled this quickly, many cannot. Particularly in those cases when choices are narrowed by the target, his own selected mediator (the father with whom he wants to play football) either must do it or a much less powerful reinforcer must be chosen. The statement of probability which the staff must make about this father's ability to consequate can never be totally accurate. On the other hand, it does not occur in total darkness. If the issue seems in the balance, we have found a useful technique: ask him. If he says, "No," one might be advised to opt for another plan. If he says, "Yes," the issue may still be in doubt. In these matters, there is always art. There is always "clinical" skill.

Besides, the empiricism of behavior modification leaves us a ready and reliable resolution. We can always try it. We can begin.

References

Homme, L. Contingency management. *Clinical Child Psychology Newsletter,* 1966, **4.** (November).

CHAPTER VI

Intervention

By the term *intervention,* we mean the institution of a new system of contingency management. As explained previously, the basic paradigm for intervention is a simple one, and virtually invariant: the rearrangement of contingencies so that undesirable behavior is no longer rewarded, and desirable behavior is rewarded. However, that simple formula, in any given case, requires unique and frequently incredible complexity of communication and logistics. In this chapter, we will report several typical patterns of Behavior Research Project intervention. Details as to specific accommodations will be illustrated by case material.[6]

Before turning to that task, however, a most interesting phenomenon must be discussed: the intervention effects of assessment.

THE INTERVENTION EFFECTS OF ASSESSMENT

No social system—at least no natural one—can be observed without the observation processes having some effect on the data obtained. The effects of the observer—and his "contamination" of the subject field—is a complex concern of the philosophy of science and indeed of the technology of every scientific enterprise. No social–psychological observations are without these effects, least of all our own. The classroom teacher, visited by an observation staff, does not emit the same behaviors as

[6] The case material in this volume has often been drawn directly from the working files and in other instances from case résumés prepared by the Behavior Analysts. Their authorship contribution is now acknowledged generally, and throughout the text where appropriate.

she did on the day prior to the visit, so that we can never observe her unobserved behavior. Parents, after they have discussed their family life with a Behavior Analyst, no longer behave in exactly the same way toward the target. Indeed, the partial reorganization of the school–home environment, which is an automatic consequence of the mere processes of problem-recognition and referral-to-an-agency, may well alter certain of the controlling stimuli of the target's behavior. Further, many individuals who observe the processes of behavior modification in the natural environment have alluded to the "Hawthorne effect" in the results: the simple effects of attention and of being singled-out may well produce an increase in criterion performance. Detailing each of these effects, separating them, and attempting to control them are the tasks of basic science and the psychological laboratories. For purposes of social action, however, these and all similar considerations can be "summed" into the single issue of "observation effects." Furthermore, extirpation of observation effects is not even necessarily desirable.

Let us clarify. If the problem behavior persists after observation and assessment, it still requires intervention. If it desists, observation itself has been a successful intervention technique. There were six such cases in the BRP sample. Of these, we will now report three types. The six represent seven percent of those cases which survived the initial screening, parental-consent, and detailed evaluation for appropriateness.

THE FUNCTION OF OBSERVATION

For certain families, the processes of discussion with the Behavior Analyst serve to bring their family interactions into focus, and allow them to see obvious corrections which they can (and often do) institute. A simple inquiry as to the "amount of time spent with son" may make a father think, and sometimes act.

> Case #81 was referred by the Juvenile Probation Department for incorrigibility and two runaway incidents. John had a severe temper and he would turn on his mother and sisters. The father, a truck driver, was away often for long periods of time. The mother was passive and meek. John was lazy at home and would not do any chores. He would only watch television, getting fatter and unhappier with himself. His school work was poor.
>
> Shortly after interviews began, John went on a trip with his father. Since it was summer vacation, father had allowed John to go East with him and paid him to work. When John returned, an assessment interview was given and baseline recordings were started. The mother reported that there was a big improvement in John and she had only one incident recorded for a two-week period. The Behavior Analyst suggested waiting until

school started to see how John's grades developed. The first six weeks in high school John made a 2.0 average and requested a more difficult math class. He began tennis in physical education and enjoyed it so much that he joined the tennis team and played several times a week with his older sister. Because of the "miraculous" improvement the case was terminated. (Patricia Staples)

In most cases of incorrigibility and runaway, the ultimate aim of complex intervention and contingency management is to establish the parent–child relationship on a sound and personal basis which will allow the father to appropriately consequate the son's desirable and undesirable behavior. In Case #81, the father's own initiative was sufficient—following the BRP-occasioned opportunity for self-examination and self-observation.

Such an effect was also occasionally seen in the school environment.

Case #93 was referred by the school for a generally hostile attitude and lack of academic motivation. Leon, age 14, also was a problem at home: temper tantrums, aggressiveness, and "general nuisance." The mother could not describe his problem behavior accurately. She was asked to keep a narrative, written record of problem incidents.

Leon received a "5" (Fail) in science during the first six-week grading period. The Behavior Analyst immediately interviewed the science teacher, an inarticulate man who could make no suggestions as to specific improvements which Leon should make. The teacher was asked to observe Leon closely (behavior, frequency of turning in work, test grades, etc.). After two weeks, the teacher reported that Leon was improving. He was asked to continue observing. In the second six weeks Leon's grade rose to a 4, in the third six weeks to a 2, and it remained there the rest of the year.

The mother never did record a problem incident. There was no intervention. The school had no further complaints. Case #93 was terminated.

Accuracy of observation can often lead to more rational reaction. Few of us observe, directly and immediately, the events of our lives. For the most part, our beliefs about events are created by past experience, expectation, convention, our own personalities, and perceptual sets. The prime and irreducible element of scientific inquiry is accurate observation; this element is not automatically given, but must be taught, learned, and earned. Accurate observation is probably more difficult in familiar surroundings than in a fresh environment. It is more difficult to see the actions of people familiar to us than to accurately know the behavior of strangers. The most difficult thing to observe accurately is one's self.

For all these reasons, it is a rare teacher indeed who can accurately observe his interaction with his pupil. The stresses of large classes, of complex curricula, and of multiple role demands militate against careful observation. Yet it is surely indisputable that intelligent action cannot proceed in the absence of accurate perception of facts, and it is our assertion that the excellent teacher is always the accurately observing one. The inclination toward accuracy and the conviction of its necessity can be taught, and indeed it becomes most valuable to the teacher to see the discrepancy between the unreflective perception and the accurate observation.

THE FUNCTION OF RECORDING

In still other cases, the potential for self-correction within the system cannot be realized by the perceptive observation of the mediators, but can be realized by their recorded observations. During the period of baseline recording, mediators are prompted into unfamiliar observation-behaviors, for example, making marks concerning the target's behavior on a score card, learning to discriminate between "getting-out-of-seat" and almost getting-out-of-seat, and the like. These unfamiliar acts typically force a more accurate belief concerning the problem behaviors into the mediator's consciousness. This more accurate belief can have several consequences, and sometimes the results are felicitous.

Case #69 (7-26-66). After spending several weeks of recording chores and tantrums, Mrs. R. has decided to withdraw from the Project. She felt that recording baseline has altered her behavior and she cannot continue to treat her son as she did before. She also feels more confident, and feels she can better handle him.
       (10-4-66). Gary no longer presents any serious behavior problems to the school and continues to have only a reading difficulty. An application to the Reading Development Center (University of Arizona) was given to Mrs. R., and she will utilize their services. Case closed.

Another effect of recording on the target may also be observed.

Case #85. Cindy Lou was a junior in high school who had straight fours and fives all through high school, and had run away from home several times.
       Interviews were conducted and an assessment was made. Baseline recording was started and the mother insisted that there was no misbehavior to record. Cindy Lou's grades were received from school and for the first time in three years of high school she had made all threes. It was decided this was not an appropriate case and the file was inactivated.
       Six weeks later, the mother called and said that her daughter's grades had come in, and she had made all fours and fives. She wanted us to reconsider working with them.
       After the Behavior Analyst went to the home, the mother said that there were still no behavior problems in the home or in school, but the underachievement was a serious problem. The mother was sorry that we could not work with her, because she felt that we represented authority figures. We had arrived in the home shortly after the juvenile probation department had been in contact with Cindy Lou. The mother had apparently told Cindy that she would have to keep records and report them to someone. Because Cindy did not want any more trouble, she decided to be

obedient at home and work hard in school. Therefore, a change had taken place before an intervention plan could be instituted.

The case could not be reopened due to the technicality of criteria: no behavior problem was present.

In this instance, the apparent presence of an authority figure (who might administer some adverse consequence) was sufficient to deter those behaviors which were being "reported."

THE FUNCTION OF DATA PRESENTATION

The presentation of recorded data to the mediators and the targets can have a powerful function. In most instances, the rise of the data line on a cumulative graph (perhaps posted on the wall) seems to serve as a stimulus to the mediator to administer praise, or to remind him to deliver other reinforcers. In those few cases for which graphed records were the only reinforcer, we did not observe behavioral improvement; for this population, apparently, back-up reinforcers are necessary.

For some targets, indeed, the presentation of graphic data is an adverse event.

Pilot Case M.D. Baseline was taken on voluntary garbage disposal on the part of a 15-year-old boy. The frequency was less than seven voluntary completions. Disputes arose as to the definition of "voluntary" when the week's tally was discussed. Thus, a chart was tacked to the wall upon which a daily record could be entered by the stepmother. The target became enraged at "being treated like a first grader." On the second day, he offered a bargain: if the chart were removed, he would take out the garbage without failure. He did, thenceforth.

The presence of data is a powerful thing. That the valence is different for different individuals makes its use much like that of any other reinforcing stimulus.

Assessment alone prompted behavior change in only 6 cases; the other 77 required the institution of intervention plans.

MAINTAINING BEHAVIOR THROUGH REINFORCEMENT

The lists of potential reinforcers which appear in the targets' reinforcement hierarchies vary. As will become clear in this chapter, reinforcers range from slot cars to summer camp, from uncle's attention to art-class time. We restricted the use of reinforcers by only two criteria. First, any reinforcer must be available in the natural environment for dispensing on contingency; second, we declined the use of any antisocial, illegal, or immoral reinforcer. This latter point implies that we did impose an external limitation on the dictates of the reinforcement hierarchy; no matter how high we might assess the potential power of marijuana, glue sniffing, sex, or the like, we never used them. One of the difficulties presented to society by the hardened delinquent is the domination of his reinforcement catalog by this class of reinforcers. One might even propose a classification scheme for delinquency based on the social acceptability of his reinforcement hierarchy. But beyond that, we do suggest most careful attention to the specifics of the target's reinforcers; any attempts which we have made to abstract and classify reinforcers, and to base intervention upon them, have failed. One must attend to the thing itself.

The headings into which this section is divided are artificial ones, and have been chosen only to clarify this discussion. The headings are Activity Reinforcers, Material Reinforcers, and People Reinforcers.

ACTIVITY REINFORCERS

In teaching the techniques of contingency management, one frequently hears from the neophyte interventionist that there simply are no reinforcers available, that the family is too poor to use cash, that the target does not like anything and does not even want to do anything. We have all seen such targets, particularly among delinquents, who are maddening in their apparent lack of interest in people, things, or the world around them. But it is useful to remember that as long as an organism is alive, it is behaving, it is doing something. And the characteristic activity may be used as a reinforcer.

The Premack Principle

The "Premack principle" may be stated as follows: a high probability behavior may be used as the reinforcer for a low probability behavior (Premack, 1965). For our purposes, a high probability behavior may be understood as that activity in which a target will engage in the given situation, if unconstrained. For example, if left to his own devices in his own home, the target has a high probability behavior of television-watching, and a low probability behavior of studying. The Premack principle is useful in that it alerts the interventionist to the fact that television watching is a good potential reinforcer for studying-behavior, if the relationship between the two is made contingent.

Thus we are never without a potential intervention plan, because the target's preferred activity can always be used as a reinforcer—even if it is only sitting and staring at the wall. The difficulty with the use of the Premack principle in the behaviorally disordered population is, of course, that the preferred activities are typically undesirable. In most cases, the use of material or people reinforcers produces a behavioral repertoire which is more acceptable. But the following rather extreme case study illustrates that successful intervention may well be possible, even for targets who apparently have "no" reinforcers.

Case #S-13. Burton had been forced out of school because of his bizarre mannerisms, gestures, and posturing. It was generally assumed that he was a severely schizophrenic child, albeit a highly intelligent 13-year-old. He acted belligerently toward his parents and was destructive of home property. He had been known to punish his parents by such behaviors as pouring buckets of water over his head in the middle of the living room, but his high probability behaviors were to publicly assume a semifetal position, and, alternately, to lock himself alone in his room for long hours. Reading the homework assigned by his visiting teacher was low probability behavior. Neither he nor his parents rated any objects or people as reinforcing. Initially, therefore, the reinforcement of "retiring to his room" was used, contingent upon completing his homework assignment.

Later, he was returned to a special education classroom. Low probability behavior was classwork, and high probability behavior was escaping alone to a corner of the school yard. A contingency was established in which Burton was allowed to leave the class after completion of his assignment. Later, school attendance became a high probability behavior. At that point, he was allowed to attend school only contingent upon more acceptable behavior at home.

The strategy implied in the use of the Premack principle is illustrated here; by reinforcing the low probability (desirable) behavior, it becomes more frequent, more probable.

Activity reinforcers are highly important in contingency management with any target population, but activities rarely occur in isolation from material or people reinforcers. In the natural environment, action, people, and things have much to do with one another. But critics of the behavior-modification enterprise frequently charge it with materialism, mechanism, and depersonalization—probably because many reinforcers are indeed objects, and nonpersonal. Clearly this is true for us all; automobiles and cameras, a shovel or a new belt, salaries and books are all things men pursue. They are also attracted by one another. But even in the instance of the material reinforcers, the natural environment almost invariably dispenses them in an interpersonal system. Detractors most often base their criticisms on an unrealistic "armchair" assessment of the reinforcer-dispensing system of society. But one simply cannot eliminate the human element from the natural environment. The ultimate aim of all intervention plans is to so correct the deviant behavior as to make the target eligible for incorporation into the social control (reinforcement) network which shapes us all into civilization. The aim, then, is to humanize. For some disordered children, it is necessary to begin with candy or money. After all, we all begin with milk.

MATERIAL REINFORCERS

Few intervention plans will be without some material reinforcement; even when "time-with-father" is the reinforcer, there may well be a baseball, bicycle, or dog-sled involved. There are certain cases, however, in which material reinforcers are relied upon most heavily.

> Case #92. One of the school's major complaints concerning Anne was her frequent absences. Although spending money was very rewarding, the mother could not afford an extra sum in addition to Anne's small allowance. To reward her for school attendance, the BRP office sent Anne a note (anonymous) and one dollar, dispensed on a variable schedule for attending classes. The note stated which day's attendance the money was for, and encouraged her to continue attending.
>
> The first note arrived in the mail after nearly ten days attendance. The next came after four and seven days attendance. The notes were discontinued without notice after another four days. Anne continued to attend school for approximately four weeks when she became ill and then malingered for five school days. After that she became tardy frequently and asked permission from her mother to remain home. Another form of intervention was necessary.
>
> While Anne was receiving the notes, her mother reported that she was exceedingly curious about her mysterious benefactor and questioned her mother about the notes often. Her mother once said that her curiosity, not the money, was responsible for her interest in school attendance. (Diana Zimmerman)

Case #92 was experimental; we rarely attempted the use of a reinforcer not currently available in the natural environment of the target. Anne's mother was a welfare recipient, and these dollars (contributed by the BA's from their own pockets) could not be a permanent plan.

This case was also our effort to experiment with maximum depersonalization of reinforcement dispensing. It is interesting to note that the target did not allow such to occur; according to the mother, at least, her curiosity was about a person, not the dollar. Anne's heightened interest in the mail also brought about an active friendship with the mailman. Lest the reader take that friendship more lightly than he should, let us observe that the dispensing of positive reinforcers has the effect of increasing the positive value of the dispenser. This principle can be used systematically to increase the emotional bonds between mediator and target.

It has been our general experience (perhaps unnecessary to observe) that the greater the emotional distance between target and his social environment the higher will rank material reinforcers. Thus, on the principle that one must begin where the target actually is, not where we might eventually wish him to be, we have emphasized material reinforcers more heavily.

Case #63. Sal was referred to us primarily for his incorrigible behavior at home. He threatened to physically harm both parents a number of times and refused to do any work around the house.

It was very clear after interviewing both parents that neither would be effective as personal mediators. The father was very ineffective and didn't get along with Sal at all; the mother was very weak and easily manipulated. Because of these factors, we felt it necessary to rely on material reinforcers.

Sal has access to a car which was provided by his father. The intervention plan was as follows. If Sal completed chores to the satisfaction of his parents, and did not abuse his car privilege, he would obtain full use of the automobile. For each chore not completed, or for every hour Sal was late in bringing home the car, he was restricted from 15 to 30 minutes of car use.

Neither parent was personally involved with Sal in the use of the reinforcer. The bookkeeping of time penalties was done on paper, and the parents were instructed to minimize discussion with the target concerning the contingency; all penalties were to be reported to him briefly and in a businesslike way.

As originally hoped for, however, Sal did become quite personally attached to his mother, and completed more chores than were asked of him.

This technique is to be strongly advised in such cases. Dispensing of reinforcement should be "depersonalized" originally, because the present "personal" relationship between mediator and target has, as its sole content, punitiveness and contention. Instructions to minimize verbalization concerning the problem behaviors help the mediators to control their own habits of scolding and being overly emotional.

Actually, the decision to depersonalize can be determined by the mediator's ability to dispense positive reinforcement without contaminating its effects by punishment or social censure. Ideally, such a capable mediator is likely to be a positive reinforcer himself.

PEOPLE REINFORCERS

In some instances, of course, a personal relationship can be discovered which is highly reinforcing to the target. Praise, attention, or even time spent with such a mediator can be the reinforcement of choice.

Case #01. Teddy was referred to our Project for his aggressiveness and inattentiveness at school, and his rebelliousness at home. We took baseline at school on Teddy's classroom behavior. We also took baseline at home for referral behaviors, but found that these occurred very infrequently. The intervention plan was designed to reduce the more frequent school behaviors, using reinforcers at home for the contingencies.

Assessing the home for reinforcers, we discovered that for Teddy any interaction with his father was reinforcing. Such interaction was thus made contingent.

Teddy's teacher was to decide for each day whether or not Teddy's behavior was satisfactory. If he met her standards, she would dispense a note which would earn Teddy time with his father in the afternoon. If he did not bring home this note, his father would voice his displeasure and ignore him. Teddy's mother's role in this plan was different; since she was the major source of punitiveness in the home, we felt that any failure on Teddy's part would bring about aversive responses from her. We decided to have her praise Teddy for bringing home his note, but ignore his not bringing it home. Under no circumstances was either parent to spank Teddy or isolate him for failing to bring home his note.

Teddy worked very hard in the classroom to earn his note. In fact, not only did his classroom behavior improve, but also his aggressive playground behavior decreased.

Case #01 represents an instance in which the interaction of the target was determined specifically in accordance with the reinforcing value of the two parents. The aversive value of the mother's contact was minimized. For Case #50, the reinforcing value of both parents was positive, but the father seemed of greater value.

Case #50. Rena was referred by her parents who were very concerned about her inappropriate behavior at school. Rena, an elementary school student, was known throughout the school for her aggressiveness toward her peers, disruptive classroom behavior, and general defiance. After interviewing her parents, we discovered that Rena was exhibiting, on a somewhat lesser scale, the same behavior at home. The parents' primary concern, however, was her behavior at school. They felt that by stabilizing her school behavior, her home behavior would improve.

An intervention plan was set up whereby Rena's teacher could inform the parents each day her behavior was satisfactory. Since reinforcers at home were so limited, we had to rely on the positive attention her father could give her when she got home. They would play simple card games or play in the yard skipping rope, etc. Rena's father had occasionally done this with her, and by making it consistent and contingent, this interaction became very meaningful to her. When Rena's behavior was not satisfactory at school, this reinforcement did not occur.

The plan took effect rather rapidly, and before long Rena was no problem at school. And, as hoped, her behavior at home also improved.

In a population such as ours, it is rare to find instances when both parents have a preexisting pattern of interaction which is gratifying to the target. Case #67, however, illustrates such a case, and also demonstrates that adequate consequation is nevertheless vital. Let the issue be forever put to rest: love is not enough.

Case #67, age seven, was referred for disobedience and bedwetting. Charts of both behaviors were used, with reinforcers of swimming and "activities with father" (games, gardening, etc.). It became apparent that Rick did not really care for the activities, but responded well to simple praise and approval from the parents. Activities and material reinforcers were withdrawn, and replaced by this contingency: after each dry night, he was allowed to sit in bed and talk with his parents for awhile. Frequency of referral behaviors reduced to zero within three months.

Those mediators most frequently employed are the parents of the target, but parents are not the only mediators of choice. Let us recall that the sole criterion for their selection is their potential for dispensing the selected reinforcer on contingency. One need not be a parent to meet this criterion; one need not even be an adult.

Case #55. In this instance, the mother was the sole support of her family, except for a small child support allowance for Herman. She had little time to spend with her two sons and it was difficult for her to assume full responsibility for mediating the completion of Herman's school assignments.

Raoul, Herman's 14-year-old brother, offered his services. The plan required that Raoul ask Herman for his spelling assignment each day and dispense the reward. Mother shared this responsibility with him when possible, and she dispensed weekly bonuses.

Daily reinforcers available for criterion performance were 2¢, praise from Raoul, 15 or more minutes play or activity with Raoul, and evening TV privileges.

The BA offered Raoul an allowance of 50¢ for cooperating with us in the intervention, but he refused it, saying he wanted to help Herman, having gone through the same situation himself when he was little.

In this instance, two elements combined. Raoul was the logical mediator of the cash and TV reinforcers because he was there, and because he was responsible. That he was, as a person, also reinforcing to the target, allowed him to simultaneously dispense the reinforcement of his attention to Herman. We employed other siblings as mediators in a number of cases, but Case #55 also illustrates an instance of the use of the sibling as a reinforcement. Time with other family members may be a useful reinforcer also; Pilot Case MC illustrates multiple use of relatives as reinforcers.

Pilot Case MC. Since the father was frequently absent when Joey came home from school he could do little to reinforce the boy. On the other hand, there were several other persons of significance to whom Joey would express his problems and complaints. Among these was a maternal aunt and her three sons (ranging from six to ten years older than Joey), a 25-year-old half sister, and a married sister who lived nearby.

Joey had a tendency to try to play some of these people against one another in order to gain sympathy. This was not altogether ineffective in the case of the aunt because her family strongly disapproved of Joey's father, particularly when he remarried a woman whom they considered to be inappropriate.

However, these relationships were of great importance to Joey, and it soon became apparent that he would go to considerable pain to maintain them. By controlling this situation, we were able to make visits to the aunt, her sons, the half sister, and the married sister, contingent upon good performance in school. No effort was made to control the content of these visits. When Joey did not bring home a note attesting to his good performance in two particular classes he was obliged to stay at home. If he missed one slip during the school week, Joey lost the privilege of leaving home on Sunday, and if he missed two he had to spend the weekend at home.

During school Joey missed very few of his "visiting friends" tokens. (Malcolm Bissell)

It has been observed that the delinquent subculture may be characterized by the heavy orientation to peers. Indeed, the movement away from the family and toward the age-mate is a normal developmental task of adolescence. In behavioral terms, peers are reinforcing, and peer-contact is frequently ranked high in reinforcement rating of our sample. Sometimes such contact can be placed on contingency.

Case #20. In evaluating reinforcers, we found that peers were the only reinforcers of any value to Sue. Daily phone privileges and weekly dates were made contingent on daily school attendance. Previous to intervention, Sue had absences on 60% of the school days that year. Thirty-one days following intervention she had missed only twice; this included the period when phone privileges were free, and only dates were left on contingency.

Of course, it is not only during adolescence that peer contact is important. Indeed, peer contact can be powerfully reinforcing even when it is not a friendly interaction.

Case #32. Willy was the class clown and general troublemaker. Unable to stay in his seat for more than three or four mintues, he punched other children, yelled out, banged his desk, threw paper balls, made vulgar noises, started fights on the playground, and continually exasperated his teacher while alienating the other children in his fourth grade class.

An intervention plan was developed in which the teacher reinforced Willy's in-seat behavior. The teacher informed him that beginning the next day she would see if he could stay in his seat for ten minutes. If he could, she would give him a note (for which he received praise and 5¢ at home). The following morning Willy asked the teacher when she would time him. "Soon" she replied. Willy remained in his seat successfully and received not only his note but public praise. The teacher expanded the reinforcement scheme with the addition of surprises (candy and trinkets). She was able to lengthen the sessions quickly.

We then set up a similar situation for the afternoon school session, covered by a second note. As a backup, we used the supervised after-school games on the school playground, for which Willy expressed a great liking.

Willy went home after school, and if he had earned his afternoon note he was allowed to return for the supervised play period. Willy usually had the afternoon note when he came home.

An arresting aspect of this reinforcement lies in the fact that Willy had no friends in school and did not directly participate in the games. He found gratification, as he had in class, by calling attention to himself through his antisocial behavior. Willy harassed the players, ran away with the ball, danced in and out of the games, yelled uncomplimentary comments at the players, and generally wore himself out making a thorough nuisance of himself. The other children tried to ignore him, but Willy's actions and taunts often aroused responses, and sometimes the entire assembly would chase Willy around the playground. Willy was the playground pest.

It has been our general experience that those cases in which peer contact is the exclusive potent reinforcer require continuing control in the form of contingencies.

Case #54. During the year that we worked with Jack, the only effective reinforcers we found for him were those involved with peer interaction. For example, Jack worked for weekend nights-out and Tuesday night Scout meetings. When he didn't earn his reinforcers, and thus missed weekend activities with his friends, he was quite sulky and unpleasant, but without fail he did work quite hard the following week to insure activities for the coming weekend. When the contingency was discontinued, Jack would revert to his former behavior. When this occurred, we would reinstitute the contingency plan, and he would improve within a short period—usually no longer than a week. (Diana Zimmerman)

This is not particularly surprising, since adult society is that from which the complaints emanate, and for peer-valuing adolescents the "normal" adult-society reinforcement schedules have little power. Thus, behaviors considered desirable by adult society required continued proctoring and the consequation of peer-oriented reinforcers. That is to say, in some cases, "intervention" plans may have to become a permanent form of family limit-setting.

In summary, then, parents, siblings, peers, teachers, and other adult friends have all been used as reinforcers. In one case, #79, we experimented with the introduction of an "artificial" relationship.

Case #79. David had been picked up for stealing hubcaps and for entering an apartment and dismantling a phone. He was also under suspicion of setting a fire and stealing a large check from a nearby house. David had been getting professional help from Child Guidance agencies, counselors, and probation officers since the first grade, when he began stealing. Family disorganization prevented the parents from consequating. David was the family scapegoat: the father resented him, felt no responsibility for him, and was physically abusive.

A pattern became apparent when analyzing data. When the father was particularly hostile to David, he in turn was aggressive with his sibs, and invariably reports of his stealing rose during these periods.

For several months we made fruitless attempts to shape the father's mediating behavior. Realizing the necessity of a male reinforcer we introduced an external mediator—a male college student volunteer—who took David out on Saturdays if he met the criterion of not bullying his sibs for a specific length of time.

David bullied his sibs on 94% of the baseline days. The 89 days following intervention he engaged in this behavior on 62% of the days. After the introduction of the external mediator, this behavior decreased to 20% of the following 75 days. Diana Zimmerman)

In cases such as this, when the natural-mediator patterns of stimulus control are not altered, other significant behaviors cannot be expected to improve. Our contact with Case #79 was terminated when he was apprehended by the police for stealing from a grocery store and referred to the juvenile court for management. He was subsequently placed in a residential institution where, incidentally, his problem behaviors subsequently disappeared.

In two other cases, experimentally conducted, the impossibility of modifying the behaviors of the naturally available mediators led us to use the Behavior Analyst himself as the reinforcer. Procedures, such as that in Case #79, create for themselves many of the same problems inherent in psychotherapy and personal counseling, i.e. the impermanence of the relationship, the failure to modify the controlling environment, and the like. If the natural environment truly cannot consequate, then some pattern of artificialization may be justified and, indeed, necessary; but we continue to recommend such procedures only when the natural-environmental system has totally failed. Thus, the preferred procedure in an environment where the significant others are not reinforcing, and not consequating, is to bring about new learning experiences for the target so that we can create people reinforcers. This is a significant element of behavior modification in the natural environment.

CREATING PEOPLE REINFORCERS

The reader will have perceived that during the consideration of material reinforcers, and in the section on people reinforcers, there has been the systematic intention of developing the relationship between mediator and target. We aim for a relationship which will be impunitive (or at least only appropriately punitive), reliable, and differentially reinforcing with heavy emphasis on positive control. Several techniques can be derived from the above and from laboratory data and have already been illustrated.

One general principle is that the target who comes to associate a mediator with positive reinforcement will then endow that mediator with reinforcing value.

Case #21. The target was described by all of his teachers as a sullen, moody, and unhappy boy. He was generally quiet in class and gave minimal responses to his academic work. The wood shop teacher reported several aggressive acts which were directed at him. The growing dislike between teacher and student was furthered by an incident in which the teacher commented on the boy's chopped-up haircut. The boy reported the comment to his father, and then told the teacher that his father had said that when the teacher "starts paying for the haircuts, then he can criticize, but in the meantime the boy can wear his hair in any style he wants."

A plan was introduced whereby weekend activities with father would be contingent on a specified number of weekly points to be earned in shop class. The teacher would be required to simply tally the weekly points on Friday and sign his name to a typed note stating that the boy had achieved the required number of points. At the end of the first week the boy had obtained the required number of points, and the teacher fulfilled his duty by signing the note. He noted that the boy's attitude had greatly improved during the first week, and he remarked that the parents must really be co-operating. At the end of the second week, the boy again met the criterion, as he did in the three following weeks. The boy ended up with a grade of 3 for the six weeks and passed the class for the semester. The teacher was happy with the boy's improved grades, but mostly with the clear display of effort.

When asked to fill out a second misbehavior checklist after termination, the teacher could not check any misbehavior, while prior to intervention he had checked 19 items of misbehavior. The teacher said the boy had changed remarkably in the last six weeks and he just couldn't observe any of the previous misbehaviors. The teacher could even sense a change in his own teaching behavior.

As a final note, as late as $2\frac{1}{2}$ months after intervention, the subject would informally visit his former shop teacher and they would engage in friendly chats. The teacher reported the boy's positive attitude remained unchanged and that the intervention plan seemed to have a lasting effect on their relationship. (Patricia Staples)

These effects have been observed repeatedly, and seem to characterize those cases in which the behavior changes are of great duration. This is as it should be; that environment which changes will maintain changed behaviors in the target.

Of course, some instances are peculiarly dramatic, and sometimes touching.

Case #98. Cowboy Gaines operated a riding stable on the outskirts of the city. Cowboy and his plump, fortyish wife were warm, homespun people, and they enjoyed the role of counselors to mixed-up youths. Cow-boy himself was full of rustic figures of speech, and he dispensed his rough and ready ranch philosophy generously. Cowboy and his wife, Irma, proved to be highly effective mediators.

Case #98 was an extraordinarily truant seventh grader who was powerfully attracted to animals, especially horses. There was no adult person with whom he had a positive relationship.

The Behavior Analyst asked Cowboy and Irma if they would help with Billy, and they at once agreed. The arrangement was simple: Billy could earn time at Cowboy's stables by staying in school. Billy was allowed to ride the horses in return for attending to minor chores when he was not riding.

Billy responded perfectly and thereafter never missed an hour of school. Cowboy and Irma had a little trouble with him at first because the undersized boy complained in smart-alec terms when he felt he wasn't getting enough riding. Cowboy gave him a few bits of rough advice and Irma was obliged to become a disciplinarian. Billy sulked and made plain his displeasure, but the horses and riding were too important to give up.

About two months later, just as Billy's grades made a dramatic improvement the family moved to a distant part of the city. Nevertheless, Billy appeared at 7:30 Saturday mornings, having ridden across town on several buses.

"He's turning out to be a nice kid," Cowboy observed to the BA about a month after the plan's inception.

Billy also said that things were "real fine." Billy stated that he liked Cowboy, as well as riding the horse.

Here the processes of interaction worked to strengthen a reinforcement. Originally Cowboy was simply the man who dispensed horseback riding, but he became a powerful rienforcer himself, and Billy treasured his sincere and warm attention. (Malcolm Bissell)

In neither of the Cases #21 or #98 did we attempt to control any of the specific elements of the interaction between the target and the mediator, save the contingency. Neither mediator was a trained "relater"; one began with antagonism toward the target and one with no acquaintance whatsoever with the target. We asked only that they dispense the reinforcer on contingency. This "mechanistic," "dehumanized" approach yielded a pattern of relationship which looks operationally very much like affection. The targets and the mediators believe that it is.

DEVELOPING NEW BEHAVIORS

SHAPING: THE METHOD OF APPROXIMATIONS

Up to this point, we have directed our discussion to the issue of reinforcers and contingencies. Equally important in the task of modification is careful attention to the behaviors of the target.

Common sense tells us that we cannot expect an individual to produce behavior which is not now in his repertoire; that is, behaviors not now possessed by a child must be taught to him. Simple though it may be, this principle is regularly violated, and never more often than in the case of the problem child. We know that new and complex behaviors rarely emerge spontaneously in their complete form. Rather than awaiting such an improbability, the wise interventionist will begin the teaching process from that point in the behavioral repertoire which is the closest, if still imperfect, approximation to the ultimate criterion.

There are several strategies in behavior modification for discovering the behavioral potentials in the current repertoire of the target. The tactic employed most often has been observation. Other tactics, such as the use of *prompting,* and the systematic use of imitative learning through the use of *modeling,* will be discussed below. At any rate, regardless of how the first approximation to the ultimate goal is produced, we know that if these approximations are reinforced, they will become the secure base from which the next and improved approximation will be launched. This process—the reinforcement of successive approximations—is known as *shaping.*

Most problem children have very narrow ranges of responses, and these are emitted to a wide range of situation-stimuli. Thus, aggression, withdrawal, anxiety, or tantrums may be the only "skill" which the child has in responding to the full range of classrooms' and teachers' complex stimuli. Because these children never emit the fully perfected criterion behavior of, say, courtesy, homework-neatness, or fully silent study hour, they are never rewarded. Not only does this produce further withdrawal or counteraggression in the problem child, but it also means he never learns to improve. In order to reverse these misfortunes, the child must be brought into society's reward-systems.

Many mediators are reluctant to praise or otherwise reward behavior which is patently undesirable. Even though the first approximations of improvement are frequently still in the "undesirable" range, they must be rewarded nevertheless. The child who has never studied quietly for the required 15 minutes will never do so unless his successive approximations—3 quiet minutes, 5, 12—are reinforced. Simply bringing a pencil to class may be the first approximation to completing an assignment. The first approximation to courtesy may be the absence of abusive language.

The general rule for the selection of the initial criterion-behavior, then, is very simple: it must exist in the repertoire of the target. Whether or not a given behavior exists in the repertoire (or potential repertoire) may be judged by observation during baseline recording.

Case #33. Based on her baseline performance of two to three daily
assignments completed, Rosita was awarded a note at school each day if she
completed three or more daily assignments; the note was redeemed at home
for evening TV privileges. During the first 17 days, she never missed her
note. In addition, she began completing not only three, but all her daily
assignments. Reference to her grades during these 17 days allowed us
to estimate that Rosita was then capable of finishing three or more assignments a day with 75% accuracy. On the 17th day we instituted this new
requirement. Rosita continued to perform well in school and showed increased enthusiasm, evidenced by the fact that she stayed after school to
help the teacher with chores and to begin the next day's assignments.

In another 16 days, we raised the criterion to 80% accuracy on three
or more assignments. The reinforcer remained the same. Rosita continued to
work diligently. However, it soon became apparent that we had pushed
her too far: she began cheating. Also, she was reported for stealing for the
first time since intervention. Based on this evidence, we changed the requirements for receiving the note to a "3" on three or more assignments.

In a period of four months, Rosita moved up from "probable retention
group" to "passing."

This case illustrates the full range of vicissitudes of the shaping process.
Baseline assessment correctly identified the current behavioral potential;
successive approximation reinforcement raised the frequency of completed
assignments above operant level. This case also illustrates a technical error,
in that one choice of a further approximation exceeded the current behavioral potential of the target. Stepping down in criterion level allowed
the reinstitution of the shaping process.

PROMPTING

We always wish to establish the behavioral improvement very rapidly,
and thus begin with initial behaviors which are as close as possible to
the ultimate criterion. One may await the random appearance of an approximation, and quickly reinforce it; learning of this sort is entirely possible, and has been carefully studied in the laboratory. In working with
human beings, however, more economical strategies are possible; people
respond better to verbal instruction than do our animal friends. Thus,
through prompting by the mediator, many targets will emit new and complex behaviors not previously in their repertoire. This is not to say that
prompting is a technique sufficient in itself; if we had only to tell problem
children to behave themselves, there would be no problem children. Furthermore, the disaffected problem child is less likely to be prompted by
verbal instructions than is the "good" one, because the "bad" child—being
so often punished by the environment—does not see the prompter as a
source of positive reinforcement. One of the great advantages of instituting a

system of positive reinforcement is that the problem child comes to associate the person of the mediator with the good things in his life, and then gradually becomes more receptive to taking verbal instructions from him. Thus he is made eligible for a wide range of adaptive learning from the subsequent prompting of his parents and teachers.

All intervention plans, and especially the criterion-behaviors, are carefully explained to all targets, regardless of their ages. Our early experimental work demonstrated that, even in the natural environment, it is possible to shape the behavior of the targets without their awareness of the details of the intervention, either of the contingency or the criterion behaviors. But such tactics are uneconomical, cumbersome, and artificial. Careful explanations to the target of precisely what was wanted of him constituted the controlled use of prompting in the BRP demonstration; these instructions were given by the mediators according to the advice of the staff. But the mediators carried out informal and "uncontrolled" prompting continuously, as is characteristic of normal interaction in their social roles. As the intervention plans took hold, this prompting was more often accepted.

The use of prompting is in no way exclusive of the shaping process; it is merely one way in which an initial approximation can be produced, so that the shaping process can begin. Prompted behavior, if not reinforced, will no more continue than will any other approximation.

MODELING

Somewhat similar to the techniques of prompting are those of *modeling*. Exhibiting desired behaviors to a target under certain circumstances produces emulated behaviors in him. Modeling is a specific technique in behavior modification; by its proponents it is argued that the imitative processes may be as fundamental a form of learning as the reinforcing processes (e.g., Bandura, 1965). By this argument it might be assumed, for example, that because a mediator would positively reward a desired behavior, the target's attention would become focused on the mediator as a model, and a wide range of "modeled" behaviors might then occur through vicarious processes, such as imitation. The authors have reported, elsewhere, their own use of modeling techniques with this same population of behaviorally disturbed (Martin *et al.,* 1968). The Behavior Research Project did not systematically manipulate the behavior of models. Throughout the section on *People Reinforcers,* it can be seen that the aim was rather to make those mediators who could and should be models into effective and appropriate ones. In a controlled, institutional, or arti-

ficial environment—a residential school, a sheltered workshop, a hospital—the interventionist has the option of controlling a target's social interaction to the end of presenting him with desirable models. But still the
interventionist must face the difficulties of the return to the natural environment and the creation of acceptable models for the target in the
real world. In our view, then, the more appropriate task of natural-environmental intervention is to create more acceptable behavior in the natural
model—the parental or teacher mediator.

INCOMPATIBLE RESPONSES

The following case is presented at some length in order to illustrate
two principles simultaneously: *shaping* and the *use of incompatible responses*. The shaping procedure in this case, #08, follows the suggestions
already outlined, and may be studied with that in mind. The behavior
chosen for shaping here, however, appears to be low on the complaint
list: Billy's most obnoxious behaviors were those of classroom disruption
and defiance, and the chosen target behavior was *academic performance*.
The logic is this: adequate academic performance is incompatible with
classroom disruption.

Case #08. Billy was a constant trouble-maker in his high school classes,
and he rarely completed any of his schoolwork. He nearly always came to
class late, announcing his arrival by various noisy means—pinching other
students, tripping loudly over chairs, yelling, whistling, etc. He often came
in wearing some outlandish clothing—a hat with ostrich plumes, a red
shirt with Christmas tree decorations, etc.
Once seated he would begin a series of annoying actions—banging his desk
top, shifting his chair, going to the pencil sharpener and poking other students in transit, yelling loudly, etc. He rarely made any effort to study or
do his work.
Intervention began under difficult circumstances; Billy had been expelled
from school, and the principal agreed to allow him to stay for a trial period
to see if we could effect a change in his behavior. Billy's English teacher, an
eager young woman, agreed to help carry out our plan and we began in that
one class.
We used a daily note for staying in his seat redeemable at home for
allowance and social activities and received with substantial parental praise.
Billy caused less trouble in English than in other classes but he never did
any work, usually refusing to open his book and never turning in written
assignments.
We stipulated that to earn his note Billy should "pay attention to his
studies." For the first three or four days the teacher agreed to accept the
opening of his book as "paying attention" to schoolwork. Under these terms
Billy received his note two or three times and the teacher encouraged Billy

to read at least a few paragraphs but did not make a point of his reading the whole lesson. From this position we advanced to a new condition for winning his note: in addition to the previous requirements Billy had to give some evidence that he had read at least a part of the lesson. At the end of the period the teacher would ask Billy a very simple question about the content of the reading and if Billy could answer it he received his note. If he could not, he was allowed a reasonable amount of extra time to read a few paragraphs.

As Billy continued to earn his note we raised the level of accomplishment, always advising Billy how the new requirements could be met. Thus, we gradually moved from the simple act of opening his book to answering a simple question about the content of the first paragraph, and from that we moved on from questions covering the first page to matters that involved more complex understanding of entire chapters.

After a couple of months of progress, Billy, who had been in the lower or "basic" section of the class, was doing the same amount of work as the other students. He asked to be transferred to the regular or "standard" group where he had more work to do. He succeeded in staying with this group for the remainder of the school year. (Malcolm Bissell)

INCREASED COMPLEXITY

Many strategies for behavior modification in the natural environment derive directly from laboratory work. Shaping is an example. Others derive from simple logic and are consistent with laboratory findings, such as the choice of incompatible responses. Still other strategies draw inspiration from laboratory-research constructs, but are not identical to them: for instance, "chaining." Animal work has produced a rather precise technology for increasing the complexity and the temporal length of a given response sequence. Roughly, the experimenter makes the discriminative stimulus (for an already learned response) contingent upon a new response, thus linking them into a "chain" of behaviors, the reinforcement for which follows the completion of the last behavioral link. Thus, the organism engages in more behavior of greater complexity, and comes to be rewarded not only by the same reinforcer for which he originally produced the simpler behavior, but also by the several stimuli associated with the responses in the chain which have acquired reinforcing properties. Thinning of the original reinforcement schedule may accompany chaining, i.e., reinforcement may not be delivered as frequently as previously. Thinning is often part of the termination operation. Thus the organism learns to engage in more behaviors for delayed (and sometimes less) primary reinforcement payoff.

The establishment of response chains is difficult to observe in the natural environment. Nevertheless, we steadily learn to work longer and harder.

Natural social teaching processes achieve this goal for most of us, but for the problem child it must also be taught. Let us return to Case #08 to illustrate one of these processes: delayed and intermittent reinforcement. The achievement of more desirable behaviors in English class was a beginning; but greater time duration and more complex good behavior was needed.

> Case #08. Billy settled down to an acceptable level of accomplishment in English class, where he was earning a daily note for good behavior and classwork. At home the note was redeemed with praise and the payment of 10¢.
>
> We then extended the range of the program so that Billy did twice as much work for the same rate of reinforcement. Instead of getting a daily note in English, Billy would earn "multi-day" notes in English, one on Tuesday, and a second on Friday. Billy also now had a new class, Biology, added to his note program, and there he received multi-day notes on Monday, Wednesday, and Friday.

Case #54 illustrates a process somewhat more similar to chaining: the opportunity to engage in other reinforced behavior as the reward for a desirable behavior.

> Case #54. Jack lived in a section of the city known for its "tough" kids. He was an underachiever and a classroom control problem. The intervention took place in the last six weeks of school; in that short period of time his academic performance improved, and the more serious problems disappeared.
>
> A few months after school reconvened the next September, Jack began presenting behavior problems in his English class. We instituted a note system. Jack earned two weekend nights out for the following criterion: a "3" average for the week's work in English, plus the acquisition of five daily good-behavior notes. Within a month he was no longer misbehaving in that class and his grades had risen from an average of 4 to 3. However, he was still failing Civics. Therefore, the plan was modified as follows: if Jack maintained a 3 and continued to behave in English, he could then earn the right to work for rewards in Civics. Friday nights out were put contingent on a grade of 3 in Civics; scout meetings on Tuesday nights were kept contingent on the previous criteria for English class behavior. As long as he earned Tuesday night out, he also earned the right to work for Friday night out. If he failed to perform adequately in English class, the contingency-system reverted to the original plan for the following week: daily notes in English to earn Tuesday out. And, of course, Jack stayed in Friday night. (Diana Zimmerman)

INDIRECT EFFECTS

Generalization refers to an organism's responding with like behavior to similar stimuli (stimulus generalization) or with similar behaviors to like stimuli (response generalization). Several operations and processes are being identified in the laboratory to account for the phenomena. As with chaining, behavior modification in the natural environment draws suggestions from generalization research by analogy, rather than by direct application. For instance, while one might often intervene directly in but one of a target's high-school classes, we would hope and expect that some stimulus-generalization might occur, so that habits learned to English class stimuli might generalize to other classes. In some cases they did; in others, they did not.

Nevertheless, intervention in one area of behavior often has correlated effects in other areas of behavior. This is entirely predictable, from the effects of reincorporating the target into the positive-reinforcement control nexus of the natural environment. Thus, "goodness" may be said to sometimes "generalize," in the definitional (though not laboratory) sense.

Case #86. The referral behaviors for Trish and Tom K., eight- and nine-year-old products of a broken home, were burglary, breaking and entering, and incorrigibility. The intervention was on chores, school behaviors, and bedwetting. In the 71 days following intervention, Trish and Tom improved considerably. No intervention was mounted on stealing and destroying property. When measured, Tom stole on 35% of baseline days (with one serious offense) and destroyed property on 50% of baseline days. Trish stole and engaged in some form of property destruction on every baseline day. After intervention on chores, all these behaviors for both children decreased to zero.

The point to be made here is that every problem behavior does not require specific intervention; the indirect effects of making the child even a bit more civilized are reliable enough to make partial intervention often the strategy of choice. This is particularly true when the problem behaviors include illegal acts, which are impossible to record (see the discussion in Chapter VIII, under Police Contact Data).

It may be true that in some instances one need intervene only to the extent necessary to establish a viable pattern of positive control. With the increase in frequency of the desirable behavior, several other less directly manipulable processes begin to have influence. The mediators prompt and model in ways no longer aggressive and destructive. The emerging behavior is reinforced in the presence of complex stimulus arrays resulting in the appearance of the behavior in an increasing variety of settings. New sources of reinforcement emerge through the pairing of events with the functional reinforcement. Variations in the new response patterns are reinforced. Thus, through these and other complex processes, socialization "generalizes" across behaviors and situations. The ability of behavior modifiers to insure such generalization will be directly proportional to their understanding and manipulation of these diverse underlying processes. There is nothing automatic about generalization. Interventionists must continually look to the basic research for direction in the development of techniques which will produce the maximum socialization effects of their intervention operations.

EXTINCTION AND PUNISHMENT

Although extinction and punishment are different operations with different outcomes, they share a common effect, namely, a decrease in the frequency of behavior. To avoid confusion in behavioral management techniques it is important to understand the differences and the procedures by which extinction and punishment reduce response frequencies.

Extinction is the operation whereby the reinforcing stimuli which have been maintaining a behavior are no longer available. The contingency between a target behavior and its maintaining positive reinforcers is disrupted. Learning theory predicts that operant responses with no reinforcing consequences will eventually disappear from the repertoire. Research literature suggests that the process of extinction may produce at least two side effects. One is a temporary increase in the frequency of the target behavior during the early stages of extinction prior to the decrease in frequency. The other is the appearance of certain emotional and other behaviors during the course of extinction. These accompanying behaviors are sometimes called collectively *frustration behaviors* (e.g., crying, aggression, changes in intensity of target behavior, etc.). These side effects do not always accompany extinction, and their appearance and nature are functions of the schedule of reinforcement maintaining the target behavior as well as the general repertoire of the individual. For example, the more intermittently the behavior has been reinforced the longer the behavior will continue without the appearance of the frustration behaviors. Although laboratory work is establishing the relationship between these variables and extinction characteristics, one seldom knows enough about the previous history of an individual's behavior to be able to specify exactly what will happen during extinction. One can at least be prepared for a temporary increase in the target behavior and the appearance of other "frustration" behaviors. Thus, the mother advised to ignore bedtime tantrums might also be counseled not to be upset if the tantrums increase in frequency and intensity during the early stages of her attempts to extinguish the behavior.

Extinction is commonly used in laboratory procedures to demonstrate the effects of nonreinforcement. As an intervention technique, however, it should almost never be used except in combination with the positive reinforcement of an acceptable alternative to the behavior being extinguished. Usually, the reinforcement which has been maintaining the behavior being extinguished is made contingent on the alternative behavior. The mother may ignore tantrums but attend to appropriate bedtime responses. The teacher may ignore speaking out of turn but attend to hand raising. The Behavior Research Project has no cases in which extinction alone was used to decrease the frequency of a target behavior. Let us explore some of the reasons that extinction alone is both a difficult and hazardous procedure for reducing the frequency of target behavior.

First, identification of the maintaining reinforcer may be difficult. Schedules of reinforcement as well as the nature of the reinforcing consequences may obscure the maintaining event from the observer. Often a response is maintained by several reinforcing events. Second, even when the reinforcing event seems clear, the behavior modifier may not be able to arrange the disruption of the contingency. It is difficult, for example, for parents to extinguish delinquent behavior which is maintained by peers. Also, other behaviors cannot be separated from their reinforcing consequences. This is true of sex, aggression, and the use of narcotics. Since extinction requires the identification of maintaining events and the disruption of the reinforcing contingency with undesirable behaviors, these conditions make it a difficult operation to engineer.

There are also hazards to the use of extinction as a single engineering operation. Once an extinction regimen begins, the mediator must see the process to the end no matter how frequently and for how long the undesirable target behavior occurs. A reinforcement during the course of extinction, however accidental, may result in prolonged occurrences of the behavior. Since the mediator is the person who has been maintaining the behavior in the first place, it may be especially hard for him to tolerate the initial increase in target behavior and the frustration behaviors. The mother who cannot tolerate the initial increase in tantrum frequency and intensity may reinforce it at such a time that she makes the tantrum response both more intense and more resistant to extinction. This possibility always exists with an extinction procedure.

As an intervention technique, extinction alone does not specify the alternative to the response being extinguished. If a response is decreasing in frequency, some other behavior will replace it; if extinction is the only technique in use, the behavior which increases in frequency is left to chance. (Actually, learning theory suggests that it is not chance that determines the new behavior but the individual's history of reinforcement.) It is completely possible that the new behavior will be just as undesirable as the behavior being extinguished. In fact a host of undesirable behaviors may appear, each one replaced by another as they successively extinguish. This phenomenon is called *symptom substitution* by certain observers;

it is likely to result from the failure to specify and reinforce an alternative behavior.

Extinction without reinforcement of another behavior also results in the diminution of available reinforcement to the individual, a situation which can elicit a variety of emotional responses. A mother who is advised to ignore bedtime tantrums may find that the crying and kicking diminish only to be replaced by head banging. Head banging may be replaced eventually by somatic complaints, somatic complaints by fear, fears by bedwetting, and so on. This string of behaviors ("symptom substitutions" or "regression") may go on interminably because the mother fails to reinforce a desirable bedtime behavior. If she does not attend to acceptable alternatives she is, in effect, attending to her child less than previously. She has removed some reinforcement from the total system. This in itself may prolong the emotional and/or frustration reaction.

Thus, there are several reasons why extinction is seldom used singly as a technique for decreasing the frequency of behavior. When a mediator is asked to consequate his attention, he is asked to ignore one behavior but attend to another. This last is crucial to prevent a decrease in delivered reinforcement and the appearance of concomitant emotional behavior.

Most often the alternative behavior which is reinforced is incompatible with the target behavior. If the mother is reinforcing the child's going to bed peacefully, then bedtime tantrums will naturally decrease. A teacher may reinforce staying in the seat so that being out of the seat will obviously decrease in frequency. Is this decrease in out-of-seat behavior a function of the teacher's ignoring the behavior so that it extinguishes, or a function of the positive reinforcement of an incompatible response? Most behavior modification studies employing extinction confound these two operations so that examples of extinction as a single operation are difficult to find outside of the laboratory (although one study strongly suggests that ignoring alone is not very effective, see Madsen, *et al.,* 1968). The Behavioral Research Project had no cases of extinction which did not involve simultaneous reinforcement of incompatible behavior.

Two separate operations, both of which decrease the frequency of behavior, are commonly designated by the term *punishment.* In one, a negative reinforcer (painful, or pain related stimulus) becomes contingent on the behavior, e.g., spanking, scolding, threats. In the other, the removal of a positive reinforcer becomes contingent upon a target response, e.g., take away privileges, favorite objects, remove money. Although there is controversy among researchers about the specific effects of punishment, there is ample evidence that under the appropriate conditions these operations can reduce the frequency of behaviors quickly and effectively.

In view of the fact that punishment can be an effective means for reducing target behavior frequency, one may ask why it is not more frequently recommended as an intervention technique. As in the discussion of extinction we must consider some of the potential effects punishment can have in addition to the reduction of target behavior frequency. The appearance of counteraggressive behavior is frequently observed to follow the punishment operation. This is a characteristic of many delinquent and predelinquent children. Such children may have extensive repertoires of counteraggression which have been developed over the years in response to the various forms of punishment to which they have been exposed. Most children also have learned several undesirable responses to make to punishing stimuli; these responses have been reinforced at one or another times by termination of the punishment. For some children almost any adult interference may evoke these counteraggressive responses. The behaviors may be rather mild topographically, such as passive refusal to comply, or they may be violent, such as physical attack on the punishing agent. These counteraggressive behaviors often force the punishing agent to intensify the punishment so that a spiraling interaction develops in which both individuals emit increasingly severe punishing behaviors. Several parents of our research group had had police contact for beating their children, not an uncommon recourse for parents who understand only punishment as a technique of behavioral control and whose children have developed repertoires of resistance and counteraggression.

Punishment can also elicit undesirable respondent behaviors which can interfere with additional learnings. Anxiety and fear may come to be elicited by the punishing agent himself, and if he is also an important teaching agent, such as teacher or parent, his effectiveness as shaper of desirable behaviors can be considerably reduced. Repertoires of *avoidance behaviors* are also developed under punishment regimens, and the individual may learn to avoid important sources of socialization and education if they are also sources of punishment. Some of these avoidance responses involve actual physical avoidance, but others may be much more subtle, such as the student's "turning off" or "tuning out" on the punishing classroom teacher. Punishment can also generate escape behavior, of course, and usually underlies truancy, running away, skipping class, and the like.

Since neither of the punishing operations necessarily involves the removal of the positive reinforcing stimuli which may be maintaining behaviors, the punishing stimuli must offset the functional value of the maintaining events. The more positive reinforcement maintaining a behavior, the stronger or more intense the punishing situation required to offset it. Since the reinforcing contingency is not disrupted by punishment, there is always the possibility that the punished behavior will eventually return. It is often said that punishment only suppresses behavior temporarily, although research (Solomon, 1964) suggests that some forms of punishment will result in long term decrements of response frequencies. The decrease of response frequencies by mild forms of punishment is likely to be temporary since the punished behavior may again come under the control of the maintaining positive reinforcers. To illustrate, a delinquent behavior such as tire slashing may be under the control of the approval and admiration of gang members. Although authorities and parents may restrict, isolate, spank, and in other ways punish, only temporary suppression may be achieved if this is the principle means of winning peer attention. Powerful punishment indeed is required to offset the powerful reinforcing value of peer approval.

Finally, punishment as an intervention technique may not teach any new behavior. As with extinction, an alternative behavior is frequently not specified. Punishment may decrease the frequency of undesirable behavior, but not guarantee at all the increase of a desirable response. Unless the adolescent finds socially desirable ways of gaining peer approval he may return to delinquent forms simply because desirable alternatives are lacking in his repertoire. Most punishing agents assume that the punished child will automatically avoid undesirable responses in the future, but there is nothing about punishment which will ensure this.

The population of the behaviorally disturbed is by and large a group of children who have been on punishing schedules of control in both the home and school. They have extensive repertoires of counteraggression, avoidance, and escape. The parents of these children have little knowledge of positive means of control and tend to rely on punishment because it is quick and appears to be effective. For this reason, punishment was an infrequently recommended technique of intervention in the Behavior Research Project. No plan of intervention ever recommended the consequation of pain and pain-related stimuli. When a "punishing" operation was recommended it always took the form of the removal of positive reinforcers contingent upon the target's undesired response. Before discussing this operation further it might be well to distinguish it from the operation of withholding positive reinforcement until a desired behavior occurs.

When a contingency is established between reinforcement and one or more target behaviors, that positive reinforcement does not occur (is withheld) until one or another of the target behaviors occurs. If the individual engages in another behavior he may not be reinforced, but he does not lose positive reinforcement. (He does not gain, but he does not lose.) If watching TV is contingent upon finishing homework, then reading comic books results in no TV. An existing positive reinforcing stimulus is not removed, it simply is not presented. Reading comic books is, of course, maintained by some other positive reinforcer. In punishment, on the other hand, a currently available reinforcer is removed contingent on the behavior. If the TV set is turned off every time the child picks up a comic book, then he is being punished. When the parent threatens by saying "if you do that you cannot watch TV" he is threatening to remove a positive reinforcer understood to be otherwise currently available.

Punishment as the removal of positive reinforcement differs from extinction in a similar way. In extinction the reinforcement which has been maintaining a response is no longer contingent upon the response. In punishment, a positive reinforcer, not necessarily the one maintaining the behavior, is removed contingent on that behavior. In extinction the operation is withholding and the reinforcer withheld is the one maintaining the behavior. In punishment the operation is removal and the reinforcer removed is any functional positive reinforcer.

Although these operations are similar and the differences subtle, their effects are different. In general, schedules of (positive) reinforcement of desirable behaviors always involve the *withholding* of reinforcement contingent on undesirable behaviors. Punishment involves the removal of positive reinforcement contingent on undesirable behaviors. The operations of withholding and removal are different and may have different effects. We might hypothesize, for example, that withholding of reinforcement which is not otherwise available does not tend to evoke counteraggression and emotional behaviors as does the removal of available reinforcement.

There is at least one situation in which the withholding operations and the removal operations become almost identical. When there are amounts and varieties of positive reinforcement available which are not contingent upon any particular target behaviors, then the establishment of contingencies is tantamount to the removal of positive reinforcement. A parent, for example, may have provided his son with an automobile which the boy is permitted to use at any time. If the parent now decides to make the use of the automobile contingent upon attending school every day and coming in on time, he is, in effect, removing previously available reinforcement from the environment. Counteraggressive and other frustration behaviors may emerge when a new contingency is established with a source of reinforcement which has been previously more accessible.

Two conditions were always observed in the prescription of punishment by the Behavior Analyst. One was that punishment be used only in conjunction with the positive reinforcement of acceptable alternative behaviors. The other was that the positive reinforcement removed as punishment was never a reinforcement which the child had earned through desired behaviors. For example, we never suggested reducing the allowance earned by desired behavior as a form of punishment or never suggested taking away earned points. If fines were used as a means of punishment, the money was first provided noncontingently on a time basis.

> Pilot Case C. M. When Carl asked for an increase in his allowance the Behavior Analyst suggested to the mother that this was an opportunity to work on his use of obscene language which had been annoying her. The mother began giving Carl an extra quarter with his Saturday morning allowance, but required that a nickel be forfeited in a ceramic pig each time she heard Carl utter an obscenity. The necessity of "pigging" Carl rapidly decreased.

In the example, if the mother had given the quarter for taking on the chore of helping with the dishes in the evening, the Behavior Analyst would not have suggested the removal of his money as a punishment for obscene talk.

Another form of punishment is to require the performance of an unpleasant task contingent upon undesirable behavior. Such tasks probably not only can cause discomfort but also result in the temporary deprivation of other positive reinforcers.

> Case #65. Tony was a fifth grader referred for perpetually disturbing classroom procedures and for low academic performance. He resided with his older married sister and her family, and presented them with a number of problems too. After reviewing the possible reinforcers the following plan was devised. Tony received a note daily for good classroom behavior (staying in his seat, talking only at the appropriate times, etc.). The note could be exchanged at home for 5¢. Failure to earn the note not only resulted in forfeiting the 5¢ but also resulted in his having to do yard work for 15 minutes—a task which was extremely aversive to Tony. In addition to this, Tony was also reinforced for good school work with money, play time, and trips with mother. (Diana Zimmerman)

The most frequently recommended form of punishment, and the one used most often by the Behavior Research Project, is *time out* from positive reinforcement (isolation). Rather than remove positive reinforcers from the individual, the individual is removed from the postive reinforcers. This requires, of course, that there be no positive reinforcers in the environment to which the child is removed.

> Case #105. John's home behavior had been of serious concern to his parents for a number of years. His violent temper tantrums put the family in a constant state of unrest and tension. The parents had been particularly lenient since John had been chronically ill for some years. Also his threats of physical violence and suicide resulted in the parents backing down on their contingencies. We instructed the parents to take the following steps when John began to have a tantrum. As soon as the tantrum started John was sent or taken to his room and was told to stay there until he could control himself. After John calmed down, the parents allowed him out of the

room and praised him. If the tantrum began again, the same procedure was followed. At the parents' convenience and as an additional punishment, the parents often substituted having John sit on a chair for a specified amount of time with no family interaction. Continued disturbance lengthened the time he stayed on the chair. John found this particularly aversive. He was not able to participate in family activities that he could watch occurring and there was absolutely nothing to be occupied with as there often was in his room.

Our experiences suggest several procedures which can be used to reduce the occurrence of the counteraggression and frustration responses when extinction and punishment are used to control behavior. It is important that neither procedure results in an overall decrement in available positive reinforcement. If positive reinforcement is removed or withheld contingent upon one response, it must be readily available by some other means. This means of reinforcement must be contingent upon a response which the individual can and does perform frequently. New sources of reinforcement should be used to avoid side effects of suddenly making contingent previously noncontingent reinforcers. Instructions can minimize counteraggression and frustration. With most children it will make a difference whether the parents say "we are going to make you do better in school," or "if you don't do better in school we aren't going to give you an allowance" or "we thought it might help you do a little better if we could sit together and work out a way for raising your allowance for doing homework and bringing home improved weekly test grades." It is important, of course, to make sure the mediators do not reinforce the counteraggressive or frustration behaviors and also do not nag, beg, and cajole. If the child continues to engage in the undesirable behavior or not engage in the desirable, the parent can sympathize. Let the stated contingencies bear the weight of the control. The parent can be a sympathetic and understanding individual and still maintain reinforcement contingencies which involve consequences other than personal anger, rejection, and pain.

ORGANIZING AND MAINTAINING CONTINGENCIES

Intervention as a process is obviously more complex than the engineering of a contingent relationship between target behaviors and reinforcing events in the environment. If the effective agents of change are to be persons in the natural environment, it becomes necessary to insure that these persons do, and continue to do, what is necessary to modify the target repertoire. It is around this issue that intervention becomes less engineering and more consultation to the natural environment. Central to the role of the interventionist is the task of organizing and maintaining an intervention plan. He must monitor the system closely to insure that mediators are fulfilling their roles. Frequent contact with mediators, especially at the beginning of an intervention attempt, is the only way to insure this.

BA CONTACTS

Exactly how a Behavior Analyst monitored a given case was determined by the characteristics of a given situation. The telephone is an indispensible monitoring instrument. A mediator lacking easy telephone access considerably increases the difficulties of monitoring. With a telephone the Behavior Analyst can tap into a developing system conveniently and at important points. For example, the interventionist might remind the parent on the night before about how to present to his son the fact that the family car is going to become contingent upon school attendance and performance. He may remind the parent what to say in order to avoid arguments and lend support and encouragement to the hesitant and fearful mediator. Later the interventionist may inquire as to how it went, and praise or advise. The telephone may be used to convey important information to the mediator, such as informing the parent that the child attended all classes and should be reinforced when he arrives home. Later the interventionist may rate whether or not the mediator did reinforce, how, and what happened. He can praise, critize, instruct, and advise on a daily or more frequent basis, as required.

Personal contacts with mediators in the home or at work give the Behavior Analyst an opportunity to develop a better relationship with the mediator and to explain and discuss details of an intervention plan. The Behavior Analysts usually encouraged mediators to suggest details of the plan (reinforcers and contingencies) and used mediator suggestions whenever possible. The interventionist may prompt or model appropriate behavior to the mediator, telling him what to say, and when. In one case in which a mother could not refrain from nagging her son when he returned from the school, the BA visited the home and signaled the mother to stop talking. The BA gave the mother immediate feedback on her interaction and shaped the mother into less provocative behavior. Visits are also necessary to instruct in the collection of data, the filling out of charts, their posting, and so on.

The records of behavioral change were an important focus of Behavior Analyst contact. The Analyst had an opportunity to discuss the progress, praise the mediator for change and for his record keeping, probe for ideas if change had not occurred, and judge how the intervention plan was affecting the mediator. The Analysts encouraged the mediators to develop better and more convenient methods for recording behavioral change.

The kinds of interpersonal relationships which developed between a Behavior Analyst and his mediators were, by and large, not monitored by the supervisors. Rather, the Analysts were allowed to exercise the skills and judgment which they brought to the situation and for which they were selected. They were encouraged to report difficulties and discomforts in mediator interaction, but otherwise made their own decisions and developed their own techniques for maintaining contingencies through their contacts.

CONTRACTS

Often with older adolescents the parent–child relationship had deteriorated into a punitive interaction, and the mediators did not have the repertoire necessary to establish contingencies. These were parents who could not talk productively with their children and children who could only react aversively or sullenly to any parental overture. We discovered that the best beginning in such cases was to depersonalize the interactions and minimize the necessity for verbalization, since they were largely aversive. In a few such cases, we experimented with a role for the BA in which he had a brief direct interaction with the target, acting as negotiator or arbitrator to develop the skills of negotiation in the family members. The most formal arrangement was the *contract* (see Fig. 9) which the Behavior Analyst helped negotiate, drew up, and had signed. These contracts stated the behavioral expectations and contingencies as they affected both sides and bore the weight of maintaining the system.

Case #63. Salvador had been seen by the police after an incident in which he chased his stepfather with a butcher knife. He was a severe management problem in a home composed of his crippled stepfather, a passive mother, and an infant stepbrother. He was sullen and defiant in most parental contacts.

Sal's stepfather had provided him with an old car which Sal drove at will and for which he was repaying the stepfather with money earned on a part-time job. The basis of the intervention plan was that Sal would repay the money in the form of improved home behaviors.

From home chores, baby sitting, coming home on time, and relinquishing the car keys, Sal earned points which were converted into car payments. Car payments had to be up to date on a weekly basis. If they were not, he was restricted in car usage to the degree that he was in arrears.

The details of the expected behaviors, their value in car payments, and the details of payment were formally negotiated and written out in contract form by the Behavior Analyst. Both Sal and his father signed the contract.

CONTRACT
English Ford Automobile

Section I

Sal R. is buying a $400.00 English Ford from his stepfather at the rate of $5.00 per week. This money is to be earned in the following way:

Item	Value
1. Remaining home or bringing in the car keys on Sunday through Thursday nights by 9:30 and giving them to his stepfather or placing them in an agreed upon place.	40¢ per night
2. Remaining home or bringing in the car keys on Friday and Saturday nights by 12:00 and giving them to his stepfather or placing them in an agreed upon place.	60¢ per night
3. Mowing front and/or back lawn once a week on day and at time of Sal's choosing. This task must be completed within one day.	60¢ per week
4. Feed dog daily prior to evening meal. (Monday through Friday)	10¢ per feeding
5. Arrive for evening meal at 6:30 or at time specified by mother in the morning. Mother shall indicate any changes prior to the 6:30 meal.	5¢ per meal
6. Straighten room each morning before leaving house or by noon. Mother and Sal are to decide what straightening up room means.	5¢ per day

Total possible—$5.00

Section II

A. Penalty for failure to make car payments
   1. The penalty for payment failure shall be computed at the rate of 15 minutes of restricted car use the following week for each $.05 under the required $5.00 per week payment.
   2. These restrictions will be imposed by the current car owner, Mr. G.
   3. Failure to make any car payment at all will result in restriction of car privilege for the following week.
B. Payments are to be computed on Sunday evenings.
C. Additional car payments may be made if purchaser acquires a job and has access to additional money.

This contract can be rewritten or in other ways changed by either Sal or Mr. G. at their request and at anytime. All changes must be made in consultation with Mr. Douglass.

Signed:

_____   _____
Mr. Sal R., Purchaser   Date

_____   _____
Mr. Paul G., Owner   Date

FIG. 9. Sample Contract, negotiated by the Behavior Analyst, between Case #63 target and mediator.

A clause was inserted requiring that any changes in the contract required renegotiation in the presence of the Analyst. Although the interaction between Sal and his stepfather did not become friendly, his behavior at home became appropriate. (Lloyd Douglass)

There are several details of this case which deserve special attention. First it should be noted that the Behavior Analyst was present during negotiations. Since neither parents nor child had negotiating behaviors in their repertoires, it was necessary for the Behavior Analyst to model and guide the new interactions. In this role the Behavior Analyst asks the parent what his expectations are, asks the child what his are, explores the parental limits, negotiates appropriate reinforcers on the part of the child, clarifies the contingencies, and teaches ways of interacting that keep the negotiation open. It seemed important to include in the contracts a clause indicating that either party might change terms of the contract and renegotiate by contacting the Behavior Analyst. Case #63 was so acrimonious that the BA urged that no renegotiations be attempted without his permission. This was to insure the success of a renegotiation. The BA withdraws from the negotiations as both parties gain the negotiating skills, and indeed the BA need not and should not enter the negotiation at all, save in families of severe disruption.

Adolescents in particular were urged to take advantage of the change clause and some contracts were negotiated with terms known to be somewhat unacceptable in order to promote use of the change clause. In the case described above, the first curfew hour was set earlier than the target wished. Since he had previously simply stayed out later than permitted when he wanted to, his decision to renegotiate the curfew hour indicated both his planning ahead and a willingness to discuss change rather than enact it. Needless to say, it was extremely important to reinforce his request that the curfew hour be changed by extending it to a later time. In general, contracts are useful instruments for reducing the high degree of aversive interaction that can develop between parents and child, clarifying contingencies and wishes of both sides, and shaping more effective repertoires of interaction. The contract must be fair to both parties, agreed to, respected, and changeable. Requests on the part of either party are honored whenever possible.

THE COMMON MARKET

Similar to contracts and also useful as a system for maintaining contingencies is the establishment of token systems, point systems, and economies. Many teachers and parents use economy systems from time to time.

They must be devised with care and often can be detrimental in effect if not devised properly. They should be arranged so that the individual is reinforced for all target behaviors, but the more he does the more he gets. They should not be devised so that only infrequently occurring behaviors are reinforced, or in such a way that the target can lose all his earnings or quickly reach a ceiling of possible earnings. The terms of the economy are frequently written out in the form of charts or booklets and the tokens may be anything from gold stars to points. Usually the system states clearly how much will be paid for behaviors and how much the backup reinforcers will cost. The backup reinforcers are the events which can be exchanged or "purchased" with accumulated tokens.

Case #66. Ann was a severe truant at her high school and was eventually suspended for unauthorized absences. Being fond of horses, much of her runaway time was spent at stables in the vicinity.

Ann was readmitted to school with the understanding that she would not present the same problems of truancy. To help control Ann's poorly limited behavior we set up a point system which was to be administered by her widowed mother who, thus far, had had little control over Ann.

Attractions outside the home were reinforcing to Ann and it was decided that she could earn the right to be absent from her home. This required the cooperation of persons outside the home, particularly the owner of the stables where Ann kept her horse and spent much of her time. Since several different activities and events functioned as reinforcers, a medium of exchange was necessary to make them available in an effective manner.

A point system was evolved in which points were earned by completing chores and other obligations at home and by attending school promptly and properly. The system required that other people recognize the validity of the exchange. If Ann left home without home points distributed by her mother, the stable owner would not allow her to remain.

Points could be exchanged for almost every away-from-home activity, including school-connected activities, clubs, dances, sports, etc. The exchange universe was geographically extended and several people (adults) in Ann's environment honored it. The terms of the system were worked out in a conference between Ann, her mother, and the stable owner. A tape of this session frustrated Ann's later attempts to manipulate the program. (Malcolm Bissell)

Point systems have the same advantage which money has in society. One need not know what an individual's current most effective functional reinforcer is to be able to reinforce a behavior. The "token" can be exchanged for a range of reinforcers much as money can. Effective and noneffective token management systems probably have characteristics similar to effective and noneffective economic systems. Market analysts, economists, industrial managers, and stock brokers probably could add a great deal to our knowledge of the management of behavior through token exchange systems. The teacher whose "star chart" does not seem effective might do well to call in her local economist rather than the school psychologist.

REINFORCING MEDIATORS

The Behavior Analysts encountered little difficulty in establishing the validity of their professional role. Mediators generally accepted their competency without argument. The matter of establishing effective personal relationships was more complex. Each Behavior Analyst adopted his own style of relating to mediators and adjusted this to situations and personalities. A natural consequence of this process was the exploration of ways in which the dispensing of personal attentions by the Behavior Analyst affected mediator behaviors.

> Case #49. It was up to the Browns to maintain the token system which regulated the semidelinquent behaviors of their daughter Sally, and the Behavior Analyst found them to be negative and uncooperative. The Browns were receiving aid from welfare in supporting eight of their children. The Behavior Analyst instructed Mrs. Brown that proper execution of her mediator job would earn extra clothing every few weeks. Mrs. Brown began expressing more positive attitudes toward the Behavior Analyst and spoke more highly about her daughter. However, when she had an opportunity to send her daughter to California to live with relatives, she did so; the long-term effects of this mediator reinforcement system were not observed.

Behavior Analysts often used their attention to try to regulate mediator verbal behavior during visits. In the following manner the Behavior Analyst attempted to keep the mediator from focusing exclusively on the complaint behaviors.

> Case #101. When the Analyst finally got to see Mrs. Otto she would go through a long complaint routine about all the things wrong with the school and with Tucson. The BA would sit and systematically and intentionally say nothing while the lady raved. On the other hand, the BA would respond to pleasant conversation, especially about Mr. Otto, who was overseas, his letters, and their plans for his return. The BA reported that the introductory period of complaints became shorter and shorter and Mrs. Otto began to develop interest in devising some sort of plan for helping her son with his school problems.

Behavior Analysts in general developed a skill in ignoring long conversations about the past, efforts to blame one or other persons, long discussion of worries, marital issues, and the like. Most BA attention was contingent on present circumstances and definitive actions that could be taken with respect to a current behavior.

Case #19. It was observed that most of the conversation with Mr. M. was tied up in talking about sports. Even during the initial interview the BA (an ex-football player) discovered that Mr. M. was fond of participating in and attending athletic events. Mr. M. seemed to look forward to BA contacts in order to talk about current athletic happenings. Before very long, these discussions got out of hand and very little time was spent talking about the case.

In the interview that followed, the Analyst first discussed the current baseline measures. The Analyst would not allow Mr. M. to wander from the subject and ignored attempts to do so. When the BA felt he had all the information he needed, he would turn to current sports conversation. When the baseline was scanty or incomplete, the BA would tell Mr. M. what he needed to do to improve it, schedule a future appointment, and leave. For whatever reason the final baseline was very complete. (Lloyd Douglass)

Occasionally the Behavior Analyst has an opportunity to enlist the aid of one mediator in the reinforcement of another. The following is an excerpt from a BA's report.

Case #42. The BA redoubled his efforts to get the father to alter his attitude toward his son and stressed to the mother the importance of reinforcing Pete's father for his efforts to praise his son and to withhold criticism. Pete's mother was a sensible, compassionate woman, and she at once understood this. Afterward she frequently reported to the BA that she never missed an opportunity to congratulate her husband for his success at becoming a "good father."

No systematic experimental attempts were made to study the relationship between Behavior Analyst contingencies and mediator behaviors. It is possible that in many cases the refusal to reinforce certain conversational content helped develop the efficiency of interaction which most Behavior Analysts maintained.

LONG DISTANCE CONSULTATION

The techniques of consultation and intervention which we have been describing have several features which lend themselves to use when consultant and target are separated by distance. Since target behavior is controlled by a mediator in the natural environment, the crucial connection is between the consultant and the mediator. Sometimes the Behavior Analyst was able to find a surrogate in the environment who could take over behavior analyst functions with minimal instructions. The following case illustrates this.

Case #MS. Bobby Smith was a first grader who lived in a mining town 180 miles from Tuscon. The school referred Bobby because he would do no school work, had extremely low grades, and had difficulty interacting with his peers. Bobby would either fight with the other children or withdraw.

He spent much time daydreaming in class rather than working on his assignments.

Two of our staff members arrived at the school shortly before noon. A conference with the school principal and the school nurse was held. In the meantime, Mrs. Smith was asked to come to the school for a conference. While we waited for Mrs. Smith to arrive one of our staff members went to Bobby's class to observe him and to talk to his teacher to find out what specific problems she was having with Bobby.

When Mrs. Smith arrived, we reconvened for a conference with her. We found that Mrs. Smith was extremely punitive with Bobby and used only negative controls with him. The Smiths also put a lot of pressure on Bobby to achieve in school. This was ineffective. Bobby had few friends in his immediate neighborhood and played only by himself. Mrs. Smith appeared overly protective and kept Bobby home most of the time. We decided that it would be extremely helpful to get both Mr. and Mrs. Smith together to work out a plan. Mrs. Smith said her husband would be getting off his work shift in the mine soon, but she was afraid that he would not come in for a meeting until he had time to bathe and change his clothes. Since we wanted all of the school personnel to get together with them, we encouraged her to bring him straight to the school and we stressed that everyone was aware that he worked at the mine, and no one would be concerned with his appearance.

While Mrs. Smith left to get her husband, and the school continued until the end of the school day, the staff members devised an intervention plan for Bobby Smith. When we returned we asked the principal, the nurse, and Bobby's teacher to meet with us and with the Smith's. The first plan we set up was one involving his school achievement. Mrs. Gray, Bobby's teacher, indicated that she graded daily papers turned in with a plus or a minus, indicating satisfactory or unsatisfactory work. The Smiths mentioned that Bobby found pennies very reinforcing and presently received no allowance. The Smiths agreed that they would be willing to dispense pennies for every paper which Bobby brought home with a plus. Nothing would be said for the minuses, but he would not earn the penny.

Mrs. Smith was also made to see that she could use positive control, such as allowing Bobby to go out and play or watch television after his chores rather than punishing him for chores undone. Mrs. Smith also agreed that she would take Bobby out to play with friends in the neighborhood, and she would visit the other mothers, which would be good for her.

Because of the distance of this community from Tucson, it was apparent that it would be difficult to come back often to check on the case. Instead we decided to use the school nurse as the "Behavior Analyst," and the Project would consult with her or supervise her by mail. The nurse was given recording sheets which she was to dispense weekly to Mrs. Smith. When Bobby brought home his school papers, the pluses and minuses were recorded, and at the end of the week the chart was returned to the nurse. The nurse was to meet weekly with Mrs. Smith to be sure that pennies were dispensed daily, to check on Bobby's visits to friends' homes, and to continue to stress positive control.

The plan worked well. Out of 217 school assignments possible, Bobby earned pluses on 163 and minuses on only 54. His report card went from straight "4's" and "5's" to all "2's" and "3's." His teacher reported that "his work is improving in both amount he is getting done and the quality of his work." The nurse reported that Mrs. Smith was "very pleased with the way Bobby was improving, everyone in the family was enthusiastic in helping Bobby, and he seems much happier." Toward the end of the school year it was recommended that the schedule be thinned to one of receiving pennies only once or twice a week.

When school closed, Mrs. Smith and the nurse had set up a summer "chores chart." Each child in the family was to be given a star for each completed chore. When the chores were all completed they would be allowed out to play. The nurse felt that the star would remind Mrs. Smith to praise the children, and it would be a systematic way of keeping track of the chores done. This plan was set up in about three hours, and only occasional letters were necessary to maintain it. This might be recommended as a useful approach for outlying communities which are difficult to reach, but which also need as much help as the metropolitan areas. (Patricia Staples)

If contact with mediators is by telephone, distance in miles is not an issue. Over the wire a consultant can advise a mediator across town, or across the continent. The nature of the consultation is identical. Instructions, graphs, progress reports, tokens, point systems, and reinforcement hierarchies can all be converted to forms which can be telephoned, telegraphed, cabled, radioed, and mailed.

The issue of lack of local professional resources should not halt all efforts to help, as is often the case. Distance no longer should be estimated in miles, but in terms of the possibilities for distortion of information between consultant and target. The more people required to pass on information, for example, the greater the distance. A Behavior Analyst giving instructions to father to give to mother is "farther away" from mother than the BA who speaks to her himself. (However, if father speaks his language and mother does not, he is closer!) The concepts of the behavioral approach and the clarity of instruction based upon them make it particularly useful for long distance consultation. The following notes formed the basis of our longest long distance consultation attempt:

Case #Bert O.   *Address:* Alaska
                          60 miles from Kotzebue by bush plane
                 Birthdate: 2/12/60

7/7/62—Itinerant Public Health Nurse
The O's home is small, bare two-room frame house which doesn't look clean. Mrs. O was taken to Nome after having convulsions; she continued to be lethargic so was transferred to Anchorage for further care.

6/1/64—Public Health Nurse
Bert's mother Rugh, has an undiagnosed disease of the nervous system. She has been aphasic for some years now. She does not appear fit mentally to take proper care of her children and the responsibility is left to the father and older girl—age 11—only.

The family lives in a 1½ room hut in the village. Income is from occasional labor, hunting, dog-racing, and fishing. The family receives welfare as the father is required to be at home most of the time because of the condition of his wife.

Bert appears an active and healthy little boy. His nose deformity is becoming more apparent, although it does not seem to bother him.

4/20/67—M.D.

"The patient appears to be something of a hyperactive youngster. He had bilateral scarred tympanic membranes without perforation. He has a deformity of the nasal bridge on both sides. This has been observed on yearly field trips and evaluated hereon 6/1/64. At this time it was felt that plastic repair was indicated but not until after adolescence. Because of the grotesque appearance of the nasal mass, and his rapidly developing behavior problem in the village, I felt he should be reevaluated for a possible attempt at plastic surgery at this time."

1/67—Teacher

Unmanageable in Head Start—wouldn't stay in seat. Talked to other children, grabbed things, hyperactive. Kicked out of school. (Killed dog, butchered it in 1964?) Unable to play with other children, teasing, fighting.

6/10/67—BRP staff

Visited with welfare worker, BIA social worker. Home: disorderly, drying fish and seal meat everywhere. Dogs wandering at will. Mother did not appear to understand. Boy, about 6, said Bert and his father were across the lake. We left.

Later, we hired a boat to cross over the lake. Father, with another Eskimo, was repairing his own boat on the beach. The several children were playing nearby, warming themselves by the scrapwood fire, then dashing down to the water. The welfare worker interpreted BRP to Mr. O, explaining that we were doctors here to help Bert if we could. He agreed to talk to us. I spoke with him privately, and he gave the following account:

Complaints:
1. Home: None. He is obedient at home, pleasant, and good.
2. School: Not understood. Bert has been sent home, but the father does not know why. Father has never spoken to teacher.
3. Peers: No complaint, as father attributes all the problems to Bert's being rejected and attacked by peers, based on his nose deformity.

Reinforcers:
1. High probability behaviors: accompanying father to fish camp, on dog sled, etc. Riding his pet dog.
2. Preferred objects: candy, food.
3. Preferred mediator: father, 16-year-old sister.

Past Contingencies:
Father has tried to get Bert to behave in school by offering him candy if he would behave. He has also tried to reason with him and plead with him to behave. (Negative reinforcers are not used in Eskimo culture, at least for the first 12 years of life.)

Past Outcomes:
Father explained that he had no way of knowing if Bert had behaved in school or not. Therefore, he would always give Bert the candy. And on those days when Bert was sent home, "well, he wanted it, he likes the candy so much" so father would give it to him anyway.

Potential of Father for Mediation:
Mr. O. loves his son and sees himself as the sole individual who supports, accepts, and nurtures the child. Positive control is used exclusively, negative is anticultural and not in the repertoire of the father. Could father withhold a reinforcer on contingency? He is passive, and would follow instructions to do so, if given enough reinforcement. I asked if he could deny a reinforcement: he paused and looked so helpless and hopeless that I'm not sure. I asked if he could say, in order to help Bert stay in school, that he must wait to get his candy until tomorrow when he *has* behaved in school. The father said he could do that.

Reinforcers for Father:
Father wants his son to go to school. Father wants to keep good rapport with welfare, because, when his dog-sled racing winnings are exhausted, he will again be eligible for benefits. He wants to please the whites.

Observation of Boy's Behavior:
He is inclined to be somewhat frantic. Agile, throws rocks a long way into the water. Seemed excited by the visitors. He did not much want to talk to Mr. Douglass, but on father's gentle instruction to do so, accompanied the BA for a stroll down the beach. Unproductive interview. If he is retarded, it is only mildly.

Suggested Intervention Scheme:
Get report from teacher. Stretch his "in-seat quiet time" by in-school reinforcers of teacher-attention or preferred activities. Use additional backup at home, with a message system fom the teacher to Mr. O., the home mediator of candy. Teacher contact: welfare worker in Nome. Supervisor: Dr. Tharp in Tucson.

Rationale:
The usual.
Nose: with or without surgery, behavioral intervention will be necessary.
(Tharp and Douglass)

EVOLVING NORMAL CONTINGENCIES

There are several ways in which a contingency can be "abnormal." For example, the abnormality may lie in the frequency of the reinforcement, as when a teacher is asked to praise a child more often than most children are praised and/or more often than she usually praises. Sometimes mediators are asked to praise more immediately and to avoid normal delays. The abnormality may lie in the nature of the reinforcement. Some reinforcers don't "fit" some behaviors, according to usual cultural standards. This is often why teachers do not approve of candy for academic work. They do not object to candy, and they do not object to reinforcing academic work, but it does not seem right to reinforce academic work with candy. Sometimes the contingency is abnormal because it is appropriate for a younger child, as when a fourth grade teacher is asked to reinforce a child for sitting in his seat as first grade teachers often do.

Many intervention techniques consist of introducing "abnormal" contingencies because the normal ones are failing for some reason. The process of evolving normal contingencies is one of shaping behaviors which will produce normal reinforcers, insuring that these are available, and fading toward "normal" contingencies. The following case is an example.

> Case #2. Bryan's misbehavior on the school bus had become a serious problem. He engaged in assorted deviltries such as fighting, throwing rocks, strewing school papers around the bus, running up and down the aisle, and keeping the bus in a state of general discord. At the time we intervened, the school bus driver had delivered his final ultimatum to the principal: either get Bryan straightened up or off the bus. The note system devised was agreeable to all parties concerned. Bryan received a note from the bus driver each day stating that he behaved himself on the bus, which was reinforced at home with a daily activity with Dad. After two weeks of perfect school bus behavior, we thinned the reinforcer to a weekend activity with Dad if Bryan received 4 out of 5 daily notes a week. Bryan only missed his note one time in the following two weeks. Based on this good performance, we thinned to receiving a note on Monday, Wednesday, and a gold note on Friday, if he behaved all the week on the bus. In the following two weeks he missed his note one time. Also, he and the bus driver became very good friends, and both seemed reinforced by this relationship. On the basis of these data we thinned down further to one gold note a week on Friday to be reinforced with a weekend activity. It was also at this time that the BA began thinning his visits to the family to every other week. Within another three to four weeks the BA discontinued visits for one entire month and subsequent visits were not in regard to school bus behavior. The parents were left to their own devices in hopes that they had learned the technique well enough to carry on themselves. Within three months the notes were discontinued entirely. Bryan had earned his gold note every week, and the relationship between him and the bus driver had become very strong. At the end of the school year (approximately two months after termination) Bryan's bus behavior continued to be very good. (Diana Zimmerman)

TERMINATION

The ideal point of termination is that at which the target's behavior is reinforcing the mediator's reinforcing behavior. For example, a good place for the Behavior Analyst to withdraw on home chores is when the boy is happy to mow the lawn for the 50¢ or the praise his father is happy to give him. Most rationales for termination of BRP cases were not so clear. Usually the Behavior Analyst terminated his intervention when things "seemed to be going well" and the mediators showed promise of maintaining the behaviors. In the following case one suspects the parents were able to establish some contingencies of their own.

Case #39. After a number of futile attempts to establish a working intervention plan for Monty M., a plan was conceived for Monty to earn the bicycle of his choice by completing four perfect weeks of household chores. The weeks were cumulative so any combination totaling 4 would earn the reward for Monty. (However, one mishap during the week would lose the entire week.) Surprisingly, Monty earned his bicycle five weeks after the plan was started. This was indeed a feat for a boy who had spent a lifetime manipulating his parents to get what he wanted when he wanted it.

The bike was delivered and Monty was free to ride noncontingent for two weeks. After this period the bike was to be made contingent if necessary. As it turned out, Monty continued performing at the same high level so we decided to wait until school started to see how he was going to respond. School was a major concern to the parents of this misbehaving and borderline child.

Monty started school in the fall and overwhelmed his teachers and his parents. His behavior in the classroom was excellent and his grades were well above average. Periodic school and family contacts were made during the semester, but not once was there a complaint. After picking up Monty's semester grades and reinforcing the parents for their part in shaping these newly acquired behaviors, the case was terminated.

Many times, of course, cases need to be reactivated as new behavioral difficulties arise and mediators fall back on old management techniques. More desirable is the case in which the mediator shows real evidence of acquiring management skill.

Case #34. Gregory H. was referred for aggressive behavior in the second grade classroom and "defiance." A token system was instituted, whereby he brought home notes daily for following instructions in the classroom which earned him an activity of his choice on the weekend. Gregory was doing fairly well but was not moving very quickly. Mrs. H. was asked to analyze the problem. She did so very accurately—Gregory was choosing activities which were not particularly important to him. Mrs. H. changed the plan. She began deciding what the activity would be and chose things Gregory really liked. He began to improve greatly. Gregory also had a classroom friend. Unfortunately, they managed to get into a lot of trouble together. Mrs. H. began including Gregory's friend in the weekend activity. If Gregory did not earn the tokens, then Joe, the friend, also missed out on the excursion. This was an excellent plan because now Joe not only began behaving in class, but would constantly remind Gregory to behave so they could go on the weekend outing.

Both of these plans worked so effectively that Gregory did not miss a single token the rest of the school year. Originally he earned 10 tokens per week. One token was earned for following instructions in the morning class session; one for the afternoon session. They were thinned to 3 per week and both behaviors were made contingent on one note. He was also inter-mittently reinforced with a bonus note on excellent days. Mrs. H. was an interested mother and wished to know more about using these principles in any situation, and with any of her children. She learned very quickly and began to function as a Behavior Analyst.

When school began in the fall the BA did nothing except check with the teacher from time to time. Mrs. H. took over the job of the Behavior Analyst very efficiently. She checked with Gregory's teacher occasionally and was ready to set up a plan the minute it became necessary. Gregory's new teacher had worked with the project before. She expressed her high regard for Mrs. H.'s interests and capability. We felt that this was the perfect time to terminate the case. A letter was written to the principal, apprising him of the situation. The school was asked to notify us immediately should any problems occur. Mrs. H. continues to check on Gregory's schoolwork and behavior. Six months later we have received no calls in regard to Gregory. We consider this case to be successfully terminated.

References

Bandura, A. In L. Berkowitz (Ed.), *Advances in experimental social psychology.* Vol. 2. New York: Academic Press, 1965.

Madsen, C. H., Jr., Becker, W. C., and Thomas, D. R. *Journal of Applied Behavior Analysis,* 1968, **1,** 139–150.

Martin, M., Burkholder, R., Rosenthal, T. L., Tharp, R. G., and Thorne, G. L. *Behavior Research and Therapy,* 1968, **6,** 371–378.

Premack, D. In D. Levine (Ed.), *Nebraska symposium on motivation 1965,* Lincoln, Nebraska: Univ. Nebraska Press, 1965.

Solomon, R. L. *American Psychologist,* 1964, **19,** 239–253.

CHAPTER VII

Resistances

Theoreticians of psychotherapy have maintained all along that the study of resistance is necessary for the full understanding of pathology and therapeutics. This is reasonable; we cleave the most doggedly to the dearest things. So too can our most central behaviors be identified by a reluctance to risk their change. At those times when the helping individual finds his helping thwarted, he knows that he is near the mechanisms which maintain the undesirable behaviors.

This form of analysis is useful—and indeed unavoidable—in any enterprise of social change, whether it be at the level of individual psychotherapy, family reorganization, community development, or political action. It is also useful in analyzing the processes of behavior modification. Certainly the reader should not suppose that the cases presented thus far have proceeded easily, smoothly, and to uniformly happy conclusions. Far from it; as any other human enterprise, intervention in the natural environment is often difficult, frustrating, and sometimes impossible. A study of those cases and conditions in which difficulty and failure occur can, however, educate the social scientist and social interventionist concerning some of the key elements in that particular environment. Thus the reporting and analysis of case "failures" and resistances to change are of an importance at least equal to that of case successes.

There are two ways of looking at cases in which we fail to modify behavior. The first is to attribute difficulty to lack of ingenuity in the interventionist. For instance, we might argue that theoretically any mediator who can be shaped into accurately consequating behaviors with sufficiently powerful reinforcers will, without fail, modify the behavior of the target. Therefore, any failure can be seen as one of two interventionist's errors: either he has failed to shape the mediator's behavior, or he has failed to accurately select the correct behavior.

In the natural environment, however, things do not work out with such simplicity. Adequate reinforcers are not always available, either for the target or mediator. Logistical problems are sometimes insurmountable. Adequate mediators may not exist.

This is not to gainsay the crucial elements of the interventionist's experience, skill, and luck. The degree to which the Behavior Research Project lacked these qualities, and thus produced its own resistances, can be judged far better by the reader than by the writers. But difficulties in the implementation of intervention plans did fall into certain categories, regardless of the particular staff members involved. Indeed, few cases did not include at least one form of these resistances, and most resisted in several ways. Just as the cases presented in the preceding chapter do not necessarily represent "successes," the case difficulties reported below do not necessarily represent eventual failure, although some were, indeed, totally unyielding. The point made here is that these resistances cannot be assumed unique to any case. They represent technical difficulties which must be faced by anyone who chooses to attempt behavior modification in the natural environment. As these patterns of resistance are presented in order, some indication will be given as to possible methods of overcoming them. The suggestions are not comprehensive, and we make it very clear that some resistances were not, and could not, be countered by us. Thus some resistances help us to perceive the limitations on the advisability of behavior modification in the natural environment.

INDIVIDUAL RESISTANCES

PHILOSOPHICAL REVULSION

To persuade others to change their ways requires a justification to them, an explanation, a theory. Our society is so heterogeneous with respect to values and beliefs that any persuader will find some people revolted by his concepts. With behavior modification, it is likely to take the following forms.

Rejection of Determinism

Scientific determinism, which a learning-theory approach implies, is unacceptable to many people. We have found it most effective to refrain from joining this argument, but simply to explain procedures. Many thoughtful critics will then find contingency management quite consistent with voluntarism; indeed a clear statement of the alternatives open to the target, and an explanation of their consequences allow him to choose. In our cases, the target's experience of the intervention plan is one of freedom to modify his behavior, or not to do so, as he wishes. But for some people, this position is unpersuasive.

> Case #99. A philosophically liberal, but personally authoritarian school principal listened uncomfortably to an explanation of the Project program. He then thundered, "I will not have any part of it! It's *Brave New World!*"

The Issue of "bribery"

A frequent complaint of mediator–teachers and parents is that the use of reward to encourage good behavior constitutes "bribery."

> Case #99. The principal also added: "I will not reward a child for doing his moral duty!"
> Case #48. The father stated vehemently, "None of my brothers or sisters or me was ever paid for being good, and no kid of mine is going to be paid for being good."

For many mediators, the issue of "bribing" is directly stated and strongly felt. It seems to arise from the assumption that behavior which is desirable to the mediator should be done "for its own sake"; it should be intrinsically, not extrinsically motivated. In other words, it should already have been learned. This view seems to ignore the responsibility which society has to teach. Otherwise, the "bribery" issue does not make much definitional sense. We have had considerable success by pointing out that bribery refers to being "paid off" for undesirable behavior. When individuals are rewarded for desirable behavior, it goes by other names: salary, commission, praise, approval, or the hope of heaven.

Of course, the bribery issue blends (many times indistinguishably) into a philosophical, habitual, or personal preference for aversive control.

A Preference for Aversive Control

The typical predelinquent child is under aversive control; his environment attempts to control his behavior by the use of punishment rather than reward. Such children, paradoxically, may find intended punishment positively reinforcing. The misbehavior of the child who is repeatedly scolded by the teacher may be reinforced by the reward of her attention—even if the attention is only scolding. But many mediators object philosophically or emotionally to the use of rewards as a technique of child rearing; the rod, they say, in effect, will prevent spoiling the child.

Case #99. The same principal admitted that he had no objections, in principle, to paddling a child who misbehaved.

In other cases, mediators cannot admit with full voice their punitive predelictions. More often, the tendency toward punitiveness manifests itself as a steady resistance, recurrent and insiduous.

Case #56. Alan's parents were fundamentalist protestants who imposed srong limitations on their son's freedom for relatively minor offenses. When his school grades began to deteriorate they reacted by almost totally restricting him to his room and depriving him of TV, the use of the phone, etc. The father was a rigid martinet whose job kept him away from home three or four days a week. Both parents felt that anything but total submission to parental authority subverted the rules of man and God.

Alan was a bright, conscientious, and mildly withdrawn 16-year-old, but this crushing limitation drove him to run away from home. He turned himself in to the juvenile probation lock-up and announced that he would rather go to the State reform school than go home. When his parents arrived he refused to go home with them and said if he were forced he would run away immediately.

Finally the boy agreed to go home after several telephone conversations among probation officers, the father, and our Project, the essence of which was that the restrictions would be lifted and our help would be immediately available.

The parents agreed to an intervention program based on weekly grade notices from Alan's teachers. On the basis of grades, Alan earned points which governed the hours he might spend away from home, watch TV, and use the phone.

The program began effectively, although the boy was suspicious since it appeared to be nonpunitive.

His suspicions soon proved well founded. Although he earned enough points to allow a greater degree of freedom than he had previously been granted, his parents meddled with the plan. Despite repeated discussions and instructions from the BA, they insisted on searching for reasons to punish Alan. One Sunday Alan had enough points to go off with some friends, but as he started for the door his father prohibited him from leaving because he had received a low grade in one subject that week. "You haven't got time to play if you can't keep up your studies," was the way his father justified the action.

The parents were obviously adding punitive features to the program, many of which were not revealed to the BA, and the boy threatened to run away again, protesting that his father and mother were not honoring their promise not to apply restrictions. When the BA deplored these actions the parents explained that they would like an "altered" program which would eliminate the reinforcement features and the point system. "We'd want to use your program as a guideline without being so formal." "We like the weekly grade notes, because we don't have to wait six weeks for Alan's report card." (To this they might have added that such an arrangement made it possible to keep *au courant* with their son's failures for punitive purposes without accepting the responsibility of rewarding his successes.)

Since the parents would not abandon their punitive point of view, the Project was obliged to drop the case. (Malcolm Bissell)

PERSONAL DIFFICULTY IN CONSEQUATION

Almost every mediator will experience some difficulty in rearranging the contingencies which he places on a given child. Before turning to the most general statement of the problem, however, let us examine the most dramatic sorts of difficulties.

Personal Disorganization

One ordinarily thinks that a parent who suffers from schizophrenia or the like is no resource for helping his child. In some cases which BRP has handled the severity of such disorders has made for failure; the mother who is hallucinating so that she cannot distinguish the reality of her child's behavior from her imaginings concerning it cannot respond differentially with accurate consequation. On the other hand, we have worked successfully with many "schizophrenic" mediators, many "psychopathic" ones, and a wide variety of "neurotics." After all, if the behavioral prescription to the mediator is clear enough and simple enough, one does not need an excess of mental health to follow the instruction. A "schizophrenic" teacher, for instance, might be asked only this: when the child completes her assignment, give her this note which she can take to her mother who will redeem it with a lipstick. Whether or not the teacher is delusional concerning her principal is irrelevant; all she must do is consequate assignment-completion with a pretyped note. Most people, of any diagnosis, are able to carry out instructions if they are simple enough. For mediators of personal disorganization we suggest maximum simplicity of requests.

External Contraints

Many mediators would prefer to cooperate with the behavior engineer, but are constrained by other people and things in their own environments. The most extreme case occurred as follows:

Case #66. Our staff strongly urged a widowed mother to call the juvenile authorities when next her daughter, Annie, sneaked out of the house at night. The mother was unable to do so, because this might have resulted in the daughter's being adjudicated delinquent. If the daughter were confined to a detention or correction home, the mother would have lost the pension which she administered for the daughter, and which was the family's major support. It was economically unfeasible for the mother to behave in her daughter's best interest.

On the other hand, we have seen only one such case. Most external constraints are in the form of pressure from the mediator's associates or family. (An example is the teacher who is reluctant to reward a child's school achievements with poker chip tokens, because other teachers would mock her, or because the principal might frown at such an irregularity.) At a child's home, the mother might be constrained from rewarding her daughter by spending some time in teaching her sewing skills because the father would be jealous of the time she spent away from him.

Such issues are frequent, but not at all insoluble. The general technique which we have developed calls for two ingredients. First, the behavior engineer must ask of the mediator only those behaviors which are commensurate with his role position, and which will not be punished. The engineer must then assume the responsibility himself for seeing that external constraints are mitigated; the program must be explained to the other teachers or to the principal or to the father; they must be encouraged to cooperate, and if necessary, the intervention plan must be negotiated with them to guarantee that the prime mediator will herself be "rewarded" for participation. Second, the engineer must see that external constraints are proctored; any backsliding must be quickly detected and the people involved must be repersuaded.

The sure guarantee against the presence of external restraints is, of course, to make the modified behavior of the child somehow rewarding to those individuals who control the mediator's reinforcers. If the daughter's improved behavior allows the father to sleep more easily at night, then he will be more likely to encourage the mother to spend the contingency-time with the girl.

The Desire to Destroy

Many of the mediators who are central to a predelinquent's world are very angry with him. This is certainly understandable, since these youngsters are (by definition) bad-actors. Let us again examine the most extreme case first.

Case #63. A very seriously predelinquent adolescent boy had repeatedly engaged in fist-fights with his stepfather. The stepfather had hated the child for years. After 4 weeks of a closely proctored intervention plan, the boy's misbehavior was rapidly decreasing. The father, fearful that the boy might stay in the home if he reformed, disobeyed every instruction which our staff gave him. The case disintegrated; the boy ran away. It was very clear that the boy's continued presence in the home was so punishing to the father that the rewards our staff offered him—praise, encouragement, attention—were swamped.

Such instances have also occurred in school settings.

Case #07 was a first-grade boy living in a foster home. The child had had many problems upon entering this home. He could not dress himself, was terrified of noisy toys, water, the dark, and had a speech handicap. The foster parents had worked very hard with Christopher and had managed to overcome all of these problems. When the BPR referral was received, the main complaints were in the school where it was said Chris bit and kicked children, refused to do any school work, and disrupted the whole class. After two conferences with the teacher, and several observations, we decided that Chris actually engaged in little, if any, of the misbehavior about which the teacher complained. She attended to his every move, reinforcing misbehaviors, and she was a very punitive woman in her approach to her whole class. She constantly complained that this child was making it impossible for her to teach and she wanted him removed immediately from her class.

An effort was made to shape the teacher's behavior. Two staff members went to the school three or four times a week. But after a month, the teacher "exploded," and she said she was tired of keeping this child in her room. She said she had no extra time to spend with him and she was tired of having no one do anything about it. The teacher was determined to get rid of the child, and would do nothing to attempt behavior modification.

It was arranged with the principal that Chris be removed to a different class; the new teacher was an effective mediator and the problem behaviors declined to an acceptable level.

For predelinquents who are older, such options may not be available. Dramatic acts by mediators can have dramatic and irreversible consequences on the target.

Case #30. Benny was a low achieving ninth grader who felt he was getting an unfair deal from his home environment as well as his school environment. He had struggled through two very inconsistent stepfathers and a number of nonmotivating teachers. The only thing that kept him in school and out of the grasp of the police was his devotion to his mother.

After overcoming a number of crises at the school, and establishing a concrete reinforcer at home, we intervened into Benny's intermittent work habits in the classroom. He began to work quite diligently in all his classes except math, where he had had the greatest teacher friction. The math teacher had been opposed to Benny and to the intervention all along. Two weeks after the intervention plan was started, Benny was suspended from math, on the slim pretext that on that day he didn't bring his book to class. The teacher accused him of stealing the book he had, and told him the homework he had been turning in was not up to par. He was called a "no-good bum" and told he would be better off out of school, and certainly out of math class. For Benny this was the last straw. He feared that the same thing would eventually happen in all his classes. He stopped coming to school. His mother, whom we had almost convinced that the school was finally giving her son a new opportunity, sympathized with Benny and did not demand that he return. She allowed Benny to get a job. Benny was a drop-out (or "push-out"); the case was terminated. (Lloyd Douglass)

Most instances of anger in the mediator do not extend to hatred of such ferocity. For the vast majority of cases, anger can be quickly mitigated, and rendered nondestructive. The technique here is to choose an original target behavior which is particularly annoying to the mediator. The immediate correction of the particular problem will thus be gratifying to the mediator and make his cooperation more likely. For instance, if a small child is annoying the teacher by getting out of his seat without permission, in addition to being bad on the playground, and is also underachieving in arithmetic, the strategy should be to focus initially on getting-out-of-seat. With that "sandpaper" removed from the relationship between teacher and child, she will be in a better position to cooperate in consequating the full range of problem behavior.

But, as in Case #30, there are some mediators who cannot be pleased by any reformation of the target. The very person of the child appears to be the offensive element.

Case #27. From the initial contact to the termination of the case, Mrs. Ellum's opinion and reaction to Barb changed very little. She described her daughter as "promiscuous, lazy, sloppy, cunning, and devious—capable of fooling the most intelligent mind." Mother stated that "Barb would make a good madam for a whorehouse!" In her estimation, Barb had a "split personality, having inherited all the bad qualities of both sides of the family." Her conclusion was "prognosis—bad!"

Mother gave little credence to attempts to improve and was quick to fall back on her preconceived diagnosis when Barb had a setback. After 41 days of a successful point system, Mother was still verbalizing her previously formed theories. On the delivery of the weekly chart, Mrs. Ellum told the BA that "Barb is one of those people born to be bad—it's in her nature." Mother admitted that she should be pleased with the success Barb was making but said "it would be extremely difficult to change Barb's defiant behavior because it is part of her makeup—she was born that way."

Only specific target behavior improved. Other undesirable behaviors in Barb's repertoire remained. For example, she lied to her mother about her school test schedule. This occurred 63 days after intervention. Mother's response was that "Barb is going down the drain and is rotten to the core. She has no sincerity and no character."

Just previous to this incident, Barb's grandfather caught her trying to get into her mother's room. At that time, Mother wrote this concerning Barb: "She has been of excellent behavior this week—I don't expect it to last! She has regard for no one, not even me, and to get anything that she might need or want, she will go to any length."

Shortly after this, the case was terminated with the decision that Barb would be better off with her grandparents who resided in another city.

For Barb, the tactic of choosing another mediator was a logical and satisfactory one. For Benny, there was no choice. To remain in school meant that he had to remain under the tutelage of his destructive math teacher, and for Case #63 there was no other home available. For such cases, behavior modification in the natural environment has reached the limits of its effectiveness. There are no mediators who can dispense reinforcement on contingency. Other strategies then become necessary: either the creation of an artificial helping relationship, or a change of environment. Benny altered his environment by excluding school and substituting a work-life. Case #63, after a brief runaway, was apprehended for breaking and entering, placed on probation, and returned to the home where the situation continues to be chaotic. In the absence of environmental change, behavioral change is absent. In extreme cases of the lack of competent mediation, institutional environments continue to be the management of choice.

INSTITUTIONAL RESISTANCES

Although it is artificial to divide resistances into individual and institutional, certain patterns of resistance can be seen to occur by virtue of occupying a particular social role, regardless of the personal characteristics of the mediators. This discussion will treat the two major institutions which impinge upon the child: school and family.

FAMILY

Parental Discord

The disorganized family which is marked by heavy marital discord presents serious management problems. In some cases, the parents can be brought to agree on a consistent intervention plan for the sake of the child. In other instances, marital quarreling is so high in the behavioral repertoire of the parents that it spills into any and every issue between them, including all phases of child management.

Case #79. Parental discord and family disorganization had marked this family for a number of years. The parents frequented counseling agencies, seeking help for their problems. More than once they engaged in heated verbal arguments in the BA's presence. The mother said "I have never been able to talk to my husband. I have tried every way to make him see the damage he's doing." On the other hand, the father stated that the mother interferred too much when he was correcting the children. Mother admitted this; she disagreed with his severe disciplinary measures.

It was very difficult to get these parents to agree on an intervention plan. When they finally did, that plan, and all subsequent plans were sabotaged. The father would promise to follow through with the agreed-upon system, but never carried it out. When his wife reminded him, the father would become irritable, completely uncooperative, and inevitably a fight resulted. The family eventually became immobilized for any intervention. The parents were then referred to a family service agency for marital counseling. After a short trial period that agency despaired of any marital accommodation. The target was placed in a residential institution, where he is manifesting virtually no behavioral problems. (Diana Zimmerman)

Case #79 illustrates a situation which is probably insoluble. With inconsistent and contradictory cues provided by the parents, and with each parent reinforcing responses which are undersirable to the other, it is inevitable that a child will be taught behaviors which are difficult for others to tolerate. In such an instance, alteration of the social environment— either by divorce or placement outside the family—is a prerequisite to behavioral modification. For Case #79 this placement resulted in consistent achievement of the Honor Roll and no observed instances of bullying, stealing, or fire-setting (the original complaint behaviors). The parents continue to argue.

The Insistence on "Equity"

"All children should be treated alike": this is a common objection to altering the environment for only one child, when there are siblings present. Some parents stated that "favoritism" should be avoided; thus, desirable things or events must not come to one child only. It is interesting that such parents rarely object to individualizing punishment.

Case #19 was referred for aggressive playground behavior (fights, tantrums, foul language) and poor grades. At home the problems were with aggression toward his four brothers and destruction of toys.

Due to the parents' divorce the five boys in the family were cared for by the paternal grandfather who stayed at home during the day, and the father, who was employed.

Prior to intervention, both grandfather and father stated that all their boys were treated equally in all ways. No boy received special attention. The grandfather emphatically stated that they all had the same amount of duties, clothes, and toys. It would be unthinkable to give one boy a toy or an article of clothing without buying the others the same. When the father went on errands, he had to take either all boys or no one. Punishments were more individualized, but on some occasions when the guilty brother could not be determined, all the boys would suffer.

An intervention plan was designed in which father and grandfather allowed the divorced grandmother to be mediator and dispense rewards. She had no objection to rewarding only one boy. With this kind of intervention, father and grandfather would not be in a position to act against their firm philosophy that all should be treated alike.

This technique of circumventing the mediators who do not wish to individualize has many disadvantages. For example, it can increase the alienation among mediators. Moreover, the introduction of a foreign element into the value system of the family and of the social network of the siblings can have unfortunate side effects. A more effective strategy is to extend the motivational scheme from the predelinquent to all the children.

> Case #19 (continued). The plan continued for several weeks successfully. The father remarried a month after intervention and all the adults involved felt that the new mother should take over the role of mediator. When interviewed, the stepmother expressed the old philosophy: all brothers should be treated alike. It was then decided that when the target met the criterion, all brothers would receive the reward. The stepmother, who was to dispense, was directed to tell all boys that when their brother did well in school then they would all be rewarded—probably with a weekend activity. This motivated the brothers to encourage and remind the target to "remember to be good this week."

With such a strategy, good behavior by the target earns rewards both for himself and for his siblings. This can produce most effective social pressure on the target from the siblings and has resulted in some of our most rapid behavioral improvements.

An alternate strategy is to employ the same intervention plan as the target's for each sibling, making each brother or sister a "target" themselves. If the sibs behave acceptably already, they lose nothing. If they do not, some intervention is desirable.

The Needed Scapegoat

This phenomenon has been discussed in casework literature and in psychoanalysis for years. In those few cases where it is present, one sees it most clearly when working with the natural environment. If the predelinquent child provides the focus for the family disharmonies, and simultaneously is the screen for them, the family will resist changing its pattern of consequation because the child's improvement is punishing to the mediator. This is never stated by the family, of course. The resistance will take other overt forms, and will thus be met by the techniques discussed under other headings. The needed scapegoat phenomenon appears after the child's behavior has improved, in the form of disturbance in other siblings, or in marital friction, or the like. Let us make clear that this is rare; indeed, the overwhelming number of successful behavior modifications has resulted in improvement in family life. In the other instances, the improvement in the predelinquent has made clear to the family that the problem lies elsewhere—in their marriage, in a personal "neurosis," or whatever.

The School

For school systems, like families, there are certain resistances which occur by virtue of common institutional practices and arise with great frequency regardless of the individuals who occupy particular school positions. Public education is managed almost entirely through aversive control: suspensions, expulsions, ridicule, loss of hall-passes or library privileges, scolding, loss of varsity eligibility, and the like. Even more alarming is the steadfast disinclination to employ available positive control. There are many reinforcers which might be used to stimulate academic performance and which incorporate imaginative arrangements for educational practice, creating a climate of positive motivation and experience. But this vision is a far cry from educational institutional practice. Thus, even the limited and correctional use of positive reinforcement meets frequent resistance.

Disinclination toward Positive Control

Pilot Case MT. A first-grade boy was inattentive and achieving well under his test IQ of 125. He could have been easily motivated through the dispensing of lemon-drops by the teacher immediately after school. The teacher was repelled by the thought of using candy as an instructional aid and reported the suggestion to her principal, who initiated complaints that ultimately lodged in the Office of the Superintendent. No intervention plan mediated at the school was allowed.

Other resistances which frequently arise on an individual basis are the feelings that all children should be treated alike, aversive control is preferable, etc.; these find strong institutional-level manifestation in the schools.

The Problem of Grades

The one positive-control feature routinely used in education is the *grade*. In this way, better work is acknowledged and, hopefully, the child is rewarded for approximations to criterion performance. It is unfortunate, however, that the only permanent-record grade is typically that for the six week grading period. This long latency between performance and consequence is insufficient for many children to maintain or improve academic behaviors. While many teachers do provide daily (or hourly, or instant) consequences in the form of comments, homework, grades, etc., the only grade which makes a difference is the one on the report card. This is a highly unreliable measure.

Case #55. The subject was referred by his second grade teacher for disruptive behavior in the classroom and underachievement.

His teacher was capable and cooperative. The intervention plan, begun after three weeks of baseline, was as follows. The target was given a daily spelling assignment. The teacher would mark "complete" or "incomplete" on the written assignment at the end of the day. His older brother would reward the subject with a great deal of praise and 2¢ for completion. In addition, the teacher would put a star on the paper if the subject had behaved in class that day (did not get out of seat, talk out inappropriately, or disturb those around him). The star earned TV privileges in the evening. From the date of intervention on April 12, 1966, to the end of school, June 2, 1966, the subject went from a 3.8 to a 2.0 average on spelling tests. Also, during three weeks of baseline he completed his spelling assignment twice. From the time of intervention to the end of school he reversed this by completing his assignment all but two times, or 84% failure dropped to 6%. There was also improvement in the subject's classroom behavior. During the baseline period he would not have earned a single star for good behavior. From the date of intervention to the termination of school (36 days) he received a star over half (60%) of the time.

Despite these marked improvements the subject's spelling grade for the six-week period remained the same. In addition, his citizenship mark went from a 3 to a 4. When confronted with the data the teacher was not able to give a reasonable account for the discrepancies in the grading.

Although this is a particularly well-documented, and perhaps extreme, example of the inadequacy of grades as a criterion-measure, it is not particularly unusual. Such nonresponsiveness of grades to target's behaviors can be very discouraging to the child and can, of course, have punishing effects. On the other hand, grades are not always lower than they should be. Sometimes they are higher. Sometimes they are both.

Case #54. The subject was referred to us on March 23, 1966, by his high school counselor, because his parents had requested help in controlling him at home. In addition the subject had been involved in two incidents with the police.

During the family interview the parents made it clear that, in their estimation, the subject was merely immature and mischievous; their serious concern was his poor school performance. Intervention was launched in three subjects: spelling, social studies, and music (band). These subjects were chosen on the basis of teacher cooperation, degree of underachievement, and the subject's personal interest. All reinforcers, other than teacher praise and attention, came from the home, contingent on the subject's practicing two hours a week for band, completing his weekly spelling assignment, and achieving good grades in social studies.

One half of the band grade was dependent on the subject's turning in his band practice slips signed by his parents stating that he practiced two hours at home that week. In the twelve weeks preceding intervention the subject had handed it in only twice (17% of the weeks). In the seven weeks following intervention he handed it in all but once (85%). His grade went up from a 4 to a 3 in that class.

In spelling, the subject had handed in his weekly assignment two times during the six weeks prior to intervention. Completing the assignment counted one-half of the spelling grade. In the seven weeks following intervention the subject handed in his assignment every week and received average to high grades on each one of them. Also, he achieved a scattering of 1's, 2's, and 3's on his spelling tests during this period. Despite this drastic improvement, his spelling grade remained the same (a 4) for this grading period.

In social studies the subject received all 4's and 5's on his tests before and after intervention. Despite a number of different contingencies, the subject made only one 3, and all the rest of his marks were failures. There was no improvement. Yet, his grade went from a 4— to a 4+.

The routine grading system then is not sufficiently reliable to serve either as a performance measure or as a reinforcer. While it is certainly true that many students will work for grades, grades cannot be used as the careful measures which corrective behavioral engineering requires. We do not suggest that this state of affairs derives from perniciousness; only rarely is it due to laziness. We do not complain of occasional errors of calculation. It seems, rather, that the grade is the only tangible reaction which schools dispense regularly to their pupils. As such, grades must carry the heavy burden of the teachers' total response to the multitude of academic and social behaviors emitted by the child for a period of six weeks. Because the grade is a reaction to everything, it is not a reaction to anything. The recent attack under which grading-systems have come seems fully warranted. At this moment in history, grades constitute an institutional resistance which militates against precise reactions from the school environment to school behaviors. When targets perceive that they have only limited behavioral control over school consequences, they are in good reality contact.

Guidance and Counseling

Most school counselors who concern themselves with problem children have been trained in the techniques of client-centered or psychodynamic therapies. In either case, such counselors are not typically concerned with the management of a child's environment. They are accustomed to a "talking cure," and in the absence of other available techniques, pursue this effort even with the predelinquent child who has been repeatedly demonstrated to be an unresponsive subject. Thus, most school counselors find behavior modification techniques foreign to their usual role performances. One elementary school counselor observed to the Behavior Analyst (and others) in a case conference, "I don't want to know what trouble the child is in—this would make counseling him more difficult." To decline facts is a clear perversion of any Rogerian position, but it is not an uncommon view for the insular counselor to assume.

We do not wish here to join the issue of the potential efficacy of "personal counseling" to disturbed children, or the linked issue of the appropriacy of this enterprise to the public schools. But this is a clear fact: so long as counseling activities are carried on in isolation from the realities of the school environment, jurisdictional or "territorial" disputes are inevitable. Thus, the academic and personal sectors of a child's life are administratively separated, and pulling-and-tugging between teacher and counselor is the consequence. Further, the guidance, counseling, psychometric, and psychological services of most school districts are bureaucratically separate from the instructional organization which tends to reify the implicit partialling-out of the child. This can result in a counselor feeling that "This is my case."

> At a conference among school counselors, administrators, and BRP staff, called for the purpose of discussing several cases which had counselor involvement, one counselor stated his position honestly and boldly: "I know counseling hasn't helped with _____, but this is my case and I don't want to turn it over to anybody."

Other instances have illustrated passive rather than active resistance.

> Case #20. Sue's school counselor was disturbed over the fact that the behavior modification approach did not involve personal counseling with Sue about her problems. But because she had regular appointments with Sue, she was included in the first intervention plan, which was organized as follows:
>
> If Sue attended school all day, she would receive a note from the counselor which would be redeemed by the mother for phone and date privileges. On the first day of intervention Sue was a few minutes late for her first class but attended school all day—a vast improvement over her previous week's attendance. (Tardiness was not a part of the criterion for week one.) Despite this, on the first day, the counselor gave Sue a lengthly lecture on tardiness, warned her she would not receive the note again if she were late, and then begrudingly signed the note and turned it over to Sue.
>
> The BA called the counselor the next morning to explain the importance of not making the afternoon note delivery an aversive experience and explained that punctuality would be added to the plan at a later date. That

afternoon Sue went to pick up her note after attending school all day. The secretary told Sue that the counselor was at a meeting, would not be returning, and hadn't left the note for her to dispense to Sue.

The following week a new plan was devised. Sue picked up her note in a sealed envelope directly from the attendance officer's desk.

This "solution" to Case #20, and to similar cases, is partial at best. Sue's counselor was understandably chagrined at being eliminated from the case management and demonstrated her hostility in continuing subtle denigrations. The BRP staff became annoyed with the counselor, and no doubt communicated this annoyance to the other case mediators. The jurisdictional dispute was thus compounded by adding still another contending element—the BRP staff—into an already disputatious social environment.

Let us make clear that not all schools and not all counselors exhibit these resistances. Many counselors perceive the necessity of participating in the social realities of the child's life and have been enthusiastic for a theory and technique which allows for a coherent plan of behavioral amelioration. For them, knowledge of behavioral modification methods has been sufficient to instantly wipe away the problems of bureaucratic insularity which were previously perpetuated by theoritical positions requiring insular action.

In fact, the school counselor is in an ideal position to assume the role of behavior engineer himself. With access to teachers, administration, and pupil, with access to parents, and with responsibilities to the "whole child," the counselor is in a far better position to administer intervention plans than is an agent of still another external agency, such as the BRP. Such arrangements will no doubt increase in the coming years.

The Bureaucracy

The structure of organizations is not designed for allowing an individual to experience the consequences of his own behavior. The staff, line, and communication patterns within a school district are created for the convenience of the staff and frequently do not allow for much modification in order to deal with the problems of an individual child. This does not make schools different from other complex organizations, but procedural uniformity—without which large-scale organizations would no doubt go beserk—creates gross, if unintended, absurdity for the individual problem child.

Case #11. An intervention plan was proposed to a school in which Case #11 would be allowed to participate in the after-school football program as a daily reinforcer for his good behavior in the morning section of his elementary school. The school administration objected to this on two grounds. First, they did not believe they could make after-school football contingent for this one child, when it was a noncontingent opportunity for all the other children. Second, and undoubtedly most important, the school had no way of forwarding information from the morning teacher to the coach of the afternoon activity. Since no communication channel existed, the school pronounced the plan impossible. Nowhere in the school was there an individual whose normal role included carrying such a message. Both the teacher and the coach would have considered it a violation of their job descriptions to seek out the other. It was necessary in this instance, as in many others, to have the BA fill in the interstices in the organization and become the communication channel himself. The BA either called or came by in the morning to verify criterion performance with the teacher and delivered the report to the coach.

It should be reported that the administration of Case #11's school was not at all opposed to continuation of behavior modification programming for the child once they had some concrete demonstration of its efficacy. The behavior engineer cannot ask for more open-mindedness or opportunity than that; but even with the philosophical support of the principal, still the organizational structure did not allow for these two positions—teacher and coach—to regularly and directly communicate over an individual child. This difficulty was entirely independent of the personalities or values of these two mediators; both were reliable, cooperative, and interested professionals. There was simply no time, no moment of spatial proximity, and no habit which would allow for the transmission of information.

A further complexity, created by a lack in the organization of reasonable communication channels, can also be illustrated by Case #11.

Case #11 (continued). The boy lived at some distance from the school. When he did not play football, he rode the school bus home. When he earned the after-school game, the family had to come to the school to get him an hour later. Thus his mother had to know whether or not he earned the reward in order to plan for transportation. Things were complicated further by the mother's employment. On afternoons when she worked, the maternal grandmother had the transportation responsibility, and a telephone was not available to the mother. Neither the teacher, nor the coach, nor the principal's secretary were willing to master the scheduling and informational complexity required to notify the family of the boy's daily post-school status. Their position was clear and consistent: schools did not (and could not be expected to) expend such time and effort for individual problems. Again, the BA provided this daily service.

This role—akin to the ombudsman—is a frequent one for the behavior engineer in the natural environment; Case #11 is typical, not unusual. The engineer thus becomes the advocate of the individual child; advocacy is particularly important for the problem case—the case which has been demonstrably failed by the standard system. But the system resists, thus maintaining its own self-created problems.

The task of the behavior engineer in overcoming this resistance is compounded if he is an agent external to the organization. The BRP was always an external element since it constituted a separate agency which had, as its openly avowed task, the modification of the procedures of the organizations to which it was consultant. This is no happy position for the school, nor for the consultant. Again we are reminded of the potential which exists in the position of school counselor or school psychologist, already possessing something of the ombudsman's role. Operating within the system, they would be more likely to be seen as sympathetic to the very real problems which schools face in their efforts to individualize instruction; thus they would encounter one less resistance.

The problems inherent in the behavior-modification agency as an independent entity are not confined to the school. Territorial disputes—as in politics and in the jungle—are rampant in the community.

COMMUNITY RESISTANCES

Some of the patterns of resistance to marshaling the forces of the natural environment occur on a level of community organization, or in the ways in which institutions relate to one another.

Individual Jurisdictional Problems

All natural relationships are not simply organized. For instance, both school and police bear a preexisting relationship to a given child, and the behavior engineer must take both into account. If the engineer chooses to work with the teacher rather than the policeman, the latter may see the intervention plan as objectionable. The objections can take two forms. The first exists when the intervention is antagonistic to the usual performances of the mediator's role, as when the use of positive controls are incommensurate with the value-system of the officer. The second form will occur when the behavior engineer suggests that one or more individuals relinquish their primary intervention on a case, in favor of a potentially more powerful relationship. Then a simple matter of jurisdiction—the territoral imperative—becomes a problem, as illustrated previously by the example of the school counselor.

The preferred technique in such instances is to involve all interested natural relationships in the decision-making process, preferably in the form of a "case conference," but minimally in the form of full discussion.

Thus, even when some relationships are not employed, the excluded ones can legitimize the intervention by their participation in decisions.

The Mental Health Establishment and the Problem of New Services

Perhaps the most vigorous and vocal resistance has arisen from those individuals of the various professions who are trained in psychotherapy. Although there has been opposition within the field of clinical psychology, the general position of behavior therapy within the profession of psychology has mitigated the opposition markedly. The objections from mental health practitioners have been uniform and predictable. First, they object to the use of nontraditional personnel in dealing with the families of disturbed children. Second, they object to BRP techniques as being directed to symptom removal only, without regard to the "cause." Naturally there has been wide individual variation on this issue. Many psychiatrists and social workers, particularly those who have seen the program effective in cases with which they are familiar, have even adopted some aspects of behavior modification techniques. But the most vigorous opposition has indeed come from other agencies in the same area who are accustomed to handling the same population with a different set of techniques. The opposition in these quarters has probably been on a jurisdictional basis; a new service can no more invade old territory unchallenged than can a new hummingbird, though there be ample nectar.

> Dr. A. attended a community study committee session along with representatives of other children's services agencies. The BRP program was presented publicly there for the first time. Dr. A. first proposed that it was inappropriate for this mental health center to begin to offer services for children (!) since there were many adult patients available for treatment. This position being of no avail, Dr. A. then suggested that the methods of BRP might well be a fit subject for an investigation committee of the state psychiatric association.

The establishing of new services is always difficult and requires careful negotiation to avoid jurisdictional disputes; careful interpretation is also required to avoid genuine misunderstandings. The problem is worst with the creation of a new agency; when new services must be integrated into an existing agency, the problems lessen.

We have seen this particularly in our program of consultation to outlying and rural areas. In these operations, the task has been to assist existing institutions—welfare offices, school nursing, government agencies, or whatever—to improve their services to the predelinquent child. In these instances, resistance has not occurred on an institutional level.

The course of events supports the view that interagency opposition to BRP operations is territorial in origin. As a case in point:

> Three years later Dr. A. regularly referred behavior-disordered children to the BRP. Territories were reboundaried. There continued to be cases enough for all.

Community Supports for Problem Behavior

The most massive forms by which problems resist their own solution, however, are those which have the most subtle camouflage—those whose protective colors are the community's own.

One type of such resistance can be observed in the community which is organized to support a specific form of behavior, and which then defines that very behavior as deviant for certain of its members.

> In one city which the BRP staff has consulted, gambling is legal. Vitually the entire economy—jobs, institutions, social services—is dependent upon the prosperity of the gambling and entertainment industry. The city is alight from dusk to dawn with fantastic and effective stimuii; an electric and human circus exists which is impressively engineered to evoke staying-out-late behavior. The most frequent "predelinquent" complaints in this city are curfew violations.

To produce effective counter-supports for such "offenses" would indeed tax the ingenuity of the helping professions. Contradictions in a community's goals may surface in its designated "deviates."

Other forms of environmental support for problems are part human and part geographical.

> In rural communities of Hawaii, school absences may be expected to rise when the call is sounded from one adolescent to another: "Surf's up!"

While regular school attendance is as highly valued in the Islands as elsewhere, a detectably less severe reaction may be expected from these communities for "ditching" on those rare days of high and perfect form surf. In situations such as this, a community may decline to label as deviant those juvenile behaviors which are prompted by recognized blessings; in such a way, the community declines to socially manufacture another problem for itself.

Other communities may not have choices quite as apparent. Indeed, they may be totally concealed from community awareness.

> BRP case consultation was performed in a northern coast town whose principal product is canned seafood. After a typical escalating conflict between the school and the target, a 15-year-old girl, she dropped out and began to work part-time at the cannery. The income was valued by the family, but the court was determined that she return to school. In investigat-

ing the possibilities of making part-time cannery employment contingent on school attendance, we were confronted with the discovery that several adolescent drop-outs, school "withdrawals," and flunk-outs were part of the cannery peak-season work force. The reason given for this pattern was that such "kids like to make the money." Only as we began to explore alternatives for the cannery–school arrangement did it become clear that the community could not, with impunity, change things very much. There was a critical labor shortage during the brief peak-season.

These communities have not been cited as "bad examples." Rather, the behavior engineer should be alert to contingencies structured by total community interactions, and he should understand that these issues obtain in every community. They are always present and often least obvious at home.

In the Southwest, Mexican-American children are, like other ethnic minorities of the United States, seriously overrepresented in such statistics as drop-out and underachievement, and in the experience of educational meaninglessness. At least at the time of this writing these students are more likely than their Anglo-American counterparts to be passive, nonparticipating, and "fatalistic" in their awareness that few responses in their repertoires will bring rewards. There still are teachers who insist that the Spanish-speaking first grader speak only English and, in effect, punish him for all available verbal behavior. It is little wonder that a common "problem" Mexican-American adolescent is one who sits silently in the back of the room, continues to underachieve, and does "nothing." Since blatant school misbehaviors, though not absent, are disproportionately low, our own referral criteria and procedures automatically excluded intervention in this major community problem. Hence we participated in a resistance to our own aims.

CHAPTER VIII

Evaluation

All individuals engaged in the modification of human behavior have a dual responsibility. Not only must they develop and implement an intervention technology, but they must also assess the effectiveness and outcomes of their interventions. The first task, the development of intervention techniques, has received by far the larger share of professional effort. For some, it is the more rewarding of the two tasks; for others, the more glamorous. For whatever reason, our evaluation methodology is seriously underdeveloped. We are just now turning our attention to a fundamental problem in assessment: the observation and report of change.

To the social scientist the charting of change provides both challenge and consternation. During the course of our contact with the cases described in the previous chapters, many changes occurred—bad behaviors decreased, academic achievement altered, teacher and parental attitudes modified, some boys went to jail, and some boys did not go back to school. We attempted to chart these things. At the same time, sibling relationships improved or worsened, girls fell in and out of love, some got work, some lost it, some people worried more, some less. These things we did not chart. To describe change, certain aspects are selected and others, rejected. We chose to chart those aspects that seemed meaningful to the intervention, those aspects for which we could develop means of observation, those aspects whose change we could communicate to others and in some way explain.

We are not submitting a "solution" to the problem of charting change, any more than we propose a "solution" to the problem of youthful misbehaviors. It is, rather, that we have defined our tasks as including the development of a research as well as an intervention methodology. The techniques and organization of this project were guided in part by research requirements. It is clear that behavioral analysis requires different forms of data and presentation than traditional clinical work has provided. New

147

forms of organization are required to develop new forms of research. The Behavior Research Project was an attempt to provide such organizational form. We have not solved the problem, but to declare these problems insoluble is to adopt a position that is at the least uninteresting. To join the issue is to foreordain at least partial failure; decades will be required to achieve refinement.

THE SINGLE SUBJECT DESIGN

ISSUES IN EVALUATION

The evaluation of therapeutic intervention is notoriously difficult. Indeed, the absence of clear-cut data makes it possible to suggest that traditional therapies have no effect whatsoever (Eysenck, 1952). The problem is twofold. First, it must be determined whether or not there has been a change. Second, the sources of the change, i.e., the therapeutic agents or ingredients, must be identified. Both issues have presented severe difficulties to past attempts at therapeutic evaluation.

An effective barrier to the determination of change has been the lack of definition and absence of agreement as to what is changing. Depending upon the therapist's point of view, change may be expected in personality variables, ego strength, emotional stability, marital relations, perceptions, defenses, work habits, frequency of hospitalization, dream contents, and a host of similar variables. Some of these expected changes are more easily observed and defined than others, but whatever the difficulties, therapeutic intervention has not been carefully monitored in the past. The traditional account of process, the case study, does not generate precise change statements.

Attempts to determine the important therapeutic ingredients have been equally frustrated. Treatment and control groups are difficult and expensive to establish. The therapeutic variables under study are frequently ill-defined (e.g., personality of therapist). Systematic manipulation of therapeutic variables is seldom attempted. It is not surprising that most of the therapeutic work which takes place daily is not evaluated and, indeed, often is recorded inadequately.

Behavior modification techniques place heavy emphasis on both the recording of change and the determination of the active therapeutic variable. This is because these techniques stem directly from the research methods of the experimental analysis of behavior. These research methods stress the precise definition and measurement of an observable behavior and the systematic manipulation of potential variables affecting it. When applied to human problem behavior as a therapeutic device these research methods often appear simple and unimportant. In comparison with the complexities of traditional procedures they are indeed simpler (at least briefer). Their importance lies in the mind of the beholder. Here we shall describe the nature of the evaluation procedures.

Their common denominator is *observable behavior*. Whatever human elements intervention is designed to affect must have a behavioral referent. The process of determining change becomes the process of counting behaviors, either automatically or with human observers. Sometimes the rate at which the behavior frequency changes over time is observed, as in a cumulative record. Sometimes the differences in frequency between two or more points in time are observed (the latter shows the amount but not the rate of change). The constant or periodic counting of behavior yields therapeutic process data, and thus a means of monitoring and evaluating the efficiency of intervention procedures.

Most of the therapeutic work in behavior modification is based on a particular research design which examines the behavior of a single organism. The purpose of this design is to identify variables which influence the individual subject's behavior frequency. In many cases the identification of a variable influencing the frequency of a "problem" behavior is tantamount to identifying a therapeutic agent.[7] The most common form

[7] In the single organism, within subject design the comparison is not made between the performance of two or more groups treated differently, as is traditional in much therapy evaluation. Rather, the comparison is made between the performance of the same individual during two or more periods of time in which he may be treated differently. Since the same individual is being observed, the problems which individual differences introduce into evaluation are eliminated. This automatically eliminates the necessity for many of the control groups traditionally used in therapy research. Two other problems still remain, however. One is the sequence effect which the order of the treatments may produce. The other is the degree to which the observations have general value. Sidman (1960) has suggested several techniques for dealing with treatment effects and argued that the within-subject design can ultimately contribute more to generality than between-groups research. He suggests that statistical averaging and statistical variable elimination (e.g., balancing) obscure actual processes and he maintains that, "As we identify more precisely the conditions under which a phenomenon will occur, we automatically increase its generality (Sidman, 1960, p. 243)." However it may be judged, the procedure is an integral part of behavior modification techniques. Gelfand and Hartmann (1968) have suggested several procedures which, if followed, enable the single organism within-subject design to yield powerful demonstrations of behavior control. Bijou *et al.* (1969) give probably the best statement to date concerning the application of experimental techniques to the study of behavior in the natural environment.

of the single organism-within-subject design includes (1) a period of observation of the behavior frequency (baseline); (2) the introduction of some factor believed to influence the behavior frequency (experimental period); (3) a return to the baseline condition; and (4) reintroduction of the influencing factor. Changes in rate concomitant with the introduction, withdrawal, and reintroduction of the experimental factor lend credence to the hypothesis that the rate of the behavior is a function of the experimental variable.

As an example, let us assume that the frequency of school attendance in a junior high student is very low. We hypothesize that the frequency of this behavior is influenced by teacher attention, and we wish to demonstrate it. We first record the baseline frequency; we then ask a teacher to praise when the boy attends. Let us say the frequency increases and we suspect that the teacher praise is reinforcing. We return to the baseline condition, i.e., no praise. Let us say the frequency decreases. We again ask the teacher to praise. We now have some good evidence that teacher praise can affect attendance frequency and, if attendance is a problem behavior, we have identified a therapeutic variable.

BASELINES

The baseline period of observation is required to observe the behavior in the "stable state." A stable state is a period of time during which behavior does not change its observed characteristic, usually frequency. Exactly what constitutes a stable state is open to question since behavior frequency is subject to some variation under the best of control conditions. Sidman (1960) warns against *ad hoc* definitions and suggests several criteria of stable states for use in experimental analyses of behavior. The important factor is that change in frequency as a result of a subsequent experimental manipulation be measurable beyond the variation in the baseline observations: ". . . the demonstration that a variable is effective does not require the attainment of a stringently defined stable state as long as the demonstrated change is large enough to override the baseline 'noise' (Sidman, 1960, p. 268)."

In a therapeutic application of this research design, the baseline observation records the frequency of the problem behavior prior to any therapeutic intervention. This baseline period is often defined *ad hoc* and usually terminates when the therapist-researcher feels he has a reliable observation of the frequency of the behavior. Baseline observations are not a part of traditional evaluation techniques, although their counterparts are the reconstructions and retrospections of the historical section of a case his-

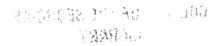

tory. Gelfand and Hartmann (1968) point out that observation of problem behavior frequency should also be accompanied by baseline observation of prosocial behaviors, and they underscore the need for reliable, quantitative baseline measures.

In the Behavior Research Project the establishment and recording of baseline rates for behaviors occurring in the natural environment proved difficult, at least as a standard procedure. There was much pressure from the environment to intervene rather than take baseline recordings. School personnel and parents would not easily tolerate observations over long periods of time if the behavior was a disturbance to them. Behavior analysts usually stated that these initial observations were valuable and intervention was difficult to assess without them. Most often this helped mediators tolerate delay in intervention, though not always.

The behavior category for which it was most difficult to develop adequate records was disruptive behavior in the classroom. Because teachers would not tolerate the baseline recording period, no adequate records exist for 9 of the 21 referred case instances[8] of classroom disruption. If other behaviors of the child were under study, behavior analysts aided in intervention in order to maintain rapport; otherwise the case was dropped. Of the 13 instances of defiance, mediators would not accept delay of intervention in 5. Of 10 cases of truancy and/or tardiness, school personnel refused to develop baselines for 3 (although school records were often adequate sources for baseline data).

It is interesting to note that persons in the natural environment were willing to accept baseline recording procedures on behaviors less directly annoying to them than the above, although such behaviors were often of greater social significance. Baselines were developed for the 3 cases referred for stealing, the 5 referred for property destruction, and 7 of the 8 referred for fighting. Two circumstances made this possible. One is that the behaviors were of relative low frequency to begin with; the other is that they are difficult to monitor and hence, were not always the target of direct intervention.

In all, there were 28 case instances for which interventions were designed and for which no adequate baseline records were obtained. Without clear information on the frequency of the behaviors prior to intervention, the degree to which the interventions were effective is difficult to assess. In such cases we must fall back on BA and mediator reports.

Initially, behavior analysts collected baseline observations over a two-week period regardless of the behavior. This tended to produce reasonably good records of behaviors for which there was frequent and regular oppor-

[8] A case instance may include more than one behavior. A case of classroom disruption, for example, might involve several distinct behaviors.

tunity for occurrence, e.g., homework, chores, coming home on time. However, for some behaviors a two-week period is inadequate because the behaviors are low frequency and irregular, e.g., fighting, cleaning the corral, lawn mowing, lying. *Ad hoc* baselines, i.e., baselines recorded until they "looked stable," became more prevalent. Actually, the *ad hoc* records tend as a group to be shorter than two weeks and may reflect a drift among the Project staff away from adequate record keeping and data-based decisions.

CHANGES

In the technique of experimental analysis a variable assumed to be related to behavior frequency is introduced when the baseline rate has stabilized. The variable most often introduced in behavior modification precedures is a *change in the reinforcement contingencies* with the aim of increasing the frequency of prosocial behavior, and with the aim of decreasing the frequency of problem behavior. In some demonstrations the change in reinforcement contingencies is reversed back to the baseline condition to see if the behavior frequency also shifts. If it does, tradition has it that the behavior is regarded to be controlled by the reinforcement. A reversal does not prove, but lends credence to, the identification of a factor controlling behavior frequency.[9]

Contingency reversal was not routinely employed in the procedures of the Behavior Research Project. There are several reasons, two of them being that not many parents or teachers are willing to return to a condition which may increase the frequency of a problematic behavior and some value characteristic of the behavior may militate against producing it, e.g., stealing or playground aggression. The absence of reversals means that the observed changes can not be attributed with complete reliability to the change in reinforcement contingencies. The frequent correspondence between contingency changes and rate changes certainly suggests a causal relationship, but other variables may be equally important (for example, the interaction between parent and child when the parent explains the

[9] There are other means for identifying the agent of change. Gelfand and Hartmann (1968) suggest several. A yoked-control subject, receiving exactly the same treatment except for therapeutic manipulation, might be observed. Another possibility is to manipulate different parts or units of a complex behavior independently to observe whether the changes are concomitant with the manipulations. Changes in certain aspects of the reinforcement, such as schedules, or reversal of only a limited segment of the total behavior, are also possible. Bijou *et al.* (1969) describe several techniques for introducing the experimental variable and its subsequent withdrawal. The latter includes not only contingency reversal but *removal* and *random scheduling* of the experimental variable.

changes in reinforcement contingency). Many researchers are exploring techniques for identifying the ingredients of change in the natural environment (see Chapter II). For most of the data from this project, the causal relationship must be inferred.

There were some cases which did resemble a contingency reversal, namely those in which, for some reason or other, the reinforcement procedures were prematurely terminated. Case #20 is representative. Figure 10 indicates that when the reinforcement for school attendance (time away from home) was again made noncontingent (by termination of program management), the frequency of absences increased.

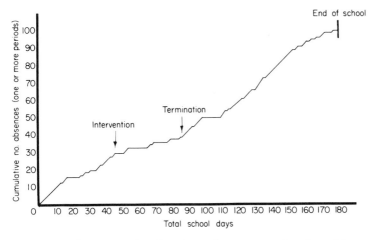

FIG. 10. Case #20: Reduction in school absences as a function of intervention. Frequency returned to early level following termination.

There were several cases in which termination of the reinforcement contingency had no effect on the frequency of the target behavior. It is often the aim of an intervention technique to arrange conditions so that a reversal is difficult. For example, it is often hoped that once a behavior occurs it will produce several natural reinforcing consequences which will maintain it. When a child's grade improves as a function of his allowance he may also be receiving the praise and attention of teachers, parents, and siblings. He may acquire skills such as reading, which produce useful information and entertainment. Under these conditions, withdrawal of the allowance will have no effect on his performance whatsoever. This might well be a pleasing outcome to the behavior modifier, in spite of (or because of) the fact that a reversal could not, in any meaningful way, be achieved. But the absence of a reversal may make the cause of a behavior change not entirely clear.

The question of whether or not a change has indeed occurred is a question of the reliability of the recorded observations. The techniques of automatic recording used in the laboratory have not yet been extended to the natural environment. Sometimes home and school records of academic performance provided an index of reliability. Occasionally a behavior analyst would record in a classroom at the same time as the teacher and both would compare records. By and large, however, the reliability of the records of the Behavior Research Project was not systematically assessed. Behavior analysts judged the reliability of the mediator's observation skill and usually assumed that the mediator's record at least approximated actual behavior change, since the mediator would have no reason to distort. This was not always true, however, as in the case where a mother believed the court would remove her child from the home if she reported that he was not doing his chores. At least the records show changes in mediator report of behavior change, and we hope they reflect actual change in target behavior. Anecdotal evidence from several sources in the natural environment suggests this is the case.

Nevertheless, five years separated the appearance of this book and those days when we chose strategy for this exploratory foray into the natural environment. Those five years have seen the development of far more sophisticated techniques and standards for assuring reliability of observations by people like our mediators. Future researchers can profit from this history of successive approximations.

The Behavior Research Project relied heavily upon the techniques of the experimental analysis of behavior for the development of intervention plans and for the monitoring and evaluation of cases. But the data are characterized by the above frailities. Keeping these in mind we turn to the problem of describing outcome. The highly individual records which characterize single subject analysis are difficult to summarize. The choice of outcome measures was based on this consideration and on matters of social significance. As with all choices they impose interpretive and procedural constraints.

OUTCOME MEASURES

At least five different criteria are appropriate to this enterprise. Two are the defining ones: *underachievement* and *misbehavior*. A third criterion would be that established by the *law of the community*. The fourth and fifth would be the *opinions of the parents* or parent surrogates, and *the opinions of the professional* interventionists. Much debate has surrounded the relative merits of these criteria as they have been used as outcome standards for psychotherapy research. There are proponents of each as the meaningful consideration: the behavior; the judgment of society; the judgment of the patient himself, or his family; or the judgment of the professional. We have elected to employ five separate outcome measures.

Change in Rate of Specific Behaviors

By specific behaviors we mean the target behaviors usually brought under mediator control through the use of a programmed reinforcer. Behavior analysts kept records of the occurrence of the behaviors and of the administration of reinforcers. These records monitored the intervention schemes and provided a detailed account of the course of change in the targets' behavior. Since the behaviors which were often selected by the mediator were those in need of change, the records also provide the mediator with a clear illustration of the consequences of his actions on the behavior of the child. The data to be presented were summarized directly from the records of behavioral rates as they were accumulated on each target's behavior by the Behavior Analyst.

School Achievement

It is clear that under rigorously controlled classroom conditions, academic performance can be modified with some precision. In this project, the teacher in the ordinary classroom was used frequently to modify both nonacademic classroom behavior and academic performance. Teachers' records, official school records, home records, and student records were the sources of these data.

Police Contact

Apprehension by the law may be a reflection of factors not fully covered in an analysis of specific behaviors or in school performance. The conditions under which a child is arrested or otherwise contacted by police are extremely varied. Although "criminal" behaviors were seldom placed under direct reinforcement control in this research project, the effects of behavior modification procedures in other areas may be expected to influence the frequency of police contact. Also, effects of police contact on various aspects of a child's life may be very significant. Juvenile court and police records provided the principal source of these data.

MEDIATOR RATINGS

The mediators rated each of the target behaviors on a 5-point scale, from 1 (very improved), through 2 (some improved), 3 (same), 4 (some worse), to 5 (much worse). These were subjective ratings based on the mediator's overall impression of the behavioral changes. They probably overlapped somewhat with the first outcome measure—change in rate of specific behaviors—since the mediator was most often the principal observer and recorder. A change in recorded rate, however, may not correlate with a subjective impression of improvement.

BA RATINGS

The Behavior Analyst rated the changes in the child on a 5-point scale in terms of likelihood of referral within two years for misbehavior as serious or more serious than that for which he was originally referred. This rating is based on many factors deriving from the BA's knowledge of the case, and is subject to all of the biases which a BA might bring to judging his own cases. The BA also rated the mediator's effectiveness. This usually involved two mediators from each case and was aided by interviews of the rated mediators.

THE SIGNIFICANCE OF THE OUTCOME

Let us anticipate our data for a moment, and report that the several measures do not correlate perfectly with one another. How then shall one judge which cases were "successes" and which were "failures"? Is an action program "successful" if it modifies referred behaviors, or only if academic improvement results? Have predelinquent tendencies been reduced if the case avoids police contact? After all, delinquency is a law-enforcement issue, and whose judgment shall we take as to whether the child has "really" improved: the parents, the interventionists, or the frequency-count data?

The answer is clear to us: "success–failure" is a category to be employed only in the absence of complex data. We do not report "success" data here, only change. The five categories of outcome will be valued differently by different readers.[10]

CHANGE IN RATE OF SPECIFIC BEHAVIORS

Since intervention frequently involved more than a single behavior per case, records were kept of 163 behaviors among the 77 intervened cases.[11] For the reasons described earlier in this chapter, not all behavior records contained adequate baselines and other characteristics which would make them suitable for outcome analysis. Of the total 163 behavior records, 135 contained at least enough pre- and postintervention information for them to be used in our outcome evaluation. Because it would not be practical to illustrate or discuss each of the 135 records we shall attempt to summarize changes which they reflect. First, however, some representative records will be described.

Figure 11 shows a working chart kept by a Behavior Analyst on four classroom behaviors of one of his cases. The data come from records kept by the teachers during the semester. The Roman numerals refer to various incidents during the course of recording. The case folder contains their explanation. This is the sort of graph which a Behavior Analyst might show to his supervisor, the teachers, or the parents. The baseline is short with some variation, but there is a correspondence between the intervention and changes in rate. The falling off at II corresponds to a change of schools. Though the improved deportment was maintained, the improvement in academic behavior was never recovered in spite of new and additional contingencies.

Figure 12 represents data collected by the Behavior Analyst himself in bimonthly time samples of 20 minutes each. These are the sorts of data which could be used to assess teacher reliability by having the teacher record the same behavior simultaneously. The target behavior for this grade-school boy is not shown here. The subject was reinforced for staying in his seat during the time allotted for working on assignments. The record

[10] Some of these data were first presented in the Final Report of Grants 65023 and 66020, Office of Juvenile Delinquency and Youth Development, Department of Health, Education, and Welfare. That report relied upon a sample of cases, rather than the total; and was necessarily restricted to a brief follow-up period. Discrepancies in data are due to these factors. The current presentation is the fuller one, and thus the more accurate.

[11] Intervention was begun with an additional 12 cases so that partial records are available on a total of 89 cases.

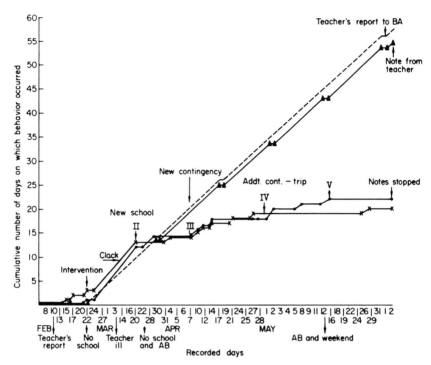

FIG. 11. *Case* #55: Behavior analyst's working chart of four classroom behaviors. Roman numerals refer to incidents recorded in the case folder. Completed spelling assignment, ×——×; completed math assignment, ●——●; behaved in spelling, – – – –; behaved in math, ▲——▲.

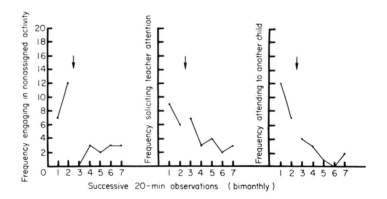

FIG. 12. Case #95: Time samples of three classroom behaviors following reinforcement of in-seat behavior (arrow indicates intervention).

suggests that this contingency affected the frequency of other behaviors: engaging in nonassigned activities, soliciting teacher attention, and attending to other children. The record does not show a reversal, and there is no direct evidence that the factor responsible for the change in these three behaviors was the reinforcement of in-seat behavior. These records plus teacher reports, however, do indicate a clear post intervention frequency change.

Figure 13 is typical of a record suggesting a substantial response to the intervention. A short baseline weakens this interpretation, although five days without completing assignments is not repeated during the re-

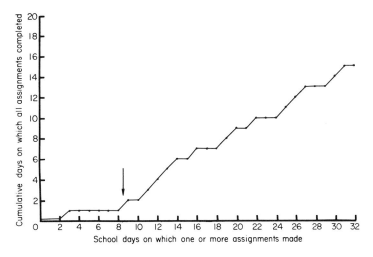

FIG. 13. Case #113: Increase in completed assignments following intervention (arrow). Reinforcement consisted of notes exchanged at home for activities and privileges.

corded period. The absence of a reversal prevents us from specifying the precise variables responsible for the change in rate of completing assignments. There is a correspondence between the intervention (notes sent home redeemed by activities and privileges) and rate change.

Fighting is the behavior recorded in Fig. 14. To be most meaningful to parents, the chart shows the number of days on which fighting did not occur. The figure suggests a rather dramatic response to intervention. Although the baseline is short, the parents regarded the rapid reduction in frequency of fighting to be amazing since they held the problem to be of long standing. According to them this change was "significant."

Figure 15 shows the predefined two-week baseline which, for bedwetting behavior, was very stable. The reinforcement for dry nights which

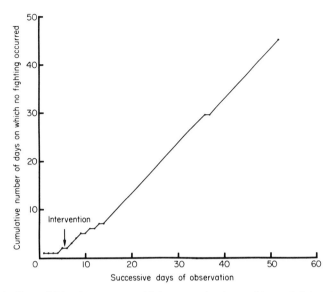

Fig. 14. Case #84: Apparent rapid increase in days without fighting incidents following reinforcement of restraint.

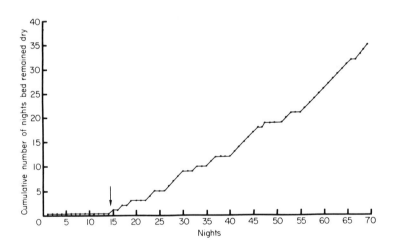

Fig. 15. Case #86: Increasing dry nights in a case of enuresis. Intervention (arrow) consisted of both holding urine for increasing time during the day and reinforcement of dry nights.

began at the arrow was preceded by several days of parental praise for holding the urine during increasing periods of time. This intervention, therefore, involved much more than changes in reinforcement contingencies for the target behavior.

Figures 16 and 17 show the response of a sister and brother respectively to intervention on home duties. In brief, this rather punitive mother began to reinforce chores and other "good" behaviors with toys, trinkets, and other surprises. Figure 16 shows the reduction in tantrum behavior

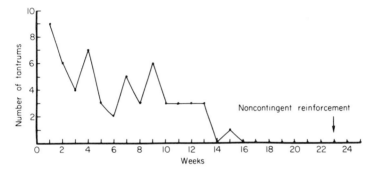

FIG. 16. Case #86: Reduction of tantrums concomitant with positive reinforcement of household chores. Noncontingent availability of the reinforcers (arrow) did not effect tantrum rate.

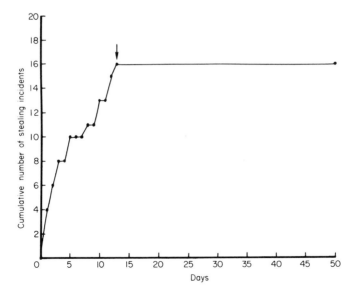

FIG. 17. Case #86: Abrupt reduction in stealing incidents following positive reinforcement of other behaviors (arrow) by an otherwise punitive mother.

of the sister over several weeks. At the mother's suggestion the reinforcers were made noncontingent for a time and the reversal affected neither the tantrum behavior nor the chore and "good" behavior (according to the mother). The stealing shown in Fig. 17 was intense. This young boy would swing through the housing project in which the family lived picking up "odds and ends" from family, friend, and stranger alike. At referral, the rate was high and the mother frantic. The abrupt cessation following intervention is probably the most dramatic change in our 135 behavior records.

The rather bizarre behavior shown in Fig. 18 consisted of eating handfuls of sugar at such high frequency that the parents became concerned

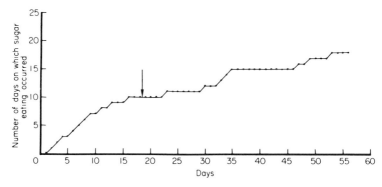

FIG. 18. Case #70: Change in behavior frequency prior to intervention (arrow). Effect of intervention is questionable.

for the target's health. The record indicates that the number of days on which the behavior occurred began to decrease during the baseline recording session. This is an example of poor correspondence between intervention and rate change, and suggests that the factors responsible for the decrease in sugar eating were introduced sometime during the baseline recording period. A lack of close correspondence between intervention and change is also illustrated by Fig. 19. In this case, there is a two-week lag between intervention and deflection. Hence, it is difficult to attribute the change to the intervention.

The length of time over which observations were made vary considerably from behavior to behavior. Our recorded behaviors have in common the fact that they were regarded to be problems worthy of attention by some referring agent. Different referring agents specify different criteria for success. Often a small reduction in behavior may be regarded as significant by the environment; at other times absolute disappearance is required. We did not perform statistical analyses to determine whether the observed frequency and rate changes were significant. Rather, we depended upon the mediator's criterion. A mother, for example, was very pleased when her son's refusal to take out the trash was reduced from 71% to 12% of the time. This reduction may or may not have been statistically significant. It was maternally significant.

Table 1 summarizes the changes observed in the 135 behaviors for which reasonable records are available. The simplest grouping would be, of course, *change* versus *no change*. We attempted to present some indication of the amount of change in the following way. The baseline rate was determined by dividing some measure of the number of responses by time units. Very often this was the accumulated number of days on which one or more instances of the behavior occurred divided by the

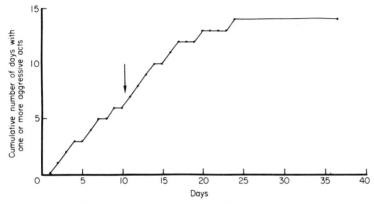

FIG. 19. Case #50: Records show a lack of correspondence between the reduction in aggressive behavior and intervention (arrow). Without a return to baseline conditions, the effect of the intervention is questionable.

number of days of observation. Occasionally baseline rate was calculated by dividing the total number of responses by days. The *during intervention rate* was calculated in the same manner, i.e., number of responses divided by time units. The *change in rate* was represented by expressing the rate during intervention as some percentage of the rate during baseline. For example, a behavior might occur on four of eight possible days yielding a baseline rate of one response (or more) every two days, or a ratio of .5. The post-intervention rate might be eight response days out of 32 possible, yielding a rate during intervention of one response every four days, or a ratio of .25. The during-intervention rate in this hypothetical case would be reported as 50% of the baseline rate.

Table 1 also shows the number of behaviors during intervention falling into each of four categories of baseline rate percentage. The first category,

0% baseline, indicates that the behavior did not occur during the intervention period. *Less than or equal to 50%* indicates that the behavior rate was reduced during intervention to either less than, or equivalent to $\frac{1}{2}$ of the baseline rate. *Greater than 50%* indicates that the behaviors were reduced but not to $\frac{1}{2}$ of the baseline rate. A behavior classified in this category might have been reduced to nearly $\frac{1}{2}$, or just slightly under the baseline rate. The final category, *equivalent,* means that there was no change in the rate following intervention. For example, Table 1 shows that two of the recorded home-chore failures were reduced to zero. Thirty-five were reduced to less than, or equal to 50% of the baseline rate; two were reduced to something greater than 50% of the baseline rate, and one showed no change.

TABLE 1

CHANGE OF RATE OF BEHAVIOR DURING INTERVENTION

	Rate during intervention expressed as percentages of baseline rates[a]				
Behavior category	0% (behavior does not occur)	Less than or equal to 50% of baseline	Greater than 50% of baseline	Equivalent[b] (no change from baseline)	Total
1. Home-chore failure	2	35	2	1	40
2. Poor academic work	6	28	2	0	36
3. Disruptive	0	16	3	1	20
4. Defiance	2	7	1	1	11
5. Fighting	1	5	1	0	7
6. Truancy and tardiness	2	2	1	2	7
7. Property destruction	5	1	0	0	6
8. Bed wetting and soiling	2	3	0	0	5
9. Stealing	1	2	0	0	3
	21	99	10	5	135

[a] The numerals refer to the number of behaviors in each category of rate during intervention.

[b] No recorded behaviors worsened during intervention.

The behaviors represented in the categories are as follows:

Chores: Refusal or failure to
1. Set dinner table
2. Mow lawn
3. Baby-sit
4. Maintain bedroom and belongings
5. Care for pets

6. Wash dishes
7. Clean horse corral
8. Take out garbage

Academic Behaviors
1. Poor seat work and test grades
2. Noncompletion of classroom assignments
3. Noncompletion of homework assignments
4. Failing to dress for physical education class

Disruptive Behavior
1. Out-of-seat
2. Talking out-of-turn
3. Throwing objects in classroom
4. Inappropriate noises made in classroom

Defiance
1. Not following instructions
2. Lying
3. Tantrums
4. Obscence language

Fighting
1. Fighting safety patrols
2. Fighting peers on playground
3. Fighting with siblings at home

Truancy and Tardiness
1. Frequency of failing to attend one or more classes
2. Frequency of failing to attend one or more days
3. Tardiness to individual classes

Property Destruction
1. Playing with matches
2. Setting fires
3. Destroying articles belonging to siblings
4. Destroying family car

Bed Wetting and Soiling
1. Encopresis
2. Enuresis

Stealing
1. From supermarket
2. From parents
3. From school lockers

A small number of cases in any one category does not necessarily mean that other targets do not engage in that behavior but, rather, that behavior was not recorded. For example, the fact that only three cases involved stealing does not mean that only three of the BRP population stole, but that stealing records were kept on only three. If, for a stealing referral, the target behaviors were school work and home chores, the records for that child would be kept under those categories rather than under stealing.

The results shown in Table 1 reflect considerable change in frequencies of response. The social significance of a particular rate change depends upon the behavior in question and the setting in which it occurs. Occasionally, as in property destruction, a response rate of zero is important. Most commonly, among the behaviors considered in the present project, a reduction to less than half the baseline rate was considered socially desirable by both project staff and persons in the natural environment of the child. Defiance, for example, is most appropriate when it occurs from time to time rather than always or never. But some may dispute this value judgment; for that reason, we have used the arbitrary 50% point as the categorical division regardless of the behavior. The reader may judge "success." There is no doubt, however, that much change in specific behaviors did in fact occur during intervention.

Follow-up frequency counts were obtained on only a few behaviors. These data indicate that

> One of the two home-chore failures increased from 0% baseline to greater than 50%
>
> Five of the less than 50% baseline chore failures decreased to 0%
>
> One of the two 0% defiance behaviors returned to the baseline frequency
>
> One of the two 0% truancy and tardiness behaviors returned to baseline frequency
>
> One of the two less than 50% stealing behaviors decreased to 0%
>
> One of the three less than 50% bed-wetting behaviors decreased to 0%

Other follow-up data are presented in a later section. In general, follow-up frequency counts over two or three months after termination were difficult to engineer. Behavior analyst case loads, moving, parental disinterest, and other changes made this an impractical measure to obtain.

SCHOOL ACHIEVEMENT

School performance is reflected in several behavioral categories of Table 1 (e.g., disruptive behavior, truancy and tardiness, and academic behavior). The most common measure of school achievement, *grades,* is not included in that summary since grades are not measures of any known specific behavior. In this section we will present the grade changes of the project population. Teachers, parents, school administrators, and students were cooperative in giving the project staff access to grade records. Partial grade records of 64 children are included in this analysis. They are drawn from a total subject pool of 117 since we were able to obtain grade records for some children for whom we have no adequate behavioral records.

It is probably of no surprise to anyone to learn that grades are unreliable and do not measure necessarily academic performance. Project staff frequently found the teacher's records inaccurate, found that the grade awarded did not correspond to the teacher's record, or found that the teacher kept no record at all. Our case files include samples of teachers recording poor academic performance from children on days they were absent. For one target, both the BRP records and teacher records showed a semester improvement of 1.8 grade points in a spelling class. According to these records, the student had improved his performance from a high "D" to a "B." The BRP records further showed that during this period the student's homework performance improved from 18% assignments completed to 95% assignments completed, yet the report card of this student showed a course grade of "C" in both semesters. The teacher, when confronted with this material, saw nothing particularly unusual about this and explained that grading is often based on other considerations than academic performance. In another class where good citizenship was rewarded with paper stars, a student got a grade of "C" during a semester when he earned no stars, and a grade of "D" in citizenship during a semester in which he earned 60% of the available stars. Although these are extreme cases, the frequency with which lack of objectivity in grading was encountered by BRP staff was both sad and frustrating. For this reason, we cannot regard grades and grade changes as totally accurate reflections of change in academic behavior by the BRP population, and certainly not as reflections of academic learning. Nevertheless, grades are of great social significance, and the analysis of grade change is presented herewith.

Table 2 summarizes the semester grades for all target subjects whose intervention plans involved the schools, whether or not academic-achievement behaviors were directly intervened. Due to variable termination dates, the periods of "follow-up" are different lengths, and were classified into 6-month, 12-month, and 18-month periods. The time-lengths of baselines also vary; they were determined by the availability of school records, and average 1.17 years. So, too, do the time-lengths of "intervention." Included here are cases of only one month of contingency management, as well as those which experienced formal plans for as long as a full year.

It can be seen that no significant changes in grades occurred for the overall group. For directly intervened courses, during intervention, there was mean improvement of about one-quarter point—surely an insignificant change, and most of this small improvement is lost by the time the six-month follow-up occurs. There is no significant difference between intervened and nonintervened course performances. Correlations of grade change with several other variables did not prove to be statistically significant. (Comparison with IQ, for example, gave a tetrachoric correlation coefficient of $r_t = .26$; for school grade, i.e., year levels, $r_t = .15$; for BA

TABLE 2

COURSE GRADE CHANGES FOR 64 BEHAVIOR RESEARCH PROJECT SUBJECTS

			Follow-up (months)		
	Baseline	Intervention	6	12	18
Intervened courses[a]					
No. of S's	45	45	29	9	4
Average grade[b]	3.60	3.36	3.47	3.92	3.22
Nonintervened courses					
No. of S's	43	39	25	16	11
Average grade[b]	3.41	3.25	3.31	3.13	3.15

[a] Intervened courses are those in which the intervention plan involved an academic achievement behavior.
[b] A "1" is equivalent to "A" and "5" equivalent to "F."

rating of referral in two years, $r_t = .33$; for mediator rating of improvement, $r_t = -.28$)

These results are totally unsurprising in view of our experience with the insensitivity of course grades to changes in pupil behavior. The issues were discussed in detail in Chapter VII. We are now in a position to document the insensitivity. Consider again the data in Table 1: *disruptive* classroom behaviors were improved; frequency of *truancy* and *tardiness* was reduced in 5 of 7 cases; data suggest that for 25 cases, an appreciable improvement occurred in *test grades, homework,* and *classroom assignments* for 34 of 36 targeted behaviors. It is not that those targets whose school-relevant behavior did improve also had improved grades; all possible permutations occurred, including instances of grossly nonrational grading such as illustrated in the case studies of Chapter VII.

Our juxtaposition of these data should not be judged entirely as a means of explaining away "no results." It is clear that for the overall group, BRP techniques were not successful in significantly changing the grades received by the targets. Because grades are socially important, regardless of their unreliability and questionable validity, we must conclude that additional forms of intervention are required to alter them.

While overall analysis of the data supports the view that the interventions made major improvements in the specific behaviors purported to be relevant to awarded grades, overall grades did not change as a function of improvement of behavior. This is final support for the rule that grades should not be used as the criterion when academic behaviors are to be modified.

POLICE CONTACT

An important outcome measure is the course of police contact for intervened cases. This predelinquent group did not contain adjudicated delinquents; but many nonadjudicated cases have had recorded police contacts, ranging from "adjusted" cases (on which the contact officer makes some disposition) to cases involving charges, court appearances, and convictions. Of our 77 intervened cases, 26 (ranging in age from 7 to 17) had police records of one sort or the other. These records included from 1 to 13 offenses, as are shown in Table 3, and range from armed assault

TABLE 3
FREQUENCY OF OFFENSES

Number of offenses	Number of cases
1	10
2	4
3	5
5	2
6	1
7	2
10	1
13	1

to curfew violations (see Table 4). These offenses were not usually intervened directly; for example, two cases involving burglary had as their targeted behavior an increase in chore-completion. It is very difficult to consequate acts which occur infrequently, and which are difficult to detect and observe. Illegal acts fall within this description. Further, as a general guide, the BRP attempted modification on desirable behavior, rather than undesirable, and tended to intervene on behavior rather than on nonbehavior. Our typical strategy for those cases involving illegal acts was to attempt reincorporation into the social-control nexus of positive reinforcement by establishing, in the target's repertoires, desirable behaviors which

TABLE 4
CLASSIFICATION OF OFFENSES

Offense	Number of cases
1. Simple assault (weapon)	1
2. Robbery (weapon)	1
3. Burglary	10
4. Shoplifting	7
5. Bicycle theft	4
6. Petit larceny	3
7. Breaking and entering	2
8. Malicious mischief	1
9. Possession of stolen property	1
10. Mischief	6
11. Violation of liquor laws	1
12. Disturbing the peace	1
13. Fighting	5
14. Trespassing	2
15. Setting off fireworks	1
16. Loud and profane	2
17. BB gun	1
18. Runaway	5
19. Wayward	9
20. Incorrigible	2
21. Habitually disobedient	2
22. Improper conduct	1
23. Curfew	3
24. Truancy	2
25. Violation of parole	3
26. Violation of probation	7
27. Review	3

would provide entrée into more civilized interactions. Thus, for a child who vandalized, we might have targeted "doing arithmetic homework"; for one who "violated liquor laws," we might have targeted "school attendance." On a few cases, notably "fighting," we did directly reward its nonoccurrence. But for most cases, the interventions' effect on police contacts may be viewed as indirect.

Comparisons were made between police records and other variables. There was no relationship between police record and (1) birth order,

(2) number of children in family, or (3) father's occupation (SES). There was, however, significant relationship between police contact and IQ measures ($X^2 = 7.6$, p less than .01). Children with IQ's less than 100 were much more likely to possess police records than were children with IQ's greater than 100.

Table 5 charts the pattern of police contacts for all cases involving one or more offenses at any time—from prior to our involvement through six months after termination. For example, the "Offenses during Intervention" chart shows that of the 26 targets who were charged with some offenses prior to termination, 14 offended only prior to intervention and 9 during intervention.

TABLE 5
DATA FROM POLICE RECORDS:
NUMBER OF TARGETS WITH OFFENSES CHARGED[a]

CHART 1
OFFENSES DURING INTERVENTION $N = 26$

Offenses prior to intervention	Number of offenses							
	0	1	2	3	4	5	6	7
0	—	3	1	1	—	—	—	—
1	9	1	1	1	—	—	—	—
2	2	—	—	—	—	—	—	—
3	3	—	—	—	—	—	—	—
4	—	—	—	—	—	—	—	—
5 or more	—	—	2	—	—	—	—	—

CHART 2
POST-TERMINATION OFFENSES DURING FIRST
MONTH FOLLOW-UP $N = 26$

Offenses prior to intervention	Number of offenses							
	0	1	2	3	4	5	6	7
0	2	—	1	—	—	—	—	—
1	12	1	—	—	—	—	—	—
2	6	—	—	—	—	—	—	—
3	1	—	—	—	—	—	—	—
4	—	—	—	—	—	—	—	—
5 or more	2	—	1	—	—	—	—	—

CHART 3
POST-TERMINATION OFFENSES DURING FIRST
TWO MONTHS FOLLOW-UP $N = 24$

Offenses prior to intervention	Number of offenses							
	0	1	2	3	4	5	6	7
0	2	—	—	—	—	—	—	—
1	10	2	1	—	—	—	—	—
2	5	—	—	—	—	—	—	—
3	1	—	—	—	—	—	—	—
4	—	—	—	—	—	—	—	—
5 or more	2	—	—	—	1	—	—	—

CHART 4
POST-TERMINATION OFFENSES DURING FIRST
FOUR MONTHS FOLLOW-UP $N = 17$

Offenses prior to intervention	Number of offenses							
	0	1	2	3	4	5	6	7
0	2	—	—	—	—	—	—	—
1	7	1	—	1	1	—	—	—
2	2	—	—	—	—	—	—	—
3	1	—	—	—	—	—	—	—
4	—	—	—	—	—	—	—	—
5 or more	1	—	—	—	—	—	1	—

CHART 5
POST-TERMINATION OFFENSES DURING FIRST
SIX MONTHS FOLLOW-UP $N = 16$

Offenses prior to intervention	Number of offenses							
	0	1	2	3	4	5	6	7
0	1	—	—	—	—	—	—	—
1	6	1	1	—	1	—	—	1
2	2	—	—	—	—	—	—	—
3	1	—	—	—	—	—	—	—
4	—	—	—	—	—	—	—	—
5 or more	1	—	—	—	—	—	1	—

[a] Relationship between pre-intervention and post-intervention offense records. Number in table indicates number of subjects, i.e., of the 9 subjects who had 1 offense prior to intervention 0 had offenses during intervention, etc.

Those offending targets for whom at least one-month follow-up data were available are entered in the second chart. The N remains 26; only three of these cases committed offenses during the first month post-termination.

The third chart describes those offending cases for whom at least two months follow-up data were available. (The N declines steadily as the follow-up period lengthens, because of the variable termination dates, and the fact that all police contact data were gathered on a single date.) Thus for the two-month follow-up group only 4 of 24 cases committed offenses and these 4 include the 3 targets who offended during the first month. In other words, only one additional target committed a second-month offense.

Chart 4 reveals a similar pattern: the N for four-month follow-up declines to 17, but only the same 4 cases are committing offenses.

Chart 5, for the six-month follow-up, shows that one additional target committed an offense between the fourth and sixth months.

One can thus observe that of the 77 intervened cases, 26 committed some offenses, and the vast majority were prior to termination. Five committed one or more offenses following termination, i.e., 5 out of 77 predelinquents, and 3 of these 5 were subsequently committed to institutions.

Which cases committed offenses? If one reads the charts by proceeding down the rows, more and more severe patterns of predelinquency are charted: the bottom row represents cases which had 5 offenses prior to intervention. It is clear that the more offenses a target committed prior to intervention, the more likely he is to commit offenses later. This unsurprising relationship is certainly not linear, but is commensurate with our general experience that the modification of a social behavior is easier when the target is not yet "hooked" on socially unacceptable reinforcers. In this demonstration program, cases were taken as they came, without regard to the probability of modification.

Three of the five targets who were repeated post-termination offenders are now in juvenile institutions: there are limits to the appropriacy of the natural environment as the setting for behavior modification.

MEDIATOR RATINGS

The following dimensions of evaluation have now been presented: recordings of behavior change, the grades assigned by the schools, and the records of the police. However, perhaps most important is the opinion of the home mediator. In the view of the parents, what has been the course of the behavioral problem?

Two separate follow-up inquiries of the home mediators were conducted. The first occurred in May and June of 1967, and the second in March of 1968. Both used a structured interview format, with ratings of improvement on a 1 to 5 scale. The numbers themselves were most often enunciated by the mediator, unless their language corresponded exactly to the numerical equivalent, e.g., "his (Problem behavior) is very much improved!" in which case the interviewer recorded a "1" without further discussion. The first follow-up was conducted by the BA who had worked with the intervention and conducted in face-to-face conversa-

TABLE 6
MEDIATOR RATINGS OF BEHAVIORS, FOLLOW-UP 1[a]

	Mediator rating on follow-up interview				
Referred behavior class	Very improved (1)	Improved (2)	Same (3)	Worse (4)	Much worse (5)
1. Bed wetting and soiling	3	—	1	—	—
2. Fighting and aggressive	2	7	2	—	—
3. Chores and irresponsibility	2	12	9	—	—
4. Truancy and tardiness	3	3	—	2	—
5. Underachievement and inattentive	8	20	6	3	1
6. Disruptive	3	10	1	—	—
7. Defiant	5	23	10	—	—
8. Poor peer association	2	5	5	—	—
9. Stealing	3	7	—	—	—
10 Runaway and out late	1	4	—	—	—
11. Property destruction	1	3	—	—	—
	33	94	34	5	1

[a] N of targets = 31; N of mediators = 30.

tion with the principal mediator. The second follow-up was conducted by a nonassigned BA, and took place by telephone. Portions of the forms employed may be found in Appendix II. We hope that the structured interview, the focus on a series of discrete behaviors, and the lengthy conversation for both follow-ups all contribute to reduction of the "hello–goodbye" effect discussed by Gelfand and Hartmann (1968). There were no instances in which a mediator's ratings were inconsistent with that mediator's previous reactions to BRP personnel. The ratings obtained from follow-ups 1 and 2 were generally consistent, although the N for follow-up 2 was larger.

The data for the follow-up are presented in two tables. Table 6 presents the mediator ratings of *behaviors* (not targets), organized by class of behavior. Mediators rated 127 behaviors as very improved or improved;

34 were rated as the same; 6 were rated as worse or much worse. Table 6 illustrates a tendency toward improvement regardless of the type of behavior being rated.

The second follow-up involved all cases located in the Tucson area. The excluded cases thus included three institutionalized targets, and one target for whom the mediator refused any contact. Two of these cases were in nonpunitive institutions and were substantially improved in their behavior; but it may be assumed conservatively that these four cases would

TABLE 7

MEAN RATINGS BY MEDIATORS OF BEHAVIOR IMPROVEMENT
AT FOLLOW-UPS 1 AND $2^{a,b}$

	Follow-up 1		Follow-up 2	
	Intervened behaviors	Non-intervened behaviors	Intervened behaviors	Non-intervened behaviors
Continue to use techniques	1.96	1.96	1.74	1.60
	(15)	(12)	(17)	(16)
No need for techniques	1.65	1.68	1.46	1.56
	(6)	(5)	(16)	(11)
Do not use techniques	2.33	2.17	2.80	2.35
	(3)	(3)	(7)	(6)
Overall	1.92	1.92	1.82	1.72
	(24)	(20)	(40)	(33)

[a] N of mediators for follow-up 1 = 30; N of mediators for follow-up 2 = 43.

[b] Numbers in parentheses indicate the number of behaviors rated in each category.

represent a lower mean improvement rating than the general population. Thirty other cases had no follow-up due to inability to locate the mediators; this is a mobile population, including wage earners who are miners, military, construction, and factory workers, and divorced mothers who remarry. No doubt, others were still in town but our staff could not locate them.

Table 7 simultaneously presents the results of both follow-ups. The cell entries are the mean mediator ratings of each separately rated behavior according to the same 5 point scale used in Table 6. The columns divide the behaviors into those which were directly intervened and those problem behaviors which were never directly consequated. The rows separate the mediators into classes: (1) those who report the continued use of contingency management verified, incidently, by the report of specific plans;

(2) those who report improved behavior and no need for further formal consequation; (3) those who prefer to no longer use behavior modification approaches; and (4) overall mediator ratings. The latter are all below 2.00.

These results obtain regardless of whether one examines intervened or nonintervened behaviors. The reported improvement in nonintervened problems is of particular interest. Such improvements (if indeed they occurred) may have occurred by several processes. For example, the successful strengthening of incompatible responses would reduce some nonintervened behaviors; instituting positive reinforcement control would reduce the problems occasioned by counteraggressive behaviors. We hypothesize that one important effect may be establishing the mediator, his associates, and more desirable peers as the sources of positive reinforcement, thus making more civilized people the child's models. Furthermore, the correction of the intervened problem behaviors might allow the targets to move into the general pattern of social control which makes most of us want to do what we should do.

It might be argued that mediator ratings do not necessarily reflect behavioral change. That need not concern us here; behavioral changes have been reported earlier. The change in mediator attitude toward the target, which the ratings represent, is itself an outcome of value and significance. Indeed, to effect such a change has been a primary goal of the natural-environmental reorganization. Apparently it did occur.

BA RATINGS

The last outcome measure to be presented reflects a "professional" opinion about the results of intervention. Each BA was asked to rate his own cases according to the following directions:

> Please rate each case according to the likelihood of the targets coming to society's attention for misbehavior, which is the same as or more serious than the BRP-referral misbehavior, at some time during the two years following case termination (excluding academic behavior). 1. Much less likelihood of misbehaviors recurring 2. Less likelihood of misbehaviors recurring. 3. The same likelihood as prior to BRP contact. 4. More likelihood than prior to BRP contact. 5. Much more likelihood of misbehaviors recurring. If two or more BA's had responsibility, decide among yourselves as to who had greatest case knowledge. One rating per case.

The mean rating of 2.43 illustrates the BA's opinion that the overall effects have been to reduce the probability of the target's undesirable behavior.

The problems of staff bias in rating the effects of their own work are so obvious and so well known as to require no discussion. It is not that we think our BA ratings are necessarily incorrect; they might even be conservative. But they do not convince, and behavioral indices must be the change criteria of the future.

QUALITATIVE CHANGES

CHANGES IN INDIVIDUAL TARGETS

The course of every case could be made to read like a novel; indeed, most human lives—particularly problem lives—need more in the telling than statistics if they are to be truly represented. As was our original conviction, the effect of behavioral intervention is, most often, to alter aspects of the target and their environments which are far more important to their futures than the simple elements of intervened behavior. It is these ramifying effects which provide the telling argument for intervention in the natural environment.

ACADEMIC ACHIEVEMENT

For many cases, the improvement in a simple behavior like "completing assignments" radically altered the relationship between child and school.

> Case #33. Rosita had barely passed second grade and was performing poorly in the third. She was in the "probable retention group" and was assessed by her teacher as still working at second grade level.
>
> Besides scoring poorly on tests, Rosita never completed assignments. Her teacher took four weeks baseline on the number of assignments completed: the average completion rate was 72.2%.
>
> Daily TV was put contingent on Rosita's finishing three or more assignments daily. The case was terminated 48 days later after she had advanced to an average completion rate of 97.4%. Also, she was scoring 3's on three or more daily assignments and improved on six subjects on her report card. Most important, she passed to the fourth grade unequivocally and was recognized at the school as a diligent and much improved pupil.

Rather than another "rebellious" and "unmotivated" Mexican-American child, launched in the classic trajectory toward junior-high drop-out, Rosita is—at least in the fourth grade—in the school's good graces.

Some instances of the secondary effects of increasing academic performance are so profound as to engender disbelief.

Case #15. Parlow was referred for lying, stealing, disturbing the class, and housebreaking. He was described by the school as a "semiabandoned waif." An unattractive, unkempt child, Parlow was the least loved, most neglected offspring of a divorcée. His teachers were mainly concerned with his academic achievement and antisocial behavior. Parlow had but one friend and rarely participated in class sessions, preferring to busy himself with various gadgets and trinkets that he hung about his neck and fastened onto his belt. Each day would see a new hoard of these trinkets which he had pilfered from neighboring stores.

Due to the mother's unreliability as a mediator, the intervention plan centered around the siblings, employing their pressure (plus money) to entice Parlow into performing academically in reading class. He responded immediately and became an interested and vocal student. This generalized to almost all of his classes.

Most important was the manner in which this success affected his social behavior. Within a month, Parlow had become the wonder of the school. Not only were there glowing reports from the mediating teacher, but his other teachers reacted similarly. "We have all noticed such change in Parlow. He is so happy. I think he is smiling for the first time in his life."

There was a marked decrease in the number of trinkets he brought to class. "He's not bringing to class so many of those little articles he steals at the stores," his teacher reported.

Mother's accounts were similar to the school's. Instead of complaining about having to earn money for his siblings, he was now chaperoning the smaller children to the store so they could "spend" pennies he had earned for them. Mother said that Parlow was now a "pleasant and friendly boy and everyone likes him." Her only complaint was that Parlow demanded a clean, pressed shirt daily. He was even taking a daily bath and rumor had it that Parlow had a girl friend. His mother was particularly proud of the fact that he was not pilfering the reward pennies, even though they were in an accessible place.

Parlow continued to perform well in school, but due to conditions of grading unreliability, he was deprived of a grade showing the improvement he had made. Despite a number of very disturbing complications in the home situation, Parlow had suffered only a minor setback at the termination of the case one month after the close of school. At the last contact mother described Parlow's behavior as "good." (Diana Zimmerman)

There are many examples of cases in which academic behaviors benefited indirectly from intervention in totally different environments. Case 46 illustrates intervention entirely at the target's home, with Barry's father mediating reinforcement for more acceptable work-habits and filial respect.

Case #46. As a result of the reduction of referral behaviors, Barry was showered with reinforcement at home, where the intervention plan was centered. Barry became accepted as an equal to his younger brother. He was delegated responsibilities never before given him when his father felt he was incompetent and untrustworthy. His ideas and feelings were more carefully considered, and he was consulted on family matters. For example, Barry was given the privilege of choosing the vacation spot he and his family visited. He was trusted to run important errands, earn and budget his own spending money, and, most important to Dad, keep and care for his infant brother.

At school, things went equally well for Barry. He was considered a very low, almost incapable, achiever and was constantly harrassed by both teachers and fellow students. The socially acceptable behavior exhibited at home "generalized" to the school. His principal, before the case was terminated, reported he was doing remarkably in the classroom. He now dubbed Barry an "overachiever." There were no more reports of harrassment by teachers or students, and no more fights. Although no direct intervention was made at school, the principal was pleased with Barry's improvement, and attributed it to the changed behavior at home.

The Removal of Misbehavior

Children who are "hyperactive" often gather to themselves the diagnosis of minimal brain damage. More than a few first and second graders who have a high probability of out-of-seat behavior find themselves shunted into Special Education and many into chemotherapy. This is a one-way track to tragedy when so often these disruptive behaviors are correctable by pathetically simple interventions.

Case #95. Rufus was a second grader who could not remain in his seat. He disturbed the classroom and his teacher constantly, and never got any work done. This pattern had persisted since early in the first grade.

"Staying-in-seat" behavior was shaped by setting a kitchen timer. Rufus was to remain in his seat from the time it was set until it rang, when he would be rewarded by a piece of candy. The plan began with ten-minute intervals; the time periods were rapidly stretched.

Rufus rarely missed staying in his seat during his timing. The teacher marveled at the success. Rufus' work improved immensely and his grades went up, though no direct intervention was employed in this area. Rufus' first-grade teacher could not believe that he could change so radically; she was invited to observe in the classroom. The school counselor made several observations and was also astonished.

Rufus responded so well to the plan that the timing period became an acquired reinforcer. The plan was changed so that he had to earn the privilege of being timed. This was accomplished by remaining in his seat before the timing period. The pretiming period was increased gradually so the actual timing period was decreased. By termination, Rufus was no longer "hyperactive."

Certainly "getting-out-of-seat-without-permission" sounds ultramild in the spectrum of predelinquent behaviors, and its correction a modest achievement. But there is no case with which the staff is more pleased, nor will anyone familiar with public school practices gainsay the importance of averting the organicity-special eduation fate of a child afflicted by the tragic ignorance of the principles of behavior in educational institutions.

Our experience does not lack instances of the dramatic correction of more "serious" behaviors, such as rampant belligerence.

Case #50. Rena was referred primarily for the inappropriate behavior she exhibited at school. Academically, she seldom finished an assignment, but more important to teacher, she was very disruptive in the classroom, and overly aggressive both in classroom and on the playground. Baseline was taken on the more serious aggressive behavior; it verified the referral opinions.

An intervention plan was negotiated with parents and teacher whereby teacher would determine daily whether Rena was aggressive or nonaggressive for that day. If she did not observe any aggressive act, or receive reports of any, she was to give Rena a note to take home stating "Rena's behavior was satisfactory today." If Rena did commit some aggressive act, she would not get the note, along with a simple explanation of why she was not getting it. The notes were to be traded for backup at home.

The teacher added other behaviors to the original contingency. Rena did not do well in the two weeks. But when these mistakes were corrected, she began bringing home a note almost every night. Rena exhibited aggressive behavior on seven of the ten baseline days. After the early problems were settled, Rena received 17 of the possible 18 notes during a three-week period. As a result of this improvement, Rena was returned to her regular seat in the classroom (she had been isolated for aggressive behavior). This new behavior facilitated her academic work. Seldom did she turn in any more incomplete assignments.

A particularly pleasing case involved the four Murphy brothers. Reminiscent of the fairy-tale tailor who felled seven with one blow, the Murphy boys alert us to the power of sibling influence.

Case #51. The four Murphy brothers ranged from 8 to 12 years of age and were notorious in their small town elementary school for pugnacity, classroom disruptions, below-average school work, and general trouble-making. Actually there were wide variations in individual behavior but all four boys stuck together in a formidable group and all were tarred with the same brush—"the worst kids in the whole school."

Mort had been socially promoted since the first grade. Now Mort found himself sunk in the mysteries of the sixth grade when he was barely capable of doing fourth grade work. Mort hated school and all connected with it.

Buck and Art were not good students but they scraped by. Although not as troublesome as Mort, both boys got into an abnormal number of fights. Donnie, the youngest, was a slightly better than average student and rarely caused trouble on his own, although he rallied to the support of his brothers whenever the fraternal battle cry was sounded.

All the boys were passionate sports participants but, although good players, their proclivity for creating rhubarbs dampened the pleasure of the games for the other participants.

The same intervention plan was employed for each of the brothers although complaints about Donnie were minimal. Each boy received a note from his teacher at the end of the school day. The note attested to the bearer's good behavior and adequate schoolwork for the date given above the teacher's signature.

At home, the parents received the notes with praise and distributed 15¢ to be collected at once or added to the week's total to be dispensed on Saturday. Failure to earn a note was to be accepted with equanimity and without threatening or disparaging parental comments.

From the beginning the plan was effective. Donnie, as anticipated, achieved an almost perfect rate, but, surprisingly, Buck, who was almost as big a troublemaker as Mort, equalled Donnie's record. Art was the least successful. He missed a little more than a third of his notes during the remaining two months of the school term. Mort astonished his teacher by his improvement in academic performance. Mort's antisocial behavior made a radical improvement and by the end of the school term he was no longer a friendless outcast.

The most dramatic evidence of the brothers' changed behavior came near the end of the term when Buck and Art suffered the humiliation of running away from a proffered fight. During the flight from temptation Art tore his pants and lost a school workbook.

The school principal explained the torn clothes to Art's mother, replaced the workbook and told Art to keep the money given him for a new one— evidence too that the Murphy's had arrived into the principal's good graces. (Malcolm Bissell)

Changes in Mediators

In it's most broad conception, behavior modification in the natural environment is an educational enterprise designed to teach skills to mediators. In this sense, all of our outcome data—which relate to changes in targets—are secondary and serve as indirect indices of the effectiveness of the mediator-education program. Ideally, one would want mediators to increase their potential for the solution of future as well as current difficulties. Data relevant to this achievement are beyond the scope of this current project, and we must be content to report examples.

Case #105. The C's are intelligent, sincere people, very much concerned with the problems they are having with their son, John. They readily accepted both criticism and praise, and quickly assimilated the principles of learning theory which they were able to generalize to many situations. A good example of their application of these principles occurred approximately three months after the BA's first contact. John began having some academic problems in school, particularly in math. Mother called his teacher and negotiated an intervention plan with her. Mother gave her index cards with the dates on them. She asked the teacher to write "yes" or "no" on the cards, depending on John's completion of in-class assignments in math. The teacher agreed to cooperate. John would be able to watch TV a half-hour a day, 15 minutes contingent on getting chores done, and 15 minutes contingent on earning his daily math note. John accepted the plan readily, and his performance in math rose to a level satisfactory to his mother.

The assumption of the BA role by the mediator is a most felicitous outcome, gratifying to observe in parents and teachers.

Case #59. Charlie was on a note system at school. earning notes for nonaggresive playground and classroom behavior, and for nondistruptive classroom behavior. The reinforcement was first programmed to be contingent on a full day of acceptable behavior. However, Charlie did not earn many notes in the first four or five weeks of the plan. Reassessment of the home revealed that the parents were seldom there, and were not correctly backing up the notes which they did receive.

The teacher, realizing the difficulty the BA was having obtaining adequate cooperation from the parents, decided something had to be done in the school to reinforce Charlie because he was making no progress. She devised a system for reinforcing Charlie's morning and afternoon behavior as well as dispensing the note he was to take home.

Many teachers have extended behavioral principles to other pupils as well as to the targeted ones.

Case #01. Teddy was a second grader, referred for aggressiveness with other youngsters, management problems in the classroom, underachievement, getting out of seat without permission, and talking out and disturbing the class.

A token system was set up with the teacher, whereby Teddy could earn tokens and cash them in for 15 minutes of playing time with his father. The notes were contingent on Teddy not talking out in class without permission. A couple of weeks later the plan was going so well it was decided that both getting out of his seat and talking out without permission were now contingent on Teddy earning his note.

A couple of months after we started work with Teddy his teacher informed us that she felt this was such a good system and she had seen such wonderful results with Teddy that she had begun sending notes home with another of her problem students. She explained in delight that the new student "has really shaped up," although she did not have a backup at home or at school for the note! Perhaps the parents' pleasure over good notes being sent home, in comparison to the "bad" notes which are a customary practice among teachers, was sufficient to elicit their positive reaction to their son.

Case #95 illustrates the extension of behavior modification principles from one target to an entire classroom. This effort is emminently rational; with little increase over the energy required for the management of one recalcitrant pupil, an entire class can be brought to greater productivity and happiness.

Case #95. Mrs. Jackson was a very attractive and dedicated teacher. The referred youngster had a problem staying in his seat. A kitchen timer was set and the youngster had to remain in his seat until the timer rang. If he succeeeded, he was awarded a piece of candy.

Mrs. Jackson was so pleased with the results that she began extending the technique. One example: she had another problem youngster with a low IQ. He also had a lot of trouble remaining in his seat. She began shaping this boy by timing him along with the target case and rewarding him. She also began setting the timer intermittently during the day. When the timer rang, all those in their seats and working hard would be awarded a piece of candy.

During a classroom observation, it was also noted that Mrs. Jackson would intermittently pick out a youngster engaging in the appropriate behavior during that time. She would verbally praise him in front of the whole class and drop a piece of candy on the child's desk.

Mrs. Jackson told the BA that she was so impressed with the system that she was now using it with her children at home. She had always had trouble getting her little girls to get through with their bath on time. She also had trouble getting them ready for school in the morning so she could drop them off and get to work on time. She now sets the timer for the time period that the children are allowed to remain in the bathtub. When it rings, they must be through and out of the tub. She also sets the timer in the morning before school. When it rings, they must be dressed and ready to go.

She also had another pupil who was affected by distractions occurring in the classroom. She used an isolation screen; he worked very well behind it. She was concerned with how to shape his work behavior without reinforcing working behind the screen. She decided to require steady work in the classroom for a certain time period, and then if he succeeded he would be allowed to use the screen. She then increased the working period within the classroom and eliminated the isolation screen entirely.

CHANGES IN THE STAFF

The modification in the behavior of the BA's and the Supervisors cannot be documented by the data collected, and their achievements must be assessed by the twice-removed indices of target's changes already presented. As we have, in speculation, turned our attention to our own reinforcement hierarchies, we are drawn to the research task of determining the patterns of control over consultant behavior which are excerised by mediators. How are they reinforcing us? For what and with what? Much of the time we do not know when our behavior is being shaped, and rarely are the reinforcers self-evident. Sometimes, of course, they are, and there are those moments more reinforcing than salary in praise or gratitude. And we can report at least one instance of a clearly labeled, though unlikely, reward.

Case #105. The parents experienced some sound improvement in the problem behavior of their 12-year-old son. They felt that, for the first time, they had available some reliable principles upon which to draw for child rearing issues. They were also taken with the energy and charm of the BA. The father had farming interests in the Midwest and rewarded the BA by a gift to the Project of 200 bushels of wheat! The consternation of an Arizona Mental Health Center, suddenly the owners of wheat stores in a Kansas silo, cannot be overstated. No administrative procedures exist for the holding and selling of grain. A solution was found through the local mental health association, who became the formal recipient. The mediator, several months later, called with advice to "sell." The project director made an unaccustomed visit to a stock broker and arranged the sale; the mental health association received the proceeds and made a gift of the cash to the Project expense fund. The wheat, thus transmogrified, blessed the behaviors of many delinquents and their mediators.

"But what reinforces you?" the authors were often asked. With some measure of self-protection, and some measure of truth, we replied, "the data." The data have certainly reinforced the continuation of the enterprise of behavior modification in the natural environment. But some of our early procedures and behaviors have extinguished, others have been shaped, and few have been impervious to changes in rate. Now that is all past and we properly turn our attention to the next and successive approximation—to what needs doing next.

References

Bijou, S. W., Peterson, R. F., Harris, F. R., Allen, E. K., and Johnston, M. S. *Psychological Record,* 1969, **19,** 177–210.
Eysenck, H. J., *Journal of Consulting Psychology,* 1952, **16,** 319–324.
Gelfand, D. M., and Hartmann, D. P. *Psychological Bulletin,* 1968, **69,** 204–215.
Sidman, M. *Tactics of Scientific Research,* New York: Basic Books, 1960.

CHAPTER IX

Implications

Based on our data and those of many others, we believe that the case for behavior modification in the natural environment has now been established in the following areas: contingencies can be managed in the natural environment; behavioral changes can be recorded and assessed; for the behaviorally disordered child, desirable changes can be effected; and, last, it is possible to work in and with the natural environment, according to an operational model derived from nonmedical learning theories.

This is not to say that the need for research and demonstration in this area has passed. Far from it. Rather, the current need is for research and demonstration in the enterprise of *implementation*. The need is not to redemonstrate that BA's can engineer school—home coordination of managed contingencies; the challenge today is for the demonstration of this achievement by school counselors, probation officers, public health nurses, and pediatricians. For example, a Behavior Research Program should be totally unnecessary in a school district whose counselors accept the challenge; equally superfluous in a Family Court district whose probation officers are willing to accept demonstrated fact; and rendered obsolescent by the creative achievements of school administrators who will organize educational establishments for the positive motivation of their individual pupils. These remarks are equally true for the full gamut of the helping professions and their agencies: psychotherapists, case workers, school counselors and administrators, rehabilitation counselors, nurses, classroom teachers, physicians, public administration officers, and all the workers in hospitals, prisons, training schools, and workshops. The time has now come for the incorporation of behavior modification techniques into each of these roles and settings.

Some readers may agree, in principle; however, the question remains as to how to begin. Bijou (1968) addressed himself to this question and concluded that if the fields of education are to profit from the scientific

185

analysis of behavior, educators must give something too; they must give some effort, some work, some experimentation. We suggest that, in the language of behavioral training, the helping professions must now "offer some behaviors." That is, he who would learn must act. The counselor or the case worker who would accept the challenge of developing new and powerful skills must risk the effort of trying. In this way the processes of learning are initiated.

The balance of this chapter suggests some behaviors which the reader may initially "offer." It is not simple to launch into unknown waters with only the accounts of other voyagers by which to navigate. And we have no illusions that the suggestions contained here will produce instant experts in the procedures of behavior modification. But neither do we have any hesitation in suggesting that the reader may begin. The behavior modification model does not concentrate on human frailty, and preach "caution, caution" lest our actions harm a client. Rather, we admit that every living organism is a learning organism, and that we are teaching something to our clients, patients, and pupils at all times. The reader is now, already, differentially reinforcing his target's behaviors. It would be well to modify these contingencies by the use of honest admission and responsible effort.

IMPLICATIONS FOR THE CHOICE OF CASES AND BEHAVIORS

The interventionist who decides to explore the usefulness of behavior modification approaches will be immediately concerned with this issue: Which individuals, which problems, and which behaviors are appropriate for the forms of contingency management and environmental control described in this volume? For a given individual, how does one choose those behaviors which should be specifically consequated? Should one intervene on underachievement, or stealing? And beyond that, are there forms of deviance, of undesirable behavior, of "psychopathology," which are *ipso facto* unavailable to behavioristic intervention or study?

As a general guide to these decisions, we would suggest that behavior modification holds promise in instances of *observable behavior*. This is not to say that the contingency management technology reported in this volume is fully developed for all ages, all behaviors, and all environments. Rather, the statement suggests that a concentration on observable behaviors will suggest to the interventionist those instances which are inappropriate, as well as those which may be advised. Many puzzles may be quickly and clearly resolved.

For example, one does not intervene on nonobservable behavior. It is from this principle that the decision not to attempt consequation of stealing and other concealed forms of undesirable behavior is derived (see Chapter VIII, p. 170). In such instances, the tactic is to select some observable behavior which is desirable, and which either (1) will be consequated so that the behavior produces the same or greater reinforcement than the undesirable concealed behavior, or (2) will occur during the same time interval, so that the undesirable behavior will cease on the general principle of incompatible responses.

> A probation officer had good though inconclusive evidence that his 16-year-old female case was "heisting" on week-day nights just prior to her 9 P.M. curfew. He arranged an intervention which would reward her with trinkets, food, etc. (her usual haul), for time spent at home at the study table during the hours 7:30 to 9:00.
> He continued, as before, to counsel her against stealing; but he did not pretend to consequate it.[12]

It also follows that one is guided away from intervention on "nonbehaviors," even though they are observable. In general, it is far more satisfactory to record, shape, and consequate behaviors than nonbehaviors, and in apparent cases of "nonbehavior" one most often has this option.

> In a day-care program for mildly retarded children, the child-care worker wished to interrupt a five-year-old girl's preferred activity of sitting on a decorated wooden chair, doing "nothing." At this point, the worker would have settled for almost any alternative to this clearly observable "nonbehavior." Her strategy was to select a behavior, however, and she chose to reinforce, as a first approximation, perambulation. Thus, any time the girl was moving about, she was rewarded. This behavior, of course, is incompatible with sitting-doing-nothing, and thus the latter is reduced. But the technique of choosing perambulation allowed control over the alternative, avoided punishment, and reduced the undesirable behaviors, simultaneously.

Of course, this suggestion is intertwined with the issues of Incompatible Responses (see p. 100, Chapter VI) and Extinction (see p. 104, Chapter VI).

There is a third guide which derives from the prescription for observable behaviors: one does not choose nonobservable nonbehaviors. This brings us to the general issue of the place of thoughts, feelings, moods, and other "internal" states with which the helping professions are often con-

---

[12] The case material included in this chapter has been drawn from the authors' experiences in consultation with a variety of individuals and agencies. The details have been changed only enough to avoid identification of the cases.

cerned. Are these aspects of the human condition a proper focus for the techniques of behavior modification now under discussion? In general, the answer should be "no"—they are not. For even though we may be vitally, and even ultimately, concerned with the thought and affect with which behavior is inextricably interwoven—such a focus may be disadvantageous. We adopt this position for simple reasons. That which cannot be seen, which cannot be discriminated, cannot be the basis for differential response. Thoughts and feelings, therefore, are inappropriate for consequation in the same way that stealing is inappropriate. Beyond that, there is substantial doubt as to whether operant analyses correctly describe emotion. Those new intervention techniques which have been most carefully developed for the reduction of anxiety or the modification of sexual excitement, for example, have been based on the *classical* conditioning paradigm rather than the *instrumental* (see p.18 Chapter I). While many— including the authors—have argued that the phenomena of "desensitization" or "aversive conditioning" can be described well by operant analyses, such work has not yet proceeded to an accurate enough state for the field worker to be advised to attempt direct mood or affect modification by contingency management. The same considerations may be applied to *thought*. It is unobservable. The great strength of the functional-analytic approach is in its demonstration that the interpolation of internal events in explanatory statements is unnecessary and often produces error. Even though scientists, notably Staats (1968), have analyzed cognition in learning-theory terms, the surfacing of cognition is always through behaviors, verbal or otherwise.

This last point raises the most interesting issue in connection with internal events: the correlated behaviors. And in the presence of the correlated behaviors lies the most persuasive deterrent to direct intervention in internal events. For example: What are strictly internal events? Are there any? If the reader reviews in imagination the range of human events, searching for those without behavior, he will have engaged in one and discovered few others. The vast majority of "internal" events—thoughts, feelings, imaginations—do have a behavorial correlate or outcome: if we feel bad, we often act differently; if we think through a problem, we often move toward action; if we become angry, we attack; if we hallucinate a threat, we cower. Thus the interventionist who describes his concerns as depressions, thinking, anger, or hallucinating, has available the characteristic linked behaviors upon which he may focus and act. Even "schizophrenia" resides only in the behavior by which it is defined. The helping vocations will be concerned only with those conditions which are behavioral.

We also suggest that we should be so limited. People cannot help but be concerned with the implications which their behaviors have for one another, and so everyone will ask from time to time that their own or someone else's behavior be modified. But for those who believe in maximizing personal freedom, those occasions should occur as infrequently as possible. And internal events, in the absence of behaviors, are simply no one else's business. Other people's thoughts, dreams, and hopes should be theirs, to hold or to share.

But what of those people who are not dissatisfied with their behavior so much as they are discontent with their thoughts or feelings, and request assistance in improvement. It is a myth of psychiatry that these are common patients, but let us consider them. Even there, the interventionist has no route to helping but on a path marked clearly by the patient's behavior. At least in his verbal behavior, the patient must learn to discriminate, to describe, and to act in ways which ramify into his complaints. And every psychotherapist knows that even such internal states as "self esteem" neither develop nor exist nor change in isolation from the patient's behavior and its consequation by the social environment. Even for the patient who just wants to "feel better," behavior and its environment are the very means by which this feeling can be achieved. One is happy by acting happy in a world which sets the occasion for and reinforces happiness.

So much, then, for admonition. We will now discuss procedures.

Thus far this volume has been more like a Baedecker than a Rombauer—more a behavior modification *Traveller's Guide* than a *Joy of Cooking*. And this final chapter will not vary in style. The prescription of specific techniques, in cookbook style, has no part in this work. The task of producing technique manuals, one for each field or profession or setting, will be left to other days and other authors. Indeed, we do not believe that a worthy cookbook can yet be prepared; and the day may never come when a reader can thumb the index for *glue-sniffing* or *paranoid ideation* or *getting-out-of-seat-without-permission* and find the tested and preferred intervention plan. People differ too much for that, in their reinforcers, in their histories, and especially in their complex social environments.

On the other hand, procedural instruction for behavior interventionists is a different matter, and the suggestions to follow may be considered a prolegomenon to a *Procedures*. The principles which guide behavior modification need no further reiteration here; general "rules" of operation which we have tested, or advocated, or derived from the work of others constitute the bulk of these pages. Now we need only suggest a few operational guides chosen specifically to answer the initial questions of the beginning interventionist. It is inevitable that the experiences of the next decade will establish volumes of detail under each of the following headings.

IMPLICATIONS FOR CASE MANAGEMENT

ESTABLISHING ASSESSMENT PROCEDURES

The first task is to achieve a clear definition of the problem behavior. In emotional and behavioral disorders, there is always (by definition) a complainant, and it is to this individual(s) that we turn for a clear behavioral description of the disorder.

> In a sheltered workshop for recent patients of a state mental hospital, the supervisor complained of 22-year-old Emily's recent "regressive tendencies"; the supervisor feared that Emily would have to be returned to the hospital. In a staff conference, the consultant psychiatrist persisted in questioning the supervisor for a behavioral specification of the "regression." It was soon apparent that Emily had been taking off her shoes with increasing frequency. This was against the rules, and was certainly inappropriate in a work-training setting. The psychiatrist suggested that prior to rehospitalization a simple contingency might be tried; Emily was advised that she could remain in the workshop if she kept her shoes on, but that she could not if she continued removing them. Emily was grateful for this information, since she had perceived vaguely that the staff was worried about something. She kept her shoes on, and proceeded through the workshop training.

The second task is that of securing baseline on frequencies of problem behavior, and of such other behaviors as may be of interest. The operational difficulty may arise with the selection of the *recorder*. The general rule might be phrased: *select the individual who can achieve reliable recording most economically.* Often this will be the interventionist himself.

> A teacher wished to reduce the frequency of bothering-classmates by a third grader. Without changing her management techniques in the class, she began to mark down a tally with each occurrence. Because the behavior often occurred while she was away from her pencil and paper, she was unsure of her record's accuracy. She purchased a golf-stroke counter which attached with a wrist band. This allowed accurate recording.

Sometimes it is not practical that the interventionist do his own recording. One then asks: Who is present when the behavior occurs? This narrows the choice sharply.

> A rehabilitation counselor, though pleased with the trade-school progress made by her 27-year-old paranoid client, was concerned that the client's parents might petition for his recommitment. The client, Clarence, reported

that his parents thought he was going crazy again, and threatened every night to return him to the hospital. After careful inquiry of Clarence, the counselor could appreciate the parents' views; while the old couple watched television at night, Clarence would intrude himself between them and the screen, grasp his throat, and gurgle and gasp thus communicating that he believed (delusionally) that his throat was cancerous. Clarence regretted this behavior to the counselor, but reported that sometimes he was doing it before he knew it. Thus the client himself was inappropriate as a recorder of gurgling-and-gasping behavior, and the choice was immediately only the mother or the father.

It is always preferrable to have the interventionist make some form of check on the behavior of the recorder, for purposes of establishing reliability, and for purposes of training in recording skills.

A YMCA Director chose a 17-year-old Youth Leader as the recorder of fighting behavior by a nine-year-old bully in the Youth Leader's swimming class. On the second day of recording, the Director visited the class and recorded the recording behavior of the recorder. After the hour was over, the Director discussed the recording with the Youth Leader, and told him that he had observed one instance of "verbal aggression" that had been erroneously tallied as "fighting." He suggested that the Leader not rely on memory for the entire hour, but mark down tallies on a tablet when, from time to time, he left the pool.

On the third day, the Director visited and recorded again; and once more on the sixth day of baseline. He was by then satisfied of the accuracy of the recorder's frequency counts.

A range of recording techniques and methods for estimating and improving reliability has been presented by Bijou and his associates (Bijou, *et al.*, 1968).

It also important to record desirable behaviors of the target, if the interventionist wishes to increase their frequency. The issue of the length of time for which baseline recording should be continued has been discussed in Chapter VIII (pp. 150–152).

During the period of time of baseline recording, the assessment of potential reinforcers and potential mediators should be proceeding apace. One detailed technique for this assessment has been the subject of Chapter IV, and Appendix II may be consulted for sample materials. In contrast to the task of problem-definition, the complainant is not usually the best source for information concerning the target's potential reinforcers. As of this date, it is our opinion that either the interventionist or another interviewer should make direct inquiry of the target along the lines of the MRB questionnaire. Of course, nothing surpasses information gathered from direct observation of behavior changes as they are functionally related to reinforcing events. But that technique for hypothesizing reinforcers is not practical in most instances. A good substitute device is to ask the target what he likes.

Neither should one neglect observation of preferred activity, for use with the "Premack principle" (see Chapter VI, pp. 86–88).

> A nurse observed that a slovenly schizophrenic patient, Patricia, invariably engaged all staff members who entered the dayroom in conversation concerning her illegal confinement, together with urging that her lawyer be contacted. The nurse correctly hypothesized this behavior was of sufficiently high probability to be used as a reinforcer; later, opportunity to speak with the staff about her lawyer was placed contingent on hair-combing and face-washing.

SELECTING MEDIATORS

The assessment of potential mediators will be partially accomplished through recording, because the recorders are often the logical mediators. Clarence's parents, or the bully's swimming teacher, would no doubt be evaluated by the interventionist as potential dispensers of reinforcement. The interest and cooperativeness of these people will become clear. In other instances, specific interviews will need to be conducted, and the interventionist must arrange such appointments. These contacts are frequently outside the usual habits of office or agency.

> A psychiatric social worker, accustomed to an office practice of individual and group psychotherapy, experimented with behavior modification techniques in a case of a particularly defiant and truant eighth-grade boy. The assessment interview had revealed time-spent-working-in-uncle's-café as a potentially powerful reinforcer. The social worker telephoned the uncle asking him to come to the agency office for an appointment, but because the little café was a one-man operation the uncle was reluctant to close his business for this interview. The social worker then volunteered to talk with him at the café. He did, over the counter, with coffee, between customers, and determined that the uncle was willing to let the boy work at the café, but only on the contingency that he had attended school that day. The social worker later opined that his original idea of an office visit had been an error. The natural setting was more informative, and allowed him to make better judgments. He also rather enjoyed getting back to social work.

This is not to say that interviews with mediators should never take place in the interventionist's office. Sometimes this is the correct place, because the task of assessment is to estimate the probable success of a given idea, and the best estimate can be made if the role-relationships between the interventionist and the mediator are made a part of the assessment conditions.

A juvenile court judge wished to determine if a particular intervention plan were sufficiently practical to form part of the probation conditions for a 16-year-old second offender. The judge called the parents into his chambers to conduct the "assessment." Because the full weight of the authority of his office would form much of the motivation for "good mediating" by the parents, the judge correctly made that motivating condition a part of the assessment situation.

The sole question surrounding mediator assessment is, of course, "Who has the target's reinforcers and can dispense them on contingency?" As has been explicated fully in Chapters III and VI, most reinforcing events are interpersonal events; thus the determination of the reinforcer will sometimes automatically determine the choice of the mediator.

A probation officer for a teen-age delinquent boy completed the reinforcer assessment, and found the target's hierarchy dominated by this single reinforcing event: diving and learning to dive for coral and rare shells in an interisland channel. This highly skilled and dangerous occupation was practiced by only one potential mediator: the boy's father. The choice of the mediator was dictated by the reinforcer.

In other situations, the opposite will be true: the choice of the mediator will determine the reinforcer.

A dormitory supervisor, for a boarding school of the Bureau of Indian Affairs, determined that there were two potentially satisfactory reinforcers available in managing the case of a 13-year-old lazy and belligerent boy. The first was probably the most powerful: time with the dormitory-owned electric guitar and amplifier. The mediator for the guitar would be a night-shift dorm aide, Walter. The other potential reinforcer was a town-pass, which would involve a ride in on Saturday morning with the mediator, Billy, the stationwagon driver. The supervisor knew that Walter was a capricious man, whose bad moods sometimes led him to lock up all the entertainment-center equipment: guitars, the stereo, and the pool cues. Billy was a steady young man, interested in "wayward youth," but not at all comfortable with the proposed intervention plan, which seemed to him like bribery. The supervisor believed, nevertheless, that he could influence Billy to dispense rides-to-town on contingency, whether or not there was philosophical agreement. Walter, on the other hand, would require supervision during hours when the interventionist was often out of the building. The mediator of choice was Billy. This eliminated the guitar from consideration, and the plan moved to the second-ranked reinforcer, town-passes.

The assessment of reinforcers and the assessment of mediators are thus intertwined processes; woven with them is the invention of specific intervention plans. For example, in the BIA-dormitory situation, the selection of Billy as mediator dictated the choice of the reinforcer, and the contingency aspects of the plan were automatically "invented": the reinforcer, town-passes, would be dispensed by Billy when and only when acceptable criterion behavior had been met.

CHOOSING CRITERIA

By "choosing criteria" we refer to the choice of the initial behavior which will be required of the target, and the steady adjustment of the criterion-behavior as the target's behavior is modified. This aspect of intervention has been discussed in full detail under the heading of Shaping, in Chapter VI, (see pp. 96–98); we will not repeat the discussion here, except to reiterate that the *interventionist should choose an initial level of behavior for the first step which can be performed by the target, and can thus be rewarded*. As a practical rule of thumb, it is far better to set the criterion "too low" than "too high". If the criterion is too high, the behavior will not occur, the reward will not be administered, shaping will not take place, and the target will not have the experience of the reward, which would draw his favorable attention to the prompting mediator. If the criterion is set "too low," the interventionist may have "wasted" a trial or two, and a reinforcer or two—in most instances, surely not a serious matter. Setting the criterion at a conservatively low point will avoid unfortunate side effects and will, in addition, allow the target to learn that improved performance is a continuing expectation.

A psychotherapist in a community mental health center used behavior modification techniques with his 22-year-old schizo-affective patient. For the fourth consecutive September, Kerry was preparing to be rehospitalized because of excessive sleeping and social withdrawal. The psychotherapist as well as others connected with the case had been encouraging Kerry to attend college because he had a tested IQ of 127. The therapist correctly perceived that urging Kerry into college was incorrect use of shaping principles since it required more social and social-system skills than Kerry possessed. Kerry and the therapist agreed that the next step should be for the patient to enroll in the YMCA's courses; Kerry thought he would like swimming, and one of the martial arts, probably judo. The therapist had only one reinforcer which he could dispense himself—and that was his own presence. The use of a contingency seemed advisable, because Kerry "talked a good game" of YMCA enrollings, but his behavior did not alter from the excessive sleeping which was alarming his parents. The therapist told Kerry that there was no point in their having further conversations until Kerry had obtained full information from the YMCA, but immediately on the performance of this task Kerry would be "dispensed" another appointment. Two hours later, Kerry was back with brochures, to collect his second interview of the day. The therapist set a second task: formal enrollment, which he expected would occupy Kerry for several days. By 4:30, Kerry had returned again, to collect the reinforcer of another interview. The therapist next asked for three days full attendance of both classes, upon which criterion another interview was made contingent.

The therapist "incorrectly" estimated Kerry's current performance potential, and "cost" himself more interview time than he had anticipated. On the other hand, Kerry was awake, out of bed, headed for the YMCA instead of the mental hospital, and rapidly and clearly introduced into the incentive system. This "error" was far less serious than the former one of setting successful college attendance as the criterion which would earn the therapist's approval.

On the other hand, shaping is not always the technique of choice. There are some instances in which the initial criterion may be the fully achieved goal behavior. One particularly dramatic example illustrates this.

A special education teacher in a residential school for emotionally disturbed adolescents attempted to devise contingency management for a seventh grade boy who was encopretic. He soiled himself several times daily, and seriously enough so that the odor was too obnoxious for public schools. This behavior had been lifelong, and the child and his family had undergone extensive psychiatric, child-guidance, psychotherapeutic, and psychopharma-cological treatment which had not decreased the frequency of soiling. Using a variety of reinforcers, the teacher set criterion behavior as steadily lengthened periods of time when the child would remain clean. The case proceeded with irregular results. The teacher called in a mental-health center psychologist for consultation, and later a university faculty psychologist. The three experimented with various forms of contingency arrangements. The records revealed wide variation in frequency of soiling across days and weeks, regardless of the reinforcers used: family trips, cola drinks, school activities, cash, etc. The conclusion was reached that the child possessed fully adequate sphincter control for remaining clean; this ability did not require further shaping, and the management issue was the discovery of a sufficiently powerful reinforcer.

The general rule, therefore, is this: *initial criteria should lie within the potential behavior reportoire, so that reinforcement can occur.* Ordinarily this will require shaping of successive approximations. However, if the behavior already can be performed, it may be asked for as fully completed. This may require a more powerful incentive than the interventionist can muster, and even potentially present behaviors should be called for in approximations. The most general rule is this: *choose to reinforce that behavior farthest along the progression toward the ultimate goal which occurs frequently enough to produce reinforcement.*

This judgment is less complex than it sounds, even though the choice will be the result of consideration of behavioral, mediator, and reinforcer characteristics. For example, the use of reinforcers which are particularly high in incentive value will allow a criterion of more fully perfected behaviors. Sometimes these reinforcers are unlikely ones.

> In the case of encopresis, described above, one of the psychologists, after four months of unsuccessful attempts at shaping and the juggling of reinforcers, suggested a new incentive; later he was unable to describe the mental processes by which he arrived at the unlikely notion. The boy was required to earn his underwear. Each day's change of briefs was earned by remaining clean during the entire day previous. After each soiling, new underwear would be withheld for 24 hours. The boy soiled once more, and experienced the contingency. At the time of this writing, there were 23 months follow-up data available. There have been no further instances of soiling. The "underwear contingency" was sufficiently powerful to induce the production of the previously fully perfected behavior of sphincter control. The child has returned to public school.

The flash of intuition plays a part in contingency management, as it does in all creative human endeavors. But the reader should notice that this is virtually the only instance cited in this volume in which the insight, intuition, or "brilliance" of the interventionist accounts for impressive results. Unlike psychotherapy, behavior modification action is guided by careful assessment, the responsible application of systematic principles, and the watchful attention of the interventionist to his own, his mediators', and his target's behavior. One does not need a gift of a "third ear" nor indoctrination into an arcane metaphysic. One does need to work.

In addition to the shaping versus nonshaping issue, there are two other points which may be reiterated concerning the issue of choosing behavioral goals and setting criteria for reinforcement. They have been fully discussed in previous chapters.

Behaviors should be chosen so that the modification will be reinforcing to the mediator (see Chapter III, pp. 52–57).

It is preferable to develop desirable behaviors rather than only remove undesirable. (For a full explication of these issues, see the sections on Incompatible Responses in Chapter VI, pp. 100–101, and the discussion of Extinction and Punishment, pp. 104–111, of Chapter VI.)

THE ARITHMETIC OF REINFORCEMENT

The overall effect of instituting an intervention plan should be to increase the total amount of positive reinforcement in the system, or at least not to reduce the total available to the target. Even when punishment or the withdrawal of positive reinforcers is employed, some alternate desirable behavior should be consequated, so that the undesirable side effects of frustration of the target may be avoided. The sum effects of the various contingencies employed should be to increase the total available reinforcement (see p. 106, Chapter VI).

The Behaviors of Mediators

One should ask for behaviors from the mediators, which are consistent with the mediator's role vis-a-vis the target (see p. 53, Chapter III).

The overall effect of the mediator's behaviors toward the target should be to reduce the aversive elements and increase the positive control features. We have discussed something of this issue in connection with "depersonalization" of reinforcement in those instances when the personal element is aversive or punitive (see Chapter VI, p. 89). It is better to be mechanically pleasant than personally aversive. Thus, in those instances when the mediator-of-choice is uncontrollably hostile toward the target, even though the hostility be mild, the personal elements of the reinforcing should be minimized.

> A sixth-grade teacher devised an intervention plan in which she served as her own mediator. She accurately assessed her own emotions toward the misbehaving target as hostility. Not being sure that she could suppress a scowl or a scolding while dispensing the reward to her provocative pupil, she "depersonalized" the reinforcing by leaving the token-note on her desk for the target to pick up after she had left the room.

This is only an elaboration of the fact that positive reinforcers must be positive, and not have their functional quality altered by the dispensing system. But if the eventual aim is to increase the positive elements of the relationships between mediator and target, as it usually is, one eventually hopes to make the dispensing itself a positive event. To rush it, though, may be to ruin it.

> (Continued): when the reinforcer had reduced the frequency of the child's provocative behavior, the teacher's irritation with the target decreased. She then altered the dispensing procedure: she handed the note to the target, smiled, and congratulated him.

Proper pacing allows the possibility that the teacher's smile or congratulation (or more slightly signaled approval) will develop functional reinforcing properties.

Another important element of the mediator's behaviors toward the target is as follows: in general, *the intervention program should be explained to the target by the mediator,* regardless of the ages or roles of the individuals or of the environment in which the intervention occurs. This has been discussed under "Prompting" (Chapter VI, pp. 98–99); and the one general exception—that of severely angry mediators—has been treated under the section on Contracts (pp. 113–115).

The details and language of the explanation vary of course with the age of the child.

THE BEHAVIORS OF THE INTERVENTIONIST

Do not argue with mediators. Argumentation is well known for its inability to bring about behavior change. A good technique for stopping an argument is to stop talking about the controversial subject.

The task of the interventionist—social worker, teacher, nurse, or anyone—*is to modify the behavior of the mediator,* not (directly) the behavior of the target (see Chapter III, pp. 56–57). We have discussed several reinforcing techniques available to the interventionist, e.g., the astute choice of targeted behaviors, enlisting the aid of the mediator's husband, etc. *The interventionist will also want to differentially reinforce the mediator with his own attention approval, etc.* Before that can be achieved, however *the interventionist must become positively reinforcing to the mediator.* This first and primary achievement is referred to in psychotherapy as "rapport building." It probably proceeds by being nice, interested in, and valuable to the mediator. Only after one has established himself as a positive reinforcer is there any point in placing his approval on contingency.

Contact with mediators should be as direct as possible. In the discussion on "Long-Distance Consultation" (pp. 118–122), we suggested that the number of individuals through which a message must pass is the real measure of the distance between interventionist and mediator. Intervention plans should include the minimum number of individuals consistent with the complexity of the social environment which must reaccept the child. One should not, in general, rely upon what a wife says that her mediator–husband is thinking and doing: one should not "leave" messages when they can be delivered directly; one should observe and interact directly with the mediator whenever it does not interfere with the viability of the social system within which the target is embedded.

The interventionist should expect to provide mediator-contact more frequently when the mediator tasks are more unfamiliar: at the inception of intervention, at changes in contingencies, when basic conditions of the environment change "accidentally," and at any points during which mediator behavior needs more propping. But the most general statement is that *mediator contact should be as infrequent as possible, while still maintaining desirable mediator behavior.* It is not a virtue to schedule regular meeting times. The development of the friendly relationship is not an end in itself; we do not suppose that frequency of time spent together increases desirable behavior. Clear specification of behavioral goals is facilitated by scheduling mediator-contract on the basis of continuous assessment of case progress.

This same guide—reduce the frequency of contact to a minimum—is also, in general, useful in considering the interventionist's behaviors toward the target. We have already stated the case for minimizing "professional" relationships, and relying instead upon the natural relationship as the vehicle for achieving behavioral amelioration. In Chapter IV we described an organizational scheme for insuring that these natural relationships were used. In Chapter VI we described several exceptions—instances in which "artificial" relationships were employed, both as primary and as adjunctive mediating vehicles. In the light of both theory and experience, we would now suggest the following: *the external interventionist should contact the target only in circumstances when natural relationships cannot be effectively employed.* When they cannot, the responsible interventionist may well seek to create or become the effective channel (p. 93). The following is an example of participation by the interventionist, probably necessary.

A welfare worker arranged that a note from the geography teacher should be backed up by a reinforcer of 5¢. The worker would have preferred that the nickle be dispensed by the child's mother; however, the mother could not have afforded an extra 15¢ per week, nor could anyone in the natural environment. The worker undertook to provide it out of her own pocket because agency funds could not be made contingent, they could only be doled. The worker would also have preferred that the mother dispense the actual coins; but because of the desperate poverty of the family, the worker feared that the mother might be sorely tempted to divert the funds. The welfare worker decided to redeem the geography note herself, at her office. The welfare worker and the target became fast friends.

MONITORING: THE USE OF DATA

Frequency data should be collected continuously from Day 1 of baseline period through the decision to terminate, and preferably well beyond termination. Reliability checks should be undertaken periodically, throughout the entire period. Action should be guided by data.

The same forms of recording may well be used during intervention as were established during the assessment period. These records should be kept by someone who is present when the behavior occurs. They should be gathered regularly by the interventionist. The data, if not recorded by the mediator, should be regularly explained to him. The intervention program should be continuously evaluated by the interventionist and, in consultation with the mediator, adjusted until the frequency counts reveal that the desired goals are being reached.

If there has been one principal burden of this volume, it is to establish the dictate: let fact inform practice.

IMPLICATIONS FOR RESEARCH

Clinical practice and research have not been convergent endeavors. Practitioners seldom evaluate the effects of their therapeutic interventions objectively, and never routinely. The demands of service, the absence of methods, and the lack of professional expectations reduce the frequency of careful monitoring and evaluation of treatment. Thus, clinical practice lumbers, hampered by untested, often outdated, theoretical concepts and inappropriate data. The practitioner remains subject to fads and unfounded claims. There is clinical research, of course. But, though it is often scientifically sound, it does not yield data appropriate to practice. Variables such as age, sex, personality, self-concept, and intelligence may be shown to be highly correlated with treatment outcome, whether they are measured in the therapist or in his client. They are not, however, variables over which the therapist has control. When treatment conditions are varied, the process is frequently so grossly and inadequately defined that a practitioner's chances of replicating a condition are extremely small. Outcome measures which are long-term, such as length of time on a job, stability of marriage, etc., do not allow the practitoner to monitor or evaluate the process of intervention. At the same time, treatment effects expressed as psychological test performance are usually of little value to a practitioner sensitive to the requests and complaints of his client. Findings are most often reported as statistical probability statements about groups of clients and have little practical value to the practitioner faced with an individual man. Thus do practice and research continue, controlled by separate events, and exercising little effect on one another. After nearly a half century of widespread professional observation and effort to change assorted aspects of human behavior, the number of reliable, data-supported, factual statements which can be made about human behavior is woefully small.

Unfortunately, practitioners have little respect for the simple facts that are known. For several reasons (not the least of which is the disease model) both practitioners and researchers have invested years of professional effort in the search for the ultimate and effective treatment. This search has generated a variety of philosophical positions, modes of therapeutic interaction, and styles of investigation. Always ahead is the phantasm of the method, the technique, the treatment which will cure, make content, happy, well, confident, relaxed, and productive, the miserable human being. The products of the laboratory, unglamorous statements about simple and isolated human behaviors, are unappreciated in the quest.

Experience tells us that real knowledge does not often develop through divine visitation. Facts accumulate slowly, in small bits, and from careful study and evaluation. The stunning breakthrough in science is rare indeed and usually follows years of study by countless researchers. Nothing analogous to the breakthrough sought by many in the understanding and control of human behavior has occurred in the history of any science. Only when the line worker can appreciate the development of a small, often impractical, fact about human behavior can he set seriously about the business of understanding the behavior of those he wishes to help.

Those involved in the effort to improve the human condition have been slow to use advances in experimental method, strategy, and philosophy. The experimental analysis of behavior and the single subject research design have been particularly neglected. Yet they are appropriate both to clinical practice and research, because it is the aim of this approach to identify those variables which determine human behavior, especially those variables over which human beings can exercise control. The techniques include a process of monitoring and, hence, evaluating the change in the behavior of a single organism—an important aim of the helping vocations. Perhaps it is the reduction of goals to simple measurable units of behavior that discourages the practitioner, or perhaps it is the analytical processes of the scientific method.

This is not to say that a complete science of human behavior lies waiting for the clinical practitioner and researcher to grasp. Far from it. Only the barest outlines are visible. But statements such as those of Sidman (1960), Dinsmoor (1966), Gelfand and Hartmann (1968), and, more recently, Bijou et al., (1969), clearly are harbingers of new thrusts in both practice and research. The Behavior Research Project upon which the material in this volume is based was an attempt to develop clinical service and research on a model provided by the experimental analysis of behavior and the single subject research design. To ask "Did it work? How many did it cure? Is it a good treatment?" is to return to the quest. We must ask instead about its strengths, weaknesses, and suggested directions for further work. It is our conviction that the fledgling science of human behavior can place scientific research and the human effort on paths which will ultimately converge. The convergence is a long way off but a comparison between the Behavior Research Project and advances in scientific method may point to next steps.

The specification of the social and physical treatment conditions is important to both research and practice, for example, but it is especially difficult in the field situation. Behavior Analysts were usually able to provide adequate descriptions of behavioral settings and environmental conditions at the beginning of a case. More difficult, however, was the monitoring of significant changes in the conditions during the course of intervention. Significant changes in the family constellation, health, finances, housing, etc., occurred and were ultimately reported by the Behavior Analyst. However, it is obvious that many such changes could be overlooked and go unrecorded. Techniques for monitoring the treatment environment need further development. Training of mediators to report certain important changes as well as the condition of the treatment variables would be desirable. What should one do if a significant extraneous change is noted? In most treatment situations the event is noted and treatment continues; the Behavior Research Project was no exception. Often the nature of the case, the situation, or the complaint behavior made this a necessity. However, when one is attempting to evaluate the effect of a particular intervention it might be important to discontinue the observation and treatment during the period of change. The researcher might prepare those in the environment of the target for such possibility; some temporary discontinuations might bring no harm to the target. In fact, as we will discuss below, it may benefit the therapist and his science.

The definition of the treatment condition varied in the Behavior Research Project from case to case and between Behavior Analysts. For example, a BA might instruct a parent to "praise," or he might specify the exact words to say. The specification of the treatment condition(s) is, of course, much easier than the monitoring of the treatment condition, especially in the natural environment. Most often BA's had to depend upon mediator report and recall, though there were occasions when the BA was able to make a direct observation of the treatment condition. Better techniques are needed here, and great effort should be made to monitor the condition when an intervention technique is being evaluated.

Probably the most challenging task in the evolution of clinical treatment and research technique is the development of reliable methods of observation. We must know whether or not an environmental or behavioral event has occurred. The Bijou *et al.* monograph discusses four central aspects of this crucial task: (1) the observational code, (2) observer training, (3) method for determining reliability coefficients, (4) techniques of observation sampling. The reader can do no better than to study that discussion carefully. The clinical situation and complexity of the human environment, its proclivities and prohibitions, make reliable observation extremely difficult. In the Behavior Research Project, BA's were occasionally able to obtain parallel observations with a mediator and thus get some measure of mediator reliability, at least in that situation. In other cases, however, the relationship between mediator records and target behavior could not be determined. In many cases, our record may document mediator recording behavior or mediator complaining behavior more than it does target behavior. Mediator behavior is not without significance, of course, but the reliable monitoring of behavioral change in significant client behavior may remain an elusive skill for some time. As we have suggested, clinical and research methods should and are growing more similar, and the rigor available to the clinician from the Bijou *et al.* (1969) work would indeed grace clinical research as well as provide the clinician with specific techniques, appropriate to clinical work as well as to research. On the other hand, there are real differences between basic, or foundational, or laboratory research and research into the techniques for the applications of the foundational findings. For example, Staats speaks of this issue:

> When we begin a study with a well-verified principle, however, we face different circumstances, at least to some extent. We require less evidence before we conclude that our results constitute a verification of the principle than we would if the study involved the discovery of a principle. When a principle has been verified so many times that it may be said to be true, we no longer see the study as a test of the principle plus a test of the specific conditions involved in the study, but only as a test of the specific conditions. If we fail to get the expected results, as a matter of fact, we are more likely to conclude that there were elements in the specific experiment that went awry. (Staats, 1968, p. 568.)

The issue is pertinent in many ways, but perhaps especially in regard to the identification of the controlling variables which constitute the treatment condition. As discussed in Chapter VIII, pp. 152–154, the traditional means of achieving this identification has been through the reversal of the treatment contingencies; Bijou *et al.* also discuss withdrawal and randomization of the reinforcers as alternatives. We would argue that such procedures are necessary to the foundational discovery—for example, that teacher attention is a reinforcer for various pupil behaviors. But this "has been verified so many times that it may be said to be true." In studies such as the BRP, which are concerned with specific applications of this fact, one need not reverse or withdraw or randomize the variable of teacher attention; to insist on this is a blind adherence to a procedure developed to solve an entirely different problem. We already know that teacher attention can be functionally related to important pupil behaviors; what we do not know are the specific techniques for systematically influencing the consequation of that attention. And to make that discovery, we may well need to employ foundational techniques, such as reversal.

Thus the researcher–clinician need not reverse or withdraw well-established reinforcers, but he would be well advised to systematically vary the techniques for the delivery of the reinforcer, until such techniques have also "been verified so many times that they may be said to be true." Following from this position, the BRP makes no apology for the small number of "reversals" contained in its cumulative graphs; we do admit serious deficiences, however, in the small number of times during which the withdrawal of other forms of the treatment condition occurred. For example, we do not know the usual effects of instructing mediators to "praise," or the effects of giving them specific words to say, or indeed whether either one had any functional relationship to mediator behavior. This discovery could only be made through systematic variation of that aspect of the treatment condition, both across and within cases. Research into the technology of behavior modification in the natural environment is in its foundational stage, and requires foundational forms of inquiry. The BRP data reported herein should be viewed only as gross indication that the enterprise is worthwhile, and should suggest some hypotheses for potential specifics of treatment. The next stage of inquiry requires precise techniques for discerning the functional relationships between aspects of consultant behavior and aspects of mediator behavior.

To do this would require that these treatment conditions be withdrawn for some period to observe the subsequent effect on mediating behavior. This is virtually unheard of in clinical practice, and ideally—when using laboratory-verified techniques—is unnecessary. The aim is not directly therapeutic. It is to ascertain the actual effect of the treatment condition. All sorts of events—in the environment, in the history and training of the therapist–researchers, and in the client—militate against this operation. But, with concentrated effort, it is possible more often than it is achieved. Clinical researchers must find the courage and the techniques. The recognition of the need is an important first step.

The above considerations obviously have great bearing on the nature of personnel and the organization of clinical work. The BRP is one suggested organization for moving these techniques into the helping professions. There are many others possible. For example, might not therapists have skilled assistants who help with recording forms, make visits to the client's environment to observe or instruct, and keep charts up to date for the therapist to examine? The incorporation of these techniques into professional practice would multiply scientific research input a thousand-fold. If all the practicing therapists kept accurate and reliable records on treatment conditions and subsequent behavioral changes, and the effects of treatment interventions and other significant environmental changes, the science of human behavior and our skills for the modification of the human condition would be rapidly and significantly advanced. Modern computer technology already provides the means for the analysis and presentation of large amounts of separate data on individual subjects. Only one consideration remains: Do we want it enough to do it?

IMPLICATIONS FOR PROFESSIONAL AND ETHICAL JUDGMENT

To a very great degree, human behavior is controlled by the behavior of other humans. For some people, this is a situation to be regretted, and if necessary denied, because they contrast control with freedom. And if given such a simple choice, who among us will not opt for those dear attributes of the latter—joy, creativity, surgency, dignity? We suggest that to make this contrast is to err. Control is not the opposite of freedom. The opposite of human control by humans might be many things. It is certainly, for example, a defining characteristic of schizophrenia. It may be hermithood. If it were possible to exist at all, it would be in some inconceivable form of nightmarish entropy. Freedom can better be viewed as the achievement of a most singular and exquisite pattern of control—one in which joy, creativity, surgency, and dignity are fostered.

Control does not mean violence for it need not be aversive nor require consciousness or intention. But individuals affect and determine classes of behavior in others, and control refers to this behavioral interdependence. What a person does is very much determined by what others around him do, and this reciprocating control is present between friends as well as enemies, extends from child to parent as well as from parent to child, and exists between psychotherapist and client, whether or not it is admitted. The behavior of the student controls the teacher's behavior which, in turn, controls the student. All of this is unavoidable. Behavioral interdependence is an irreducible existential aspect of the human condition.

So the ethical issue of the helping professions is not whether or not to control. It is, rather, a question of the form and the ends of that control. The helping professions are, and must be, controlling professions too. We must be concerned with whom to help, how to help, and what to help them do.

We do not presume to formalize an ethic for behavior modification. In what follows, we wish to describe some of the considerations of professional and ethical judgment faced by the Behavior Research Project, and which will face all those who interact with others in the name of helping.

WHOM TO HELP

The targets of the BRP interventions were children. The laws and customs of our society dictate that parents, school personnel, and others have the responsibility to socialize the child and see to his best interests in the process. Parents (and others legally responsible) may call upon the professions to assist without the child's consent. For professional intervention in the natural environment, however, the consent of parents and certain others is absolutely necessary. Not only is this technically required, because of mediator cooperation, but it seems to us to be an ethical imperative. The BRP required signed consent of the parents before any case was accepted for continued contact. The parents understood that they could terminate at any time. Occasionally additional consent was sought from physicians when removal of drugs or certain behaviors (e.g., enuresis) indicated medical advice. The consent of superintendents and principals of schools was sought to enter buildings, contact teachers, look at files, and observe the child.

In the natural environment, consent of a target adult would also be a technical requirement as well as an ethical one. The BRP adopted the same attitude toward adolescents. Although the fact of intervention was ordinarily decided by the parents alone, the content of the intervention was consented to through negotiation by the adolescent target.

It is characteristic of techniques involving the natural environment that consent from a number of individuals in that environment be obtained, since these individuals are the helpers. The mediators must be in accord both with the selection of the target behaviors and with their own roles in bringing about behavior change. With some older children and with adults, the target must agree to the selection of mediators and their role in the control of one or more of his behaviors.

Consenting parties were permitted to refuse help and to terminate at any time. Behavior Analysts often suggested a trial time, at the end of which a reevaluation would be made. The research nature of the BRP and its relationship to the sponsoring agency was explained to the consenting adults. Behavior Analysts explained their role and training, the process of supervision, the relationship between the sponsoring agency and the schools, and the expected role of the mediators.

Thus, consent was given or withheld within the context of maximum relevant information. Maximizing such information was extended to the targets, even though they might be very young children, and awareness on the part of all members of the client environment was as full as our staff could make it. The processes of information-giving, of course, varied with the age of the child. With the very young, parents were advised to explain to the child that they had decided to help him with, let us say, his problems in school. They might explain that the teacher would be sending home notes so they would know when he had done well (e.g., attempted some classwork or not hit anyone). Furthermore, they would explain that they will be increasing his allowance, or some other consequence, in order to help him. The parents are encouraged to tell the child that this is a decision on their part. They may or may not tell him that someone else is working with them to help. The older the child the more informed he is about the exact roles of all persons involved, including the BRP personnel. Adolescents were often included in all plans and negotiations from the beginning. We found no reason to conceal the planning and intervention from the target himself. We did require the mediators to explain and to assume the responsibility for deciding to initiate change. Every effort was made to prohibit mediators from feeling that the BRP was responsible for initiating change and selecting behaviors. Likewise, parents were advised not to put the responsibility on the school for home behaviors and the teachers not to shift responsibility for school behavior to the parents. Referring mediators were instructed to explain the basis for their referral to the child. Awareness, consent, contracted right to terminate, and the presence of a consenting natural helper were the principal issues in the BRP's choice of whom to help.

How to Help

A major premise upon which the BRP interventions were based is that aversive control is undesirable, rarely the most effective choice as a permanent socialization technique, and frequently so objectionable in its experiential concommitants for the target and in it's brutalizing effects on the mediator as to be distasteful and unethical. This is not to say that we would never endorse punishment as a control technique (see Chapter VI, pp. 106–111); for grossly intolerable behaviors, such as autistic-self-destruction, pain—infrequently and judiciously administered—can create conditions which allow for instituting positive control. But in any environment, particularly the natural one, such instances are rare indeed. Nevertheless, many behaviors of the targets of the BRP, prior to our involvement, were controlled by pain and pain-derived stimuli. Intervention was aimed at removing aversive control. Behavior Analysts attempted to teach those in the target's environment that the child's behavior could be developed and guided more effectively and to better ends through the use of positive reinforcing events. From this point of view the burden falls on the environment to find and recognize the functional positive reinforcers for given individuals, to provide a range of positive reinforcers for a variety of behaviors, to develop effective reinforcing events, and to provide alternatives (such as wearing hair and clothing in changing ways) to harmful reinforcers.

The arrangement of contingencies and the selection of reinforcers must involve the advice and consent of the target. He is the one most able to describe his effective reinforcers. It is the interventionist's job to find them. If the constituted environment is limited in its resources of positive reinforcers, then they must be moved in from another. Our society is faced with serious problems surrounding the distribution of reinforcers and the movements of reinforcers from one environment to another. This issue is crucial to the management of behavior of individuals, of groups, of entire subcultures. And in the absence of positive control systems, aversive devices willy-nilly appear. Thus, ethically unjustifiable management systems are continued, for the "lack" of positive alternatives.

But let us assume that positive reinforcers are discovered; decisions as to their contingent use raise controversies also. There are those, for example, who believe that behavior can and should be maintained "without" reinforcement. These beliefs are expressed in such form as demands that children be "good for goodness' sake" or "study for the love of learning." An analysis of the contingencies affecting the behavior of one who is "good" for no apparent reason will reveal that good behavior is periodically reinforced and/or that good behavior avoids certain undesirable outcomes: punishment, criticism, shame. Very often, the people who are unwilling to reinforce desirable behavior are perfectly willing to punish for its absence. This is particularly true of those around delinquents who frequently punish for bad but seldom reward for good behavior. Until we escape from the notion that good behavior is its own reward, we will be faced with failures in the socialization and educational processes.

Another common issue is that of extrinsic versus intrinsic reinforcement. "Extrinsic" reinforcers include material goods; the term often encompasses any form of reinforcement originating in the external environment. Some commentators feel that it is somehow unethical, or at least unwise, to reinforce a child's behavior extrinsically, although such commentators are rarely observed declining their own salaries. There are many members of our society who do insist that their "good" behavior is not maintained by extrinsic reinforcement, but rather by internal systems of values and desirable attitudes. This belief can arise from a sensitivity toward the internal events which are typical accompaniments of positive reinforcement, but by less acuity concerning the rewarding events external to them. For example, the reinforcer following a well-done piece of work might be identified as "a sense of pride," even though some other consequences are also praise, money, deference, or gratitude. Though the latter occur irregularly, they may still be functional, indeed, even more powerful, for their variable schedule. But even if we were to grant that certain desirable behaviors may be so well learned as to require no further extrinsic reinforcement (or perhaps are maintained on an infinitely thinned schedule), does that mean that individuals so "fortunate" as to possess these habits should then sanctimoniously decline to teach by the use of schedules richer in payoff than those which maintain their own behaviors? We must not confuse appropriate schedules for acquisition with those appropriate for ultimate maintenance. Nor need jealousy, penury, or egocentricity be regarded as the motives for opposition to extrinsic reinforcement control. More often, such opposition confuses the extrinsic issue with that truly ethical issue: the contingencies in which reinforcement is woven.

For example, it surely must be unethical to bring a client under the ultimate control of reinforcers not available to him in his natural environment, just as surely as it is wrong to dispense harmful reinforcers, such as glue to sniff or stolen goods to sell. Beyond these apparent issues, there is also the problem of the use of legitimate reinforcers, but in inappropriate contingencies.

For example, an important characteristic of reinforcers is that they be relevant to the environment and to the behavior. Reading may be shaped with candy reinforcers. However, candy is not relevant to reading because the natural environment does not sustain reading with candy. The most relevant reinforcer for reading is the information and/or entertainment value of the material. Money is also a relevant reinforcer since many environments will reinforce reading with money. On the other hand, sometimes only irrelevant reinforcers are functional. Candy and a variety of reinforcers might be used to initiate the occurrences of a behavior such as reading, but eventually the behavior must be shifted to the control of available and appropriate reinforcers.

Reinforcing consequences can be inappropriate in another way. A response and its consequences are imbedded in the social network in which the individual is enmeshed. Sometimes a reinforcer, effective for one behavior, is inappropriate because its use upsets other behavioral systems. A parent may be advised to pay handsomely for a bit of homework. He might discover, however, that the value of his affection and praise begins to decrease. Many cautions have been issued about this potential effect, most of which are not based on any evidence. However, the matter must be given the closest consideration, and the careless establishment of contingencies always avoided.

WHAT TO HELP THE INDIVIDUAL TO DO

The determination of target behavior is governed by many factors. In most situations, the choice is made by the target individual himself, and this choice is a function of his particular reinforcement history. The techniques of intervention described in the preceding chapters involve the arrangement of reinforcing contingencies so that a target behavior, once selected, will not be punished but will, indeed, be reinforced and maintained by the environment in which he operates. The order of events in this process is crucial. The target individual selects a behavior by verbalizing his choice and/or emitting the behavior. He is being helped when some agent then works to provide a nonpunishing, maintaining outcome of that behavior. A client may announce, for example, that he intends to seek employment. His helper may then work with potential employers in such a way that the seeking of employment, besides not being punished, actually pays off.

This sequence of events is different from one in which the helper first selects a target behavior and then arranges the environment to maximize the occurance and subsequent maintenance of that behavior. In this case, the choice of behavior is a function of the helper's reinforcement history. In the hospital a vocational therapist may arrange the withholding of certain reinforcing events (privileges, money, food) until a client seeks a job. When he does seek the job, the therapist arranges a nonpunishing, rewarding outcome. In the first sequence the client chooses the target behavior while in the second the helper chooses it. The later sequence is more similar to the common concept of behavioral control than the first, which is most often considered a "helping" situation.

Whether or not a behavior will result in a nonpunishing, rewarding event is in part a function of the complex system of customs, taboos, and laws determining reinforcement contingencies. The interventionist must take this system into account in advising a target to select, or in selecting particular behaviors for the target. A very important role of all therapy is to advise the client of behavioral outcomes. The delinquent needs to know what the outcome will be if he swears at the teacher or refuses to open his book. How the target responds to such information is, of course, a function of his particular history.

Another set of practices, customs, and laws determines which groups will have behaviors selected for them. Committed patients, criminals, delinquents, children, and others are groups for whom target behaviors are selected and the environment arranged to maximize and maintain them. Child rearing is a process of behavioral engineering. The society pays teachers to arrange environments so that certain behaviors will appear in the repertoires of children and be maintained. Usually the child does not select. The choice is not a function of his history but of the history of those around him. Should others choose for the criminal? Should the psychotic be committed to the choices of a staff? Should fourteen years be old enough to choose for oneself? These crucial issues of behavioral selection go beyond the scope of this book. The question of who should select target behaviors for whom is a serious and critical one which must be faced by the contemporary culture. It is generally agreed that parents may select target behaviors for their children. The contemporary times are characterized, on the other hand, by challenges to many controlling systems which are long standing and unjust. Though the inevitability of control is recognized throughout this volume, let it not be misconstrued to mean control in order to subdue, to produce conformity, or to defeat. Control can be positive and just. We must accept the responsibility of making it so. But this effort will bring us often face to face with a most difficult ethical dilemma. If the controlling systems are indeed unjust— whether they be systems of schools, of governments, or of two individual parents—shall we participate in their determinations of behavior, or shall our effort be to change the systems themselves? The BPR from time to time joined this issue. No Behavior Analyst had difficulty deciding whether or not to help a parent control his destructive child. But should a behavior analyst help a parent set up a reinforcing system for practicing the violin? Should he help a parent eliminate all arguing? Behavior Analysts were urged not to assist with target behaviors which they could not approve. Sometimes, they attempted to modify the controlling system itself by establishing negotiations between the target and his parents, or by advising the parents about likely outcomes of their controlling systems. On the other hand, changing a controlling system is difficult to achieve if it is a complex organization such as a school or hospital. In the school, if the Behavior Analyst felt that an individual teacher was maintaining a truly harmful controlling system, he was advised to see the principal. If a Behavior Analyst withdrew from a case, it was made clear what conditions occasioned his withdrawal.

Our own ethical resolution was a simple one: we declined to participate in any program of behavior modification which did not meet our own ethical and moral standards, no matter who or what system was represented. Even though we might not challenge a parent's, or a hospital's, or a school's "right" to choose behaviors and reinforcers, we maintained the prerogative of the behavior consultant not to relinquish the right of choice for his own behavior.

Still, there is a dilemma. In retrospect as we examine our participation in implementing some goals of the school, we are not altogether comfortable with participating in such educational practices as requiring silence, in-seat behavior, and tedious workbook assignments. In our view a truly educational environment provides multiple opportunities for action which lead to outcomes of maximum relevance for the learner. But the widespread modification of the educational establishment was beyond our power to achieve—indeed, that is a separate enterprise. What compromises should we make for the sake of those individual children for whom the current system is the only alternative?

These issues are important because what one does, does make a difference. Behavior modification techniques are powerful, and in the presence of power, ethical issues can become frighteningly clear. What we might choose to do for, or with, or to, a target might very well happen. There is no hiding in the ethical murk of a vaguely defined psychotherapeutic enterprise with a low probability of changing much of anything anyway. Shall we, or shall we not? The answer must often be yes or no. The behavior engineer finds himself on the cutting edge—exciting, frightening, vital—of carving a new, self-conscious ethic of socialization.

A safeguard in controlling social systems is the dispersal of reinforcers and decision making, so that systems of mutual control guarantee a measure of fairness and justice. This condition will not obtain if the controlling reinforcers rest in the hands of a few. One aim of this project was to explore ways of dispersing the helping function into the natural environment. The power and ability to control for helping must reside in many persons, and we may now ask of them all those important questions which we address to the helping professions. What behaviors are you now choosing? Are they reasonable? Are they helpful? Can you justify them, when you consider the known laws of human behavior? Our environment must oppose systems which prevent entrée to that evironment's cultural rewards. We must oppose systems which maintain behaviors through aversive controls. We must foster systems which maintain the widest possible range of behaviors with the widest possible range of outcomes. Let there be the greatest possible array of reinforcers potentially available to all individuals, and for each individual the opportunity to achieve them in varied and unique ways. This pursuit is helping. As the power for helping passes into the natural environment, so, too, does the responsibility pass to the helper.

References

Bijou, S. W. What has psychology to offer education now? Division 7 Presidential Address, American Psychological Association Annual Meetings, San Francisco, 1968.

Bijou, S. W., Peterson, R. F., Harris, F. R., Allen, E. K., and Johnston, M. S. *Psychological Record,* 1969, **19,** 177–210.

Dinsmoor, J. A., *Journal of Consulting Psychology,* 1966, **30,** 378–380.

Gelfand, D. M., and Hartmann, D. P. *Psychological Bulletin,* 1968, **69,** 204–215.

Sidman, M. *Tactics of scientific research.* New York: Basic Books, 1960.

Staats, A. W. *Learning, language, and cognition.* New York: Holt, 1968.

APPENDIX I

TABLE A.1
DEMOGRAPHIC CHARACTERISTICS OF INTERVENED BRP CASES[a]

Characteristic	Percentage
Ethnic origin[b]	
Anglo	93
Mexican–American	7
Negro	0
Religion	
Protestant	67
Catholic	23
Other	10
Marital status	
Divorce in family history	54
Parent figures in home:	
Mother only	16
Both	84
Sex of target	
Male	81
Female	19

[a] $N = 77$.

[b] Three Negro–Americans (1%) and 15 Mexican–Americans (7%) were referred initially. The remaining referrals were Anglo–American children. Tucson has a small Black population (about 4%) and a large Mexican–American one (about 30%).

TABLE A.2
CASE REFERRAL AND ACCEPTANCE FIGURES

Referral sources	Percentage
Public schools	76
Juvenile court	18
Public welfare	4
Other	2

Case fate	No. of cases
Cases referred	227
Referrals rejected[a]	90
Parents declined service	25
Case files created	112
Closed prior to intervention[b]	35
Intervened cases	77
Cases for which at least one behavior record was available	89
Behavior recorded	163
Behaviors recorded adequately for evaluation	135

[a] Identified as not meeting the criteria of underachievement, misbehavior, nonadjudication, and IQ = 90.

[b] Six of the 35 improved so significantly during assessment that no intervention was required. The remaining 29 were closed for a variety of reasons: the families moved away, more careful assessment revealed the case as inappropriate, loss of family interest in services, etc.

TABLE A.3
DISTRIBUTION OF INTERVENED BRP CASES ACROSS GRADE LEVELS

Grade	Total cases (%)
1	5
2	9
3	11
4	9
5	8
6	11
Total elementary	53
7	16
8	12
Total junior high	28
9	8
10	8
11	3
12	0
Total high school	19

TABLE A.4
OCCUPATIONAL RANKINGS FOR FATHERS OF CASES

Occupational category[a]	Intervened (%)
I. Professional, proprietors, e.g., farm and business owners	19
II. Managers (farm and business), officials	4
III. Clerical, sales, skilled craftsmen, foremen	31
IV. Skilled and semiskilled operatives, miners, services	33
V. Unskilled and household laborers	13

[a] Does not include the three families supported entirely by State Welfare.

TABLE A.5
IQ SCORES OF INTERVENED BRP CASES

IQ groups	Cases[a] (%)
Below 89	15[b]
90–99	23
100–109	34
110–119	18
120–129	8
130–139	0
140–149	2

[a] Based on 62 cases having school administered IQ scores.

[b] Accepted due to special requests by the schools, or to opinions by teachers that the IQ was grossly invalid. Acceptance of these cases insured continued referrals from these sources.

TABLE A.6
AVERAGE NUMBER OF CASE CONTACTS[a] PER QUARTER BY BA'S
IN HOMES AND SCHOOLS

Quarters	Total number of active cases	Mean number of contacts[b]	Mean contacts/ case/week	Mean Cases/BA
Home contacts				
First year				
Q_1	31	138	4.4	6.2
Q_2	48	224	4.7	9.5
Q_3	78	283	3.6	15.6
Q_4	96	314	3.3	19.2
Second year				
Q_1	105	252	2.4	21.0
School contacts				
First year				
Q_1	31	129	4.2	
Q_2	48	218	4.5	
Q_3		School vacation		
Q_4	96	255	2.6	
Second year				
Q_1	105	185	1.8	

[a] Includes telephone and personal contacts.
[b] Based on Random Sample Extrapolation.

APPENDIX II

SAMPLE FORMS

School Observation: Form I

Relations with peers

A - Aggressive

B - Fails to participate when approp.

C - Disruptive activities

Relation with teacher

A - Openly defiant

B - Actively soliciting attention

Class work (solitary) behaviors

A - Engages in activity other than test or activity assigned

B - Fails to have necessary materials at hand

C - Responds to disruptive influence

Referral behaviors

A -

B -

C -

Date:

Observer:

Class:

Teacher:

Target:

School Observation: Form II

Child's name	School	Recorder

Time period

Behavior to be recorded

Date:

1.					
2.					
3.					
4.					
5.					

Date:

1.					
2.					
3.					
4.					
5.					

Date:

1.					
2.					
3.					
4.					
5.					

Date:

1.					
2.					
3.					
4.					
5.					

Name _____

Date _____

School _____

M – R Incomplete Blank

1. My favorite grown-up (adult) is _____

    What do you like to do with him? _____

    _____

2. The best reward anybody can give me is _____

    _____

3. My favorite school subject is _____

4. If I had ten dollars I'd _____

    _____

5. My favorite relative in Tucson is _____

6. When I grow up I want to be _____

7. The person who punishes me most is _____

    How? _____

    Effectiveness? _____

    Other punishments used? _____

    Which works best with you? _____

8. Two things I like to do best are _____

    _____

    _____

9. My favorite adult at school is _____

10. When I do something well, what my mother does is _____

    _____

11. I feel terrific when _____

    _____

12. The way I get money is _____

    _____

13. When I have money I like to _____

    _____

14. When I'm in trouble my father _____

    _____

15. Something I really want is _____

    _____

16. If I please my father, what he does is _____

    _____

17. If I had a chance, I sure would like to _____

    _____

18. The person I like most to reward me is _____

    How? _____

19. I will do almost anything to avoid _____

    _____

20. The thing I like to do best with my mother is _____

21. The thing I do that bothers my teacher the most is _____

22. The weekend activity or entertainment I enjoy most is _____

23. If I did better at school I wish my teacher would _____

24. The kind of punishment I hate most is _____

25. I will do almost anything to get _____

26. It sure makes me mad when I can't _____

27. When I am in trouble, my mother _____

28. My favorite brother or sister in Tucson is _____

29. The thing I like to do most is _____

30. The only person I will take advice from is _____

31. Not counting my parents, a person I will do almost anything for is _____

32. I hate for my teacher to _____

33. My two favorite TV programs are _____

34. The thing I like to do best with my father is _____

Subject's Ranking of Reinforcers

Behavioral Research Project
Home Follow-Up Evaluation: Form I

Child's name _____   Case no. _____ Date _____

Interviewee _____   Assigned BA _____

Interviewer _____

Intervention? Yes _____ No_____

(A) Referral behaviors (home and school):

	Very impr.	Impr.	Same	Worse	Much worse
1.					
2.					
3.					
4.					
5.					
6.					
7.					
8.					

(B) Nonreferred behaviors (behaviors that have changed since our initial contact, but never referred):

1.					
2.					

Home Follow-Up Evaluation: Form II

Case No. _____

Child's name _____
Interviewee _____
Interviewer _____
Assigned BA _____

Date of first contact _____
Date of termination _____
Date of first follow-up _____
Date of phone call _____

Time lapse
_____

(A) Target behaviors intervened

	1st Follow-up	2nd Follow-up
1. _____	_____	_____
2. _____	_____	_____
3. _____	_____	_____
4. _____	_____	_____
5. _____	_____	_____
6. _____	_____	_____
7. _____	_____	_____
8. _____	_____	_____

Ratings

| | 1st Follow-up | 2nd Follow-up |

(B) Target behaviors at the time of referral

1. _____
2. _____
3. _____
4. _____
5. _____

Ratings

| | 1st Follow-up | 2nd Follow-up |

(C) Any new behaviors now occurring

1. _____
2. _____
3. _____

(D) Have you used the techniques we taught you? _____
If so, how? _____

(E) Have you had any reports from the school concerning your child's behavior? _____

(F) How are your child's grades? _____

Author Index

Numbers in italics refer to the pages on which the complete references are listed.

Subject Index

233